THE DOCTOR WHO
PROGRAMME GUIDE

Also by Jean-Marc & Randy Lofficier

The Nth Doctor
Into The Twilight Zone

THE DOCTOR WHO PROGRAMME GUIDE

FOURTH EDITION

Revised and updated
by
Jean-Marc & Randy Lofficier

Mystery Writers of America Presents
New York Lincoln Shanghai

The Doctor Who Programme Guide
Fourth Edition

All Rights Reserved © 1981, 1989, 1994, 2003
by Jean-Marc & Randy Lofficier
'Doctor Who' series copyright © 2003 British
Broadcasting Corporation

Mystery Writers of America Presents
an imprint of iUniverse, Inc.

For information address:
iUniverse
2021 Pine Lake Road, Suite 100
Lincoln, NE 68512
www.iuniverse.com

Originally published by W. H. Allen & Co. Plc and Virgin
Publishing, Ltd.

ISBN: 0-595-27618-0

Printed in the United States of America

FOREWORD

When a BBC Producer is a 142 years old (or does it just feel like that?), he regenerates and turns into an Executive Producer, or so they say; and then people from all over the world write and ask him questions; and he gets the answers wrong...

Well, perhaps I don't get them all wrong, but to be corrected by a 15-year-old about the third monster on the left in a show made before he was born can be an earth-shaking experience.

But now, thanks to the quite extraordinary industry of Jean-Marc and Randy Lofficier, I can be right every time. And so can you—and you—and you. Though you, sir, who pointed out that in the various *Doctor Who* stories there have been three entirely different and incompatible versions of the destruction of Atlantis, presumably won't need the help of Jean-Marc and Randy.

Of course, they haven't been able to put everything down; their self-imposed brief couldn't allow it even if they could have persuaded the publishers to accept a manuscript the length of the *Encyclopaedia Britannica*. In any case, a lot of it is secret.

For example, it will always remain untold that one of the monsters in an early Jon Pertwee story was familiarly known to one and all as Puff the Magic Dragon, looking as he did like an 80 foot-long pink-quilted pyjama case.

My lips will be even more firmly sealed about the various suggestions put forward concerning the interpersonal relationships of Alpha Centauri, the hermaphrodite hexapod. After all, even snails must have a surprisingly interesting social life and they don't have six arms.

Anything short of such revelations (which will only be made known 300 years after the Doctor's last regeneration) is sure to be found in this remarkable work of eccentric but dedicated scholarship.

Barry Letts
producer, *Doctor Who*

CONTENTS

ACKNOWLEDGEMENTS

I am deeply grateful to the following people who helped me in the compilation of the information included in this book: Jeremy Bentham, Christopher H. Bidmead, Eric Hoffman, David J. Howe, Barry Letts, Ian Levine, John McElroy, John Nathan-Turner, John Peel, Graham Williams, Shaun Ley, The BBC *Doctor Who* Production Office and the Members of the *Doctor Who* Appreciation Society.

Special thanks are particularly due to Terrance Dicks, whose help and advice were invaluable in the making of this book and to Andrew Pixley who compiled the information about novelisations, video and audio tapes – and did an extremely thorough job of it.

J.-M. & R.L.

TABLE OF STORIES

The title of each serial is preceded by its story production code.

First Doctor (1963 – 1966)

First Season

A	An Unearthly Child (4 episodes)
	(Also known as The Tribe of Gum and 100,000 BC)
B	The Daleks (7 episodes)
C	The Edge of Destruction (2 episodes)
	(Also known as Inside the Spaceship)
D	Marco Polo (7 episodes)
E	The Keys of Marinus (6 episodes)
F	The Aztecs (4 episodes)
G	The Sensorites (6 episodes)
H	The Reign of Terror (6 episodes)

Second Season

J	Planet of Giants (3 episodes)
K	The Dalek Invasion of Earth (6 episodes)
L	The Rescue (2 episodes)
M	The Romans (4 episodes)
N	The Web Planet (6 episodes)
P	The Crusade (4 episodes)
Q	The Space Museum (4 episodes)
R	The Chase (6 episodes)
S	The Time Meddler (4 episodes)

Third Season

T	Galaxy Four (4 episodes)
T/A	Mission to the Unknown (1 episode)
U	The Myth Makers (4 episodes)
V	The Daleks' Master Plan (12 episodes)
W	The Massacre (4 episodes)
X	The Ark (4 episodes)
Y	The Celestial Toymaker (4 episodes)
Z	The Gunfighters (4 episodes)
AA	The Savages (4 episodes)
BB	The War Machines (4 episodes)

Fourth Season

CC	The Smugglers (4 episodes)
DD	The Tenth Planet (4 episodes)

Second Doctor (1966 – 1969)

Fourth Season (continued)

EE	The Power of the Daleks (6 episodes)
FF	The Highlanders (4 episodes)
GG	The Underwater Menace (4 episodes)
HH	The Moonbase (4 episodes)
JJ	The Macra Terror (4 episodes)
KK	The Faceless Ones (6 episodes)
LL	The Evil of the Daleks (7 episodes)

Fifth Season

MM	The Tomb of the Cybermen (4 episodes)
NN	The Abominable Snowmen (6 episodes)
OO	The Ice Warriors (6 episodes)
PP	The Enemy of the World (6 episodes)
QQ	The Web of Fear (6 episodes)
RR	Fury from the Deep (6 episodes)
SS	The Wheel in Space (6 episodes)

Sixth Season

TT	The Dominators (5 episodes)
UU	The Mind Robber (5 episodes)
VV	The Invasion (8 episodes)
WW	The Krotons (4 episodes)
XX	The Seeds of Death (6 episodes)
YY	The Space Pirates (6 episodes)
ZZ	The War Games (10 episodes)

Third Doctor (1970 – 1974)

Seventh Season

AAA	Spearhead from Space (4 episodes)
BBB	The Silurians (7 episodes)
CCC	The Ambassadors of Death (7 episodes)
DDD	Inferno (7 episodes)

Eighth Season

EEE	Terror of the Autons (4 episodes)
FFF	The Mind of Evil (6 episodes)
GGG	The Claws of Axos (4 episodes)
HHH	Colony in Space (6 episodes)
JJJ	The Daemons (5 episodes)

Ninth Season

KKK	Day of the Daleks (4 episodes)
MMM	The Curse of Peladon (4 episodes)
LLL	The Sea Devils (6 episodes)
NNN	The Mutants (6 episodes)
OOO	The Time Monster (6 episodes)

Tenth Season

RRR	The Three Doctors (4 episodes)
PPP	Carnival of Monsters (4 episodes)
QQQ	Frontier in Space (6 episodes)
SSS	Planet of the Daleks (6 episodes)
TTT	The Green Death (6 episodes)

Eleventh Season

UUU	The Time Warrior (4 episodes)
WWW	Invasion of the Dinosaurs (6 episodes)
XXX	Death to the Daleks (4 episodes)
YYY	The Monster of Peladon (6 episodes)
ZZZ	Planet of the Spiders (6 episodes)

Fourth Doctor (1974 – 1981)

Twelfth Season

4A	Robot (4 episodes)
4C	The Ark in Space (4 episodes)
4B	The Sontaran Experiment (2 episodes)
4E	Genesis of the Daleks (6 episodes)
4D	Revenge of the Cybermen (4 episodes)

Thirteenth Season

4F	Terror of the Zygons (4 episodes)
4H	Planet of Evil (4 episodes)
4G	Pyramids of Mars (4 episodes)
4J	The Android Invasion (4 episodes)
4K	The Brain of Morbius (4 episodes)
4L	The Seeds of Doom (6 episodes)

Fourteenth Season

4M	Masque of Mandragora (4 episodes)
4N	The Hand of Fear (4 episodes)
4P	The Deadly Assassin (4 episodes)
4Q	The Face of Evil (4 episodes)
4R	The Robots of Death (4 episodes)
4S	The Talons of Weng-Chiang (6 episodes)

Fifteenth Season

4V	Horror of Fang Rock (4 episodes)
4T	The Invisible Enemy (4 episodes)
4X	Image of the Fendahl (4 episodes)
4W	The Sunmakers (4 episodes)
4Y	Underworld (4 episodes)
4Z	The Invasion of Time (6 episodes)

Sixteenth Season (The Key to Time)

5A	The Ribos Operation (4 episodes)
5B	The Pirate Planet (4 episodes)
5C	The Stones of Blood (4 episodes)
5D	The Androids of Tara (4 episodes)
5E	The Power of Kroll (4 episodes)
5F	The Armageddon Factor (6 episodes)

Seventeenth Season

5J	Destiny of the Daleks (4 episodes)
5H	City of Death (4 episodes)
5G	The Creature from the Pit (4 episodes)
5K	Nightmare of Eden (4 episodes)
5L	The Horns of Nimon (4 episodes)
5M	Shada (6 episodes) (not televised)

Eighteenth Season

5N	The Leisure Hive (4 episodes)
5Q	Meglos (4 episodes)
5R	Full Circle (4 episodes)
5P	State of Decay (4 episodes)
5S	Warriors' Gate (4 episodes)
5T	The Keeper of Traken (4 episodes)
5V	Logopolis (4 episodes)
	K9 and Company (50-minute special)

Fifth Doctor (1982 – 1984)

Nineteenth Season

5Z	Castrovalva (4 episodes)
5W	Four to Doomsday (4 episodes)
5Y	Kinda (4 episodes)
5X	The Visitation (4 episodes)
6A	Black Orchid (2 episodes)
6B	Earthshock (4 episodes)
6C	Time Flight (4 episodes)

Twentieth Season

6E	Arc of Infinity (4 episodes)
6D	Snakedance (4 episodes)
6F	Mawdryn Undead (4 episodes)
6G	Terminus (4 episodes)
6H	Enlightenment (4 episodes)
6J	The King's Demons (2 episodes)
6K	The Five Doctors (90-minute special)

Twenty-First Season

6L	Warriors of the Deep (4 episodes)
6M	The Awakening (2 episodes)
6N	Frontios (4 episodes)
6P	Resurrection of the Daleks (2 45-minute episodes)
6Q	Planet of Fire (4 episodes)
6R	The Caves of Androzani (4 episodes)

Sixth Doctor (1984 – 1986)

Twenty-First Season (continued)
6S   The Twin Dilemma (4 episodes)

Twenty-Second Season
6T   Attack of the Cybermen (2 45-minute episodes)
6V   Vengeance on Varos (2 45-minute episodes)
6X   The Mark of the Rani (2 45-minute episodes)
6W   The Two Doctors (3 45-minute episodes)
6Y   Timelash (2 45-minute episodes)
6Z   Revelation of the Daleks (2 45-minute episodes)

Twenty-Third Season (The Trial of a Time Lord)
7A   The Mysterious Planet (4 episodes)
7B   Mindwarp (4 episodes)
7C   Terror of the Vervoids (4 episodes)
7C   The Ultimate Foe (2 episodes)

Seventh Doctor (1987 – 1989)

Twenty-Fourth Season
7D   Time and the Rani (4 episodes)
7E   Paradise Towers (4 episodes)
7F   Delta and the Bannermen (3 episodes)
7G   Dragonfire (3 episodes)

Twenty-Fifth Season
7H   Remembrance of the Daleks (4 episodes)
7L   The Happiness Patrol (3 episodes)
7K   Silver Nemesis (3 episodes)
7J   The Greatest Show in the Galaxy (4 episodes)

Twenty-Sixth Season
7N   Battlefield (4 episodes)
7Q   Ghost Light (3 episodes)
7M   The Curse of Fenric (4 episodes)
7P   Survival (3 episodes)

THE TELEVISION STORIES

Information is presented in the following format:

Doctor (actor and years of tenure in the role)

Season

Producer   **Script Editor**
*(These are only given at the beginning of each season and when
a change occurs mid-season)*

Story Production Code and title by which the story is most
commonly known
Number of episodes
Dates of first transmission of first and last episodes (in England)

Titles of individual episodes (if given)

Writer   **Director**

Regular cast: Doctor and companions

Cast: guest cast for particular story

Story: brief plot summary

Novelisation: title, author, ISBN, publisher, year of first publica-
tion, cover artist and year of each edition, any title changes, and
Target library number

Script book: title, author, ISBN, publisher, year of first publica-
tion, cover artist and year of each edition

Video tape: title, catalogue number, year of first release and cover
artist

Audio tape: title, catalogue number, ISBN, year of first publica-
tion and cover artist

NOTE: *All video and audio tapes are published by BBC Enterprises.*

FIRST DOCTOR

WILLIAM HARTNELL
1963 – 1966

First Season

Producers:
Verity Lambert
Mervyn Pinfield

Script Editor:
David Whitaker

(A) AN UNEARTHLY CHILD
(4 episodes)
23 November 1963 to 14 December 1963

1. AN UNEARTHLY CHILD
2. THE CAVE OF SKULLS

3. THE FOREST OF FEAR
4. THE FIREMAKER

Writer:
Anthony Coburn
(Additional material
by C.E. Webber)

Director:
Waris Hussein

Regular cast: William Hartnell (the Doctor); William Russell (Ian Chesterton); Jacqueline Hill (Barbara Wright); Carole Ann Ford (Susan Foreman).

Cast: Derek Newark (Za); Alethea Charlton (Hur); Jeremy Young (Kal); Howard Lang (Horg); Eileen Way (Old Mother).

Story: Susan Foreman, 15, is the Doctor's granddaughter and goes to Coal Hill School, London. Two teachers, Ian Chesterton and Barbara Wright, go to investigate her home background. 'Home' appears to be a police box, located in a junkyard at 76

Totter's Lane. This police box is in fact a TARDIS (Time and Relative Dimensions in Space), the Doctor's dimensionally transcendental spaceship, which plunges them all back to the Earth of 100,000 BC. They are captured by a tribe which has lost the secret of fire. Two leaders, Kal and Za, are involved in a power struggle. Ian makes a fire for Za by rubbing two sticks together, but Za does not allow the time-travellers to leave as promised. By a clever trick the Doctor and his companions escape to the TARDIS now stuck in the shape of a police box. because of its faulty chameleon circuit.

In this first story the Doctor seems very much the anti-hero, and is portrayed as a tetchy, selfish old man. The working title for this story was *100,000 BC*.

Novelisation: *Doctor Who – An Unearthly Child* by Terrance Dicks (0 426 20144 2) first published by W H Allen (now Virgin Publishing Ltd) in 1981 with cover by Andrew Skilleter. New edition in 1990 with cover by Alister Pearson. Target library number 68.

Script book: *Doctor Who – The Tribe of Gum* by Anthony Coburn (1 85286 012 X) first published by Titan Books in 1988 with cover by Dave McKean.

Video tape: *An Unearthly Child* (BBCV 4311) first released in 1990 with cover by Alister Pearson. Pilot on *The Hartnell Years* (BBCV 4608) first released in 1991 with photomontage cover.

(B) THE DALEKS
(7 episodes)
21 December 1963 to 1 February 1964

1. THE DEAD PLANET
2. THE SURVIVORS
3. THE ESCAPE
4. THE AMBUSH

5. THE EXPEDITION
6. THE ORDEAL
7. THE RESCUE

Writer:	**Directors:**
Terry Nation	Christopher Barry
	(episodes 1, 2, 4 and 5)
	Richard Martin
	(episodes 3, 6 and 7)

Regular cast: see A above

Cast: Robert Jewell, Kevin Manser, Michael Summerton, Gerald Taylor, Peter Murphy (Daleks); Peter Hawkins, David Graham (Dalek voices); John Lee (Alydon); Philip Bond (Ganatus); Virginia Wetherell (Dyoni); Alan Wheatley (Temmosus); Gerald Curtis (Elyon); Jonathan Crane (Kristas); Marcus Hammond (Antodus); Chris Browning, Katie Cashfield, Vez Delahunt, Kevin Glenny, Ruth Harrison, Lesley Hill, Steve Pokol, Jeanette Rossini, Eric Smith (Thals).

Story: The TARDIS arrives on the planet Skaro. The Doctor deliberately sabotages the TARDIS to have an excuse to explore an alien city. There, the travellers encounter the Daleks, evil mutants who have survived centuries of neutronic wars and who are now encased in mobile machines powered by static electricity conducted through the city floors. Later, Susan meets Alydon, one of the Thals, the Daleks' ancient enemies, who have mutated into perfect human beings. Alydon tells her that his race is starving. Susan asks the Daleks to help, but instead they set a trap and the Thal leader, Temmosus, is killed. The Daleks then plan to detonate another neutron bomb to render Skaro totally uninhabitable. The Doctor and the Thals invade the city and destroy the Daleks by cutting off their power.

This is the first Dalek story, which turned *Doctor Who* into an overnight success with over 8 million viewers. The original title was *The Mutants*, later changed to avoid confusion with story NNN.

Novelisation: *Doctor Who – The Daleks* by David Whittaker

(0 426 10110 3) first published by Frederick Muller Ltd as *Doctor Who in an Exciting Adventure with the Daleks* in 1964. New edition published by Armada Paperbacks in 1965 with cover by Peter Archer. New edition published by Universal-Tandem (became W H Allen) as *Doctor Who and the Daleks* in 1973 with cover by Chris Achilleos. New edition published by Virgin Publishing Ltd in 1992 with cover by Alister Pearson. Target library number 16.

Script book: *Doctor Who – The Daleks* by Terry Nation (1 85286 145 2) first published in 1989 by Titan Books with cover by Tony Clark. New edition in 1994 with cover by Alister Pearson.

Video tape: *The Daleks* (BBCV 4242) first released in 1989 with photomontage cover.

(C) THE EDGE OF DESTRUCTION
(2 episodes)
8 February 1964 to 15 February 1964

1. THE EDGE OF DESTRUCTION

2. THE BRINK OF DISASTER

Writer:
David Whitaker

Directors:
Richard Martin (episode 1)
Frank Cox (episode 2)

Regular cast: see A above

Cast: No others

Story: In a desperate attempt to gain control of the faulty TARDIS's guidance system and return the two school teachers to London 1963, the Doctor decides to experiment with a new combination. There is a violent explosion and the TARDIS blacks out. Susan and Barbara are convinced this is the work of an invisible alien force but Ian rationalises it as a technical fault.

The irascible Doctor accuses the two teachers of sabotage; he suspects them of trying to blackmail him into returning them to Earth. Finally even Susan begins to suspect Ian and Barbara. However, they eventually realise that the halt has been caused by the ship's defence mechanism, which is also responsible for the psychological disturbances the crew are experiencing. The TARDIS has resorted to these measures because the Fast Return Switch jammed and the space ship was on its way back to the very beginning of Creation.

This is the only story which takes place entirely inside the TARDIS with no other cast than the regular actors. The working title for this story was *Inside the Spaceship*.

Novelisation: *Doctor Who – The Edge of Destruction* by Nigel Robinson (0 426 20327 5) first published by W H Allen (now Virgin Publishing Ltd) in 1988 with cover by Alister Pearson. Target library number 132.

(D) **MARCO POLO**
(7 episodes)
22 February 1964 to 4 April 1964

1. THE ROOF OF THE WORLD
2. THE SINGING SANDS
3. FIVE HUNDRED EYES
4. THE WALL OF LIES
5. RIDER FROM SHANG-TU
6. MIGHTY KUBLAI KHAN
7. ASSASSIN AT PEKING

Writer:
John Lucarotti

Directors:
Waris Hussein (episodes 1, 2, 3, 5, 6 and 7)
John Crockett (episode 4)

Regular Cast: see A above

Cast: Mark Eden (Marco Polo); Derren Nesbitt (Tegana); Zienia Merton (Ping-Cho); Leslie Bates (the man at Lop);

Jimmy Gardner (Chenchu); Charles Wade (Malik); Philip Voss (Acomat); Philip Crest (Bandit); Paul Carson (Ling-Tau); Gabor Baraker (Wang-Lo); Tutte Lemkow (Kuiju); Peter Lawrence (Vizier); Martin Miller (Kublai Khan); Basil Tang (Foreman); Claire Davenport (Empress); O. Ikeda (Yeng).

Story: The TARDIS lands in 1289 on the plateau of the Pamir. The time-travellers meet Marco Polo, a young Venetian emissary of Kublai Khan, who is on his way to Kublai's court in Peking, accompanied by a Tartar war lord named Tegana, a peace ambassador from the rival Mogul ruler, and a Chinese girl called Ping-Cho. Marco Polo forces the Doctor to join his caravan – he wants to present the TARDIS to Kublai Khan in the hope he will be allowed to return to Venice. But Tegana also wants the TARDIS and attempts to steal the ship, thinking it can fly; he tries to poison the party's water supply and drills holes in their water barrels as they cross the Gobi desert, then escapes on the last horse. Because of the intense night cold, condensation forms on the TARDIS so they survive. The party arrives in Peking; the Doctor meets Kublai Khan and they play backgammon. At first the Doctor wins 35 elephants, 4,000 horses and 25 tigers; then the tide turns and he gambles away the TARDIS. But when he exposes Tegana and saves Kublai's life the TARDIS's keys are returned to him.

Novelisation: *Doctor Who – Marco Polo* by John Lucarotti (0 426 19967 7) first published by W H Allen (now Virgin Publishing Ltd) in 1984 with cover by David McAllister. Target library number 94.

(E) THE KEYS OF MARINUS

(6 episodes)

11 April 1964 to 16 May 1964

1. THE SEA OF DEATH
2. THE VELVET WEB
3. THE SCREAMING JUNGLE

4. THE SNOWS OF TERROR
5. SENTENCE OF DEATH
6. THE KEYS OF MARINUS

Writer:
Terry Nation

Director:
John Gorrie

Regular cast: see A above

Cast: George Couloris (Arbitan); Martin Cort, Peter Stenson, Gordon Wales (Voords); Robin Phillips (Altos), Katharine Schofield (Sabetha); Heron Carvic (voice of Morpho); Edmund Warwick (Darrius); Francis de Wolff (Vasor); Michael Allaby (Larn); Alan James, Anthony Verner, Peter Stenson, Michael Allaby (Ice Soldiers); Henley Thomas (Tarron); Raf de la Torre (Senior Judge); Alan James, Peter Stenson (Judges); Fiona Walker (Kala); Martin Cort (Aydan), Donald Pickering (Eyesen); Stephen Dartnell (Yartek); Dougie Dean (Eprin).

Story: The travellers land on an island on the planet Marinus, where the sand is glass and the sea is acid. The TARDIS is captured by Arbitan, Keeper of the Conscience of Marinus, a machine that controls the planet, preventing crime. But four of the five keys that make it function are lost. The Doctor and his companions use watch-shaped time dials to go to some strange places in search of them: the city of Morphoton, ruled by Giant Brains who keep its population enslaved; a jungle whose flora's evolution has been accelerated by the old scientist Darius; an ice-bound wilderness; and finally the city of Millenius where Ian is framed for murder. On their return they find Arbitan dead, murdered by Yartek, leader of the Voord, who now control the island. Ian is forced to hand over the four hard-won keys, but one is a fake – which causes the machine to explode, blowing

23

itself and the Voord to pieces and freeing the inhabitants of Marinus from its domination.

Novelisation: *Doctor Who and the Keys of Marinus* by Philip Hinchcliffe (0 426 20125 6) first published by W H Allen (now Virgin Publishing Ltd) in 1980 with cover by David McAllister. Target library number 38.

(F) THE AZTECS
(4 episodes)
23 May 1964 to 13 June 1964

1. THE TEMPLE OF EVIL
2. THE WARRIORS OF DEATH

3. THE BRIDE OF SACRIFICE
4. THE DAY OF DARKNESS

Writer:
John Lucarotti

Director:
John Crockett

Regular Cast: see A above

Cast: Keith Pyott (Autloc); John Ringham (Tlotoxl); Ian Cullen (Ixta); Margot van der Burgh (Cameca); Tom Booth (Victim); David Anderson (Captain); Walter Randall (Tonila); Andre Boulay (Perfect Victim).

Story: The TARDIS lands in 1430 inside the Tomb of Yetaxa, one-time High Priest of the Aztecs. When the Doctor and his companions leave the Tomb the door locks behind them. They meet Autloc, High Priest of Knowledge, and Tlotoxl, High Priest of Sacrifice. Autloc hails Barbara as Yetaxa's reincarnation – she is wearing the Priest's bracelet, which she found in the tomb. Ian is appointed Chief of the Aztec Warriors and as a result finds himself in competition with the Chosen Leader, Ixta, who eventually plunges to his death from a pyramid after a fight with Ian. Susan is made a handmaiden but she causes a rumpus when she refuses the last wish of the Perfect Victim –

marriage. The Doctor rests in luxury with the esteemed elders and, although this seems incongruous, flirts mildly with a beautiful elderly Aztec lady, Cameca. This, however, is to learn from her a way into the Tomb to retrieve the TARDIS. Barbara is declared a fake after she tries to stop human sacrifices but the crew escape when the Doctor opens the Tomb door with an old-fashioned wheel-and-pulley, a device unknown to the Aztecs.

Novelisation: *Doctor Who – The Aztecs* by John Lucarotti (0 426 19588 4) first published by W H Allen (now Virgin Publishing Ltd) in 1984 with cover by Nick Spender. New edition in 1992 with cover by Andrew Skilleter. Target library number 88.

Video tape: *The Aztecs* (BBCV 4743) first released in 1992 with cover by Andrew Skilleter.

(G) **THE SENSORITES**
(6 episodes)
20 June 1964 to 1 August 1964

1. STRANGERS IN SPACE
2. THE UNWILLING WARRIORS
3. HIDDEN DANGER
4. A RACE AGAINST DEATH
5. KIDNAP
6. A DESPERATE VENTURE

Writer:
Peter R. Newman

Directors:
Mervyn Pinfield (episodes 1, 2, 3 and 4)
Frank Cox
(episodes 5 and 6)

Regular Cast: see A above

Cast: Stephen Dartnell (John); Ilona Rodgers (Carol); Lorne Cossette (Captain Maitland); Ken Tyllson, Joe Greig, Peter

Glaze, Arthur Newall (Sensorites); Eric Francis, Bartlett Mullins (Elders); John Bailey (Commander); Martyn Huntley, Giles Phibbs (Survivors).

Story: The TARDIS lands on the deck of a gigantic spaceship from 28th-century Earth. Its Captain, Maitland, explains they are under the control of a race called the Sensorites, who live on the Sense-Sphere. They are all physically identical, with huge, bald, bulb-shaped heads. Through telepathic communication with Susan, the Sensorites invite them down to Sense-Sphere for talks. They explain they know the spaceship has discovered the mineral molybdenum on their planet, and they are wary of being exploited. The Sensorites fear the Humans because many of them have died since another spaceship left. The Doctor discovers deadly nightshade in the city's water supply and tracks down the culprits to underground caves – three deranged spacemen left behind from the previous expedition. The Captain promises to say nothing of the Sensorites' existence.

Novelisation: *Doctor Who – The Sensorites* by Nigel Robinson (0 426 20295 3) first published by W H Allen (now Virgin Publishing Ltd) in 1987 with cover by Tony Masero. Target library number 115.

(H) **THE REIGN OF TERROR**
(6 episodes)
8 August 1964 to 12 September 1964

1. A LAND OF FEAR
2. GUESTS OF MADAME GUILLOTINE
3. A CHANGE OF IDENTITY
4. THE TYRANT OF FRANCE
5. A BARGAIN OF NECESSITY
6. PRISONERS OF CONCIERGERIE

Writer:
Dennis Spooner

Director:
Henric Hirsch
(episode 3 directed by
John Gorrie, uncredited)

Regular cast: see A above

Cast: Peter Walker (Small Boy); Laidlaw Dalling (Rouvray); Neville Smith (d'Argenson); Robert Hunter (Sergeant); Ken Lawrence (Lieutenant); James Hall (Soldier); Howard Charlton (Judge); Jack Cunningham (Jailer); Jeffry Wickham (Webster); Dallas Cavell (Overseer); Denis Cleary (Peasant); James Cairncross (Lemaitre/Stirling); Roy Herrick (Jean); Donald Morley (Renan); John Barrard (Shopkeeper); Caroline Hunt (Danielle); Edward Brayshaw (Colbert); Keith Anderson (Robespierre); Ronald Pickup (Physician); Terry Bale (Soldier); John Law (Barrass); Tony Wall (Bonaparte); Patrick Marley (Soldier).

Story: The TARDIS lands in a forest clearing. The travellers think it's England 1963 but they are in fact 20 kilometres from Paris during Robespierre's Reign of Terror. A farmhouse is sacked by Government troops; the Doctor is concussed and left for dead, the others are dragged off to prison. The Doctor masquerades as a citizen, while Ian gets involved in the counter-revolutionary plot of English master spy James Stirling.

Novelisation: *Doctor Who – The Reign of Terror* by Ian Marter (0 426 20264 3) first published by W H Allen (now Virgin Publishing Ltd) in 1987 with cover by Tony Masero. Target library number 119.

Producers:
Verity Lambert
Mervyn Pinfield

Script Editor:
David Whitaker

(J) **PLANET OF GIANTS**
(3 episodes)
31 October 1964 to 14 November 1964

1. PLANET OF GIANTS
2. DANGEROUS JOURNEY

3. CRISIS

Writer:
Louis Marks

Directors:
Mervyn Pinfield (episodes
1, 2 and 3)
Douglas Camfield (episode
4, incorporated into episode 3)

Regular cast: William Hartnell (the Doctor); William Russell (Ian Chesterton); Jacqueline Hill (Barbara Wright); Carole Ann Ford (Susan Foreman).

Cast: Alan Tilvern (Forester); Frank Crawshaw (Farrow); Reginald Barratt (Smithers), RosemaryJohnson (Hilda); Fred Ferris (Bert).

Story: The doors of the TARDIS open. All readings indicate complete normality – but the travellers are only one inch tall! A crooked manufacturer, Forester, intends to capitalise on a new insecticide, DN6, to be used to increase food production for starving nations. He realises, however, that eventually the product will destroy every living thing for its molecules are stable instead of ephemeral. A Government Inspector, Farrow, finds out but is murdered by Forester before he can reveal his discovery. The crime is witnessed by the miniaturised Ian and Barbara. The Doctor, against almost insurmountable odds – they are vulnerable to such hazards as being washed down plug holes and tumbling into matchboxes – stops Forester from publishing his bogus report on the scheme, using a gas jet and a match to cause an explosion that goes off in the evil Forester's face.

Novelisation: *Doctor Who – Planet of Giants* by Terrance Dicks (0 426 20345 3) first published by W H Allen (now Virgin Publishing Ltd) in 1990 with cover by Alister Pearson. Target library number 145.

(K) THE DALEK INVASION OF EARTH
(6 episodes)
21 November 1964 to 26 December 1964

1. WORLD'S END
2. THE DALEKS
3. DAY OF RECKONING
4. THE END OF TOMORROW
5. THE WAKING ALLY
6. FLASHPOINT

Writer:
Terry Nation

Director:
Richard Martin

Regular cast: see J above

Cast: Bernard Kay (Carl Tyler); Peter Fraser (David Campbell); Alan Judd (Dortmun); Martyn Huntley, Peter Badger, Reg Tyler, Bill Moss (Robomen); Robert Aldous (Rebel); Robert Jewell, Gerald Taylor, Nick Evans, Kevin Manser, Peter Murphy (Daleks); Peter Hawkins, David Graham (Dalek voices); Ann Davies (Jenny); Michael Goldie (Craddock); Michael Davis (Thomson); Richard McNeff (Baker); Graham Rigby (Larry Madison); Nicholas Smith (Wells); Nick Evans (Slyther); Patrick O'Connell (Ashton); Jean Conroy, Meriel Hobson (Women).

Story: The scene is London in 2167. The Daleks have invaded Earth, making many thousands of inhabitants into Robomen – Human Dalek servants – by clamping metal control helmets to their heads. Other slaves have been shipped to Bedfordshire, where the Daleks have a vast mining complex; they have discovered a fissure in the Earth's inner shell, through which they aim to remove the planet's core and replace it with a magnetic power system, so they can pilot Earth anywhere in the Universe. The Doctor and Ian are captured by Robomen and taken to the Dalek Supreme, the Black Dalek, who tries to change the Doctor into a Roboman, strapping him to an operating table in the Robotiser Chamber of a Dalek flying saucer parked at Chelsea Heliport. The rest of the TARDIS crew escape from London and head for the mining fields, where Ian confronts the Slyther, the Daleks' man-eating pet. Susan and a freedom-fighter named David Campbell manage to gain entry into the complex and destroy the Daleks' radio network. No longer under the Daleks' control, the Robomen and the Slaves are encouraged by the Doctor to rise against their inhuman masters. A bomb is detonated, which destroys the Daleks and their craft. Earth is now safe and Susan, who has fallen in love with David Campbell, decides to stay behind.

With the departure of Susan, the Doctor's granddaughter, the TARDIS' crew changes for the first time.

Novelisation: *Doctor Who – The Dalek Invasion of Earth* by Terrance Dicks (0 426 11244 X) first published as *Doctor Who and the Dalek Invasion of Earth* by W H Allen (now Virgin Publishing Ltd) in 1977 with cover by Chris Achilleos. New edition in 1990 with cover by Alister Pearson. Target library number 17. Also reprinted in *Doctor Who – The Dalek Omnibus* in 1983 with cover by Andrew Skilleter.

Video tape: *The Dalek Invasion of Earth* (BBCV 4353) first released in 1990 with cover by Alister Pearson.

Script Editor:
Dennis Spooner

(L) **THE RESCUE**
(2 episodes)
2 January 1965 to 9 January 1965

1. THE POWERFUL ENEMY 2. DESPERATE MEASURES

Writer: **Director:**
David Whitaker Christopher Barry

Regular cast: William Hartnell (the Doctor); William Russell (Ian Chesterton); Jacqueline Hill (Barbara Wright); and introducing Maureen O'Brien (Vicki).

Cast: Ray Barrett (Bennett/Koquillion); Tom Sheridan (Captain/Sand Monster); John Stuart, Colin Hughes (Didonians).

Story: The Doctor lands on the planet Dido in the year 2493. He finds a crashed spaceship from Earth with two survivors: a paralysed man named Bennett and a young girl, Vicki. Bennett tells the Doctor that the rest of the crew have been murdered by the locals and Vicki says a native named Koquillion is protecting them from the further wrath of the enraged Didonians. The Doctor is suspicious of these explanations and challenges Koquillion – to find that he is Bennett in disguise. Bennett confesses that he murdered all the spaceship crew and the friendly Didonians to conceal a murder he had previously committed on the spaceship. He had planned to take Vicki – she is unaware of his crimes – back to Earth to testify to his innocence. However, terrified by two Didonian survivors, Bennett plunges over a cliff to his death. The Doctor offers Vicki a chance to join his crew and she accepts.

Novelisation: *Doctor Who – The Rescue* by Ian Marter (0 426 20308 9) first published by W H Allen (now Virgin Publishing

Ltd) in 1987 with cover by Tony Clark. Target library number 124.

(M) THE ROMANS
(4 episodes)
16 January 1965 to 6 February 1965

1. THE SLAVE TRADERS   3. CONSPIRACY
2. ALL ROADS LEAD TO ROME   4. INFERNO

Writer: **Director:**
Dennis Spooner   Christopher Barry

Regular cast: see L above

Cast: Derek Sydney (Sevcheria); Nicholas Evans (Didius); Dennis Edwards (Centurion); Margot Thomas (Stall-holder); Edward Kelsey (Slave-buyer); Bart Allison (Maximus Petullian); Barry Jackson (Ascaris); Peter Diamond (Delos); Michael Peake (Tavius); Dorothy-Rose Gribble (Woman Slave); Gertan Klauber (Galley Master); Ernest Jennings and John Caesar (Men in Market); Tony Lambden (Messenger); Derek Francis (Nero); Brian Proudfoot (Tigilinus); Ann Tirard (Locusta); Kay Patrick (Poppaea).

Story: The TARDIS crew have been resting up in a villa outside Rome in the year AD 64, while its owner campaigns in the Gallic Wars. When Vicki and the Doctor visit Rome, Ian and Barbara are captured by slave traders – Ian is sold as a galley slave and Barbara to the court of Nero. The Doctor is mistaken for Maximus Petullian, celebrated musician and enemy of Nero, and is taken to the Emperor's palace; but it is quickly obvious that he cannot play a note of music. Ian escapes from the galley ship only to be sent to Rome as a gladiator, where he encounters Barbara. With his spectacle lens the Doctor sets fire to plans Nero has rejected for his perfect city – inspiring Nero

32

to start the Great Fire of Rome, under cover of which the crew of the TARDIS escape back to the villa.

Novelisation: *Doctor Who – The Romans* by Donald Cotton (0 426 20288 0) first published by W H Allen (now Virgin Publishing Ltd) in 1987 with cover by Tony Masero. Target library number 120.

Producer:
Verity Lambert

(N) **THE WEB PLANET**
(6 episodes)
13 February 1965 to 20 March 1965

1. THE WEB PLANET	4. CRATER OF NEEDLES
2. THE ZARBI	5. INVASION
3. ESCAPE TO DANGER	6. THE CENTRE

Writer:	**Director:**
Bill Strutton	Richard Martin

Regular cast: see L above

Cast: Robert Jewell, Jack Pitt, Gerald Taylor, Hugh Lund, John Scott Martin, Kevin Manser (Zarbi); Roslyn de Winter (Vrestin); Arne Gordon (Hrostar); Arthur Blake (Hrhoonda); Jolyon Booth (Prapilius); Jocelyn Birdsall (Hlynia); Martin Jarvis (Captain Hilio); Ian Thompson (Hetra); Barbara Joss (Nemini); Catherine Fleming (voice of the Animus).

Story: The TARDIS is drawn by an unknown force to the planet Vortis. While the Doctor and Ian are busy exploring, the force causes Barbara to leave the TARDIS. Eventually she is captured by ant-like creatures, the Zarbi, who are at war with the butterfly-like Menoptera. She is taken to a slave colony and the Zarbi drag the TARDIS to their Web headquarters. The Doctor and Ian follow the tracks and the Doctor confronts the Animus, a blinding white light concealing a large spider parasite, who is the mind behind the Zarbi. An invasion by the Menoptera to regain their planet fails, but the Doctor manages to obtain an isop-tope brought to Vortis during the attack. When the Doctor and Vicki are taken to the Animus, Barbara manages to use the isop-tope and destroys the Animus. The Menoptera return to Vortis while the Zarbi revert to mindless creatures.

Novelisation: *Doctor Who – The Web Planet* by Bill Strutton (0 426 20356 9) first published by Frederick Muller Ltd as *Doctor Who and the Zarbi* in 1966. New edition published by Universal-Tandem (became W H Allen) in 1973 with cover by Chris Achilleos. New edition published by Virgin Publishing Ltd in 1990 with cover by Alister Pearson. Target library number 73.

Video tape: *The Web Planet* (BBCV 4405) first released in 1990 with cover by Alister Pearson.

(P) THE CRUSADE
(4 episodes)
27 March 1965 to 17 April 1965

1. THE LION
2. THE KNIGHT OF JAFFA
3. THE WHEEL OF FORTUNE
4. THE WAR-LORDS

Writer:
David Whitaker

Director:
Douglas Camfield

Regular cast: see L above

Cast: John Flint (William des Preaux); Walter Randall (El Akir); Julian Glover (Richard the Lionheart); David Anderson

(Reynier de Marun); Bruce Wightman (William de Tornebu); Reg Pritchard (Ben Daheer); Tony Caunter (Thatcher); Roger Avon (Saphadin); Bernard Kay (Saladin); Derek Ware, Valentino Musetti, Anthony Colby (Saracen Warriors); Jean Marsh (Joanna); Robert Lankesheer (Chamberlain); Zohra Segal (Sheyrah), Gabor Baraker (Luigi Ferrigo); Chris Konyils, Raymond Novak (Saracen Guards); George Little (Haroun); Petra Markham (Safiya); John Bay (Earl of Leicester); Sandra Hampton (Maimuna); Viviane Sorrel (Fatima); Diane McKenzie (Hafsa); Tutte Lemkow (Ibrahim); Billy Cornelius (Soldier).

Story: The scene is 12th-century Palestine. Saracens, led by Emir El Akir, wait to ambush King Richard the Lionheart. The Doctor manages to save Richard. The King plans for peace by arranging a marriage between Saladin's brother, Saphadin, and his own sister, Joanna, but Joanna refuses. The Doctor and Vicki narrowly escape being burnt at the stake as sorcerers.

Novelisation: *Doctor Who and the Crusaders* by David Whitaker (0 426 11316 0) first published by Frederick Muller Ltd in 1966. New edition published by Dragon Books in 1967. New edition published by Universal-Tandem in 1973 with cover by Chris Achilleos. New edition published by W H Allen (now Virgin Publishing Ltd) in 1981 with cover by Andrew Skilleter. Target library number 12.

Video tape: 'The Wheel of Fortune' included on *The Hartnell Years* (BBCV 4608) first released in 1991 with photomontage cover.

(Q) **THE SPACE MUSEUM**
(4 episodes)
24 April 1965 to 15 May 1965

1. THE SPACE MUSEUM
2. THE DIMENSIONS OF TIME

3. THE SEARCH
4. THE FINAL PHASE

Writer:
Glyn Jones

Director:
Mervyn Pinfield

Regular cast: see L above

Cast: Peter Sanders (Sita); Peter Craze (Dako); Richard Shaw (Lobos); Jeremy Bulloch (Tor); Salvin Stewart (Messenger); Peter Diamond (Technician); Ivor Salter (Commander); Billy Cornelius (Guard); Murphy Grumbar (Dalek); Peter Hawkins (Dalek voice).

Story: The planet Xeros has been made into a space museum by the warlike Moroks. Among samples of their historical conquests are familiar aliens like the Daleks, and the Doctor and his friends – who have become invisible – see their own replicas in the museum. They realise that the TARDIS has jumped across a time track and to avoid ending up as exhibits they must change this possible future. They learn of a revolution planned against the Moroks and the Doctor helps the Xerons to victory.

Novelisation: *Doctor Who – The Space Museum* by Glyn Jones (0 426 20289 9) first published by W H Allen (now Virgin Publishing Ltd) in 1987 with cover by David McAllister. Target library number 117.

(R) **THE CHASE**
(6 episodes)
22 May 1965 to 26 June 1965

1. THE EXECUTIONERS
2. THE DEATH OF TIME
3. FLIGHT THROUGH ETERNITY

4. JOURNEY INTO TERROR
5. THE DEATH OF DOCTOR WHO
6. THE PLANET OF DECISION

Writer:
Terry Nation

Director:
Richard Martin

Regular cast: see L above, and introducing Peter Purves (StevenTaylor) in the last episode.

Cast: Robert Marsden (Abraham Lincoln); Hugh Walters (William Shakespeare); Roger Hammond (Francis Bacon); Vivienne Bennett (Queen Elizabeth I); Richard Coe (TV announcer); The Beatles (Themselves); Jack Pitt (Mire Beast); Gerald Taylor, Kevin Manser, Robert Jewell, John Scott Martin (Daleks); Peter Hawkins, David Graham (Dalek voices); Ian Thompson (Malsan); Hywel Bennett (Rynian); Al Raymond (Prondyn); Arne Gordon (Guide); Peter Purves (Morton Dill); Dennis Chinnery (Albert Richardson); David Blake Kelly (Captain Briggs); Patrick Carter (Bosun); Douglas Ditta (Willoughby); Jack Pitt (Stewart); John Maxim (Frankenstein's Monster); Malcolm Rogers (Dracula); Roslyn de Winter (Grey Lady); Edmund Warwick (Robot Doctor); Murphy Grumbar, Jack Pitt, John Scott Martin, Ken Tyllson (Mechanoids); David Graham (Mechanoid Voices); Derek Ware (Bus Conductor).

Story: The Doctor finds through his new Time/Space Visualiser – with which he can see scenes from any time he wishes (stock film of the Beatles is used) – that the Daleks are after him in a time machine of their own design. The two crafts engage in a frantic chase through the Cosmos. After a brief encounter on the desert planet Aridius, the TARDIS lands on the Empire State Building, the *Marie Celeste* (whose crew leap into the sea at the sight of the Daleks), a Gothic house with Dracula and Frankenstein's Monster (who turn out to be amusement-park robots), and finally on the planet Mechanus, a world overgrown with deadly vegetation, and inhabited by the Mechanoids, human-built robots sent there to prepare the planet for colonisation, but subsequently forgotten. The travellers are taken prisoner by the Mechanoids after the Doctor's victory over a robot built in his image by the Daleks. They meet Steven Taylor, the only survivor of a crashed spaceship. The Daleks and the Mechanoids fight and destroy each other, but the Dalek time machine survives intact. Ian and Barbara use it to get back to their own time. Steven stumbles into the TARDIS and stays with the Doctor and Vicki.

After the departure of Ian and Barbara, the TARDIS crew no longer contains any of the original companions.

Novelisation: *Doctor Who – The Chase* by John Peel (0 426 20336 4) first published by W H Allen (now Virgin Publishing Ltd) in 1989 with cover by Alister Pearson. Target library number 140.

Video tape: *The Daleks Limited Edition Boxed Set* (BBCV 5005) first released in 1993 with art by Alister Pearson includes *The Chase* (BBCV 5006) with cover by Andrew Skilleter.

Script Editor:
Donald Tosh

(S) THE TIME MEDDLER
(4 episodes)
3 July 1965 to 24 July 1965

1. THE WATCHER
2. THE MEDDLING MONK

3. A BATTLE OF WITS
4. CHECKMATE

Writer:
Dennis Spooner

Director:
Douglas Camfield

Regular cast: William Hartnell (the Doctor); Maureen O'Brien (Vicki); Peter Purves (Steven Taylor).

Cast: Peter Butterworth (Monk); Alethea Charlton (Edith); Peter Russell (Eldred); Michael Miller (Wulnoth); Michael Guest (Hunter); Norman Hartley (Ulf); Geoffrey Cheshire (Viking Leader); David Anderson (Sven); Ronald Rich (Gunnar).

Story: The TARDIS materialises on the east coast of England in 1066. There they are puzzled to find a modern wristwatch and an old gramophone. Their owner, the Monk, is another time-traveller from the same planet as the Doctor. He is planning to ensure Harold's victory at Hastings with atomic bazookas. It takes all the Doctor's cunning to stop the meddling Monk. Finally he removes the Monk's dimension controller, leaving his TARDIS stuck in 1066.

This is the first story in which another member of the Doctor's race appears, although they are not yet identified as Time Lords.

Novelisation: *Doctor Who – The Time Meddler* by Nigel Robinson (0 426 20312 7) first published by W H Allen (now

Virgin Publishing Ltd) in 1987 with cover by Jeff Cummins. Target library number 126.

Third Season

Producer:
Verity Lambert

Script Editor:
Donald Tosh

(T) GALAXY FOUR
(4 episodes)
11 September 1965 to 2 October 1965

1. FOUR HUNDRED DAWNS
2. TRAP OF STEEL

3. AIRLOCK
4. THE EXPLODING PLANET

Writer:
William Emms

Director:
Derek Martinus

Regular cast: William Hartnell (the Doctor); Maureen O'Brien (Vicki); Peter Purves (Steven Taylor).

Cast: Stephanie Bidmead (Maaga); Marina Martin, Susanna Carroll, Lyn Ashley (Drahvins); Jimmy Kaye, Angelo Muscat, William Shearer, Pepi Poupee, Tommy Reynolds (Chumblies); Robert Cartland, Anthony Paul (Rill voices); Barry Jackson (Garvey).

Story: The Drahvins and the Rills crashlanded on a deserted planet in Galaxy Four. The planet is about to explode so the women-dominated Drahvins plan to escape in the spaceship belonging to the alien but peace-loving Rills. The true evil nature of the Drahvins eventually becomes apparent to the Doctor, who helps the Rills escape in their spaceship, with the aid of power from the TARDIS. The Doctor manages to escape the vengeance of the Drahvins thanks to the self-sacrifice of one of the Rills' friendly robots, the Chumblies.

Novelisation: *Doctor Who – Galaxy Four* by William Emms (0 426 20202 3) first published by W H Allen (now Virgin Publishing Ltd) in 1985 with cover by Andrew Skilleter. Target library number 104.

(T/A) **MISSION TO THE UNKNOWN**
(1 episode)
9 October 1965

Writer:
Terry Nation

Director:
Derek Martinus

Regular cast: None

Cast: Edward de Souza (Marc Cory); Robert Cartland (Malpha); Jeremy Young (Gordon Lowery); Barry Jackson (Garvey); Ronald Rich (Trantis); Robert Jewell, Kevin Manser, Gerald Taylor, John Scott Martin (Daleks); Peter Hawkins, David Graham (Dalek voices).

Story: The setting is the planet Kembel, whence information of mysterious happenings has reached the Space Special Security Service. Agent Marc Cory is despatched to investigate, but almost at once disaster strikes: his crew are cut down one by one by Varga plants which infest the planet. But what Cory discovers is of vital importance for Earth's future: the Daleks are present in force on Kembel and their intention is to unify alien races to wipe out humans. Cory is exterminated by the Daleks but a tape containing the information he gathered survives.

This is the only one-episode story of *Doctor Who* except for *The Five Doctors*. It does not feature the Doctor or any other of the regular cast and serves merely as a teaser for story V.

Novelisation: Part of *Doctor Who – Mission to the Unknown (The Daleks' Master Plan I)* by John Peel (0 426 20343 7) first published by W H Allen (now Virgin Publishing Ltd) in 1989 with cover by Alister Pearson. Target library number 141.

Producer:
John Wiles

(U) **THE MYTH MAKERS**
(4 episodes)
16 October 1965 to 6 November 1965

1. TEMPLE OF SECRETS
2. SMALL PROPHET, QUICK RETURN

3. DEATH OF A SPY
4. HORSE OF DESTRUCTION

Writer:
Donald Cotton

Director:
Michael Leeston-Smith

Regular cast: see T above, and introducing Adrienne Hill (Katarina) in the last episode.

Cast: Cavan Kendall (Achilles); Alan Haywood (Hector); Ivor Salter (Odysseus); Francis de Wolff (Agamemnon); Jack Melford (Menelaus); Tutte Lemkow (Cyclops); Max Adrian (Priam); Barrie Ingham (Paris); Frances White (Cassandra); Jon Luxton (Messenger); James Lynn (Troilus).

Story: On the plains outside a besieged Troy the Doctor is hailed as Zeus and taken by Achilles to his camp. But a fellow warrior, Odysseus, is sceptical as to his authenticity and gives him two days to devise a plan to capture Troy. Meanwhile, the TARDIS is seized by Paris and Vicki is hailed as a prophetess and given the name Cressida. She and Steven are thrown into jail and Vicki is given two days to prove her supernatural

42

powers. At the Greek camp the Doctor decides his attack on Troy will be with a huge wooden horse. They wheel it into the city and the Greeks emerge from inside the horse, open the gates and take the city. Steven clashes swords with a Trojan warrior and is injured. Vicki, who has fallen in love with Troilus, is torn between taking him to safety and joining the Trojans. She finally asks Katarina to take the nearly unconscious Steven back to the TARDIS, while she remains with Troilus.

Novelisation: *Doctor Who – The Myth Makers* by Donald Cotton (0 426 20170 1) first published by W H Allen (now Virgin Publishing Ltd) in 1985 with cover by Andrew Skilleter. Target library number 97.

(V) **THE DALEKS' MASTER PLAN**
(12 episodes)
13 November 1965 to 29 January 1966

1. THE NIGHTMARE BEGINS
2. DAY OF ARMAGEDDON
3. DEVIL'S PLANET
4. THE TRAITORS
5. COUNTER PLOT
6. CORONAS OF THE SUN

7. THE FEAST OF STEVEN
8. VOLCANO
9. GOLDEN DEATH
10. ESCAPE SWITCH
11. THE ABANDONED PLANET
12. DESTRUCTION OF TIME

Writers:
Terry Nation
(episodes 1–5, 7)
Dennis Spooner
(episodes 6, 8–12)

Director:
Douglas Camfield

Regular cast: see U above, and introducing Jean Marsh (Sara Kingdom).

Cast: Brian Cant (Kert Gantry); Nicholas Courtney (Bret Vyon); Pamela Greer (Lizan); Philip Anthony (Roald); Kevin Stoney (Mavic Chen); Michael Guest (Interviewer); Julian Sherrier

43

(Zephon); Roy Evans (Trantis); Douglas Sheldon (Kirksen); Dallas Cavell (Bors); Geoffrey Cheshire (Garge); Maurice Browning (Karlton); Jack Pitt (Gearon); Roger Avon (Daxtar); James Hall (Borkar); Bill Meilen (Froyn); John Herrington (Rhynmal); Terence Woodfield (Celation); Peter Butterworth (Monk); Roger Brierley (Trevor); Bruce Wightman (Scott); Jeffrey Isaac (Khepren); Derek Ware (Tuthmos); Walter Randall (Hyksos), Bryan Mosley (Malpha); Robert Jewell, Kevin Manser, Gerald Taylor, John Scott Martin (Daleks); Peter Hawkins, David Graham (Dalek voices).

Episode 7 is a Christmas story, falling in the middle of the main plot and features: Clifford Earl (Sergeant); Norman Mitchell, Malcolm Rogers (Policemen); Kenneth Thornett (Inspector); Reg Pritchard (Man in mackintosh); Sheila Dunn (Blossom Lefavre); Leonard Grahame (Darcy Tranton); Royston Tickner (Steinberger P. Green); Mark Ross (Ingmar Knopf); Conrad Monk (Assistant Director); David James (Arab Sheik); Paula Topham (Vamp); Robert G. Jewell (Clown); Albert Barrington (Professor Webster); Buddy Windrush (Prop Man); Steven Machin, Jack le White (Cameramen); Paul Sarony, Malcolm Leopold (Keystone Cops); Harry Davies (Make-up Man); William Hall (Cowboy); Jean Pastell (Saloon Girl); M. J. Matthews (Chaplin).

Story: Many months after the death of Cory (see story T/A), the Doctor lands on Kembel and finds a new expedition from Earth led by Space Special Security Agent Bret Vyon. The Doctor finds Cory's tape and he and Vyon decide to warn Earth of the impending Dalek attack. The year is AD 4000 and Mavic Chen, Guardian of the Solar System, has just betrayed Earth by giving to the Daleks the taranium element which will enable them to power their supreme weapon: the Time Destructor. The Doctor and his friends steal the taranium element but are unable to alert Earth as Chen has them branded as traitors. In the course of their escape from the Daleks Katarina sacrifices herself to save the Doctor from Kirksen, a psychopathic criminal. Bret Vyon is killed by his sister Sara Kingdom, who subsequently finds out

44

the truth and helps the Doctor. After a chase through Time and Space the TARDIS lands on the volcanic planet Tigus, where the Doctor meets his old enemy, the Meddling Monk, who betrays him to the Daleks. The next stop is Ancient Egypt where Mavic Chen blackmails the Doctor into surrendering the taranium core. The Monk flees in his TARDIS but becomes stranded on an ice world because the Doctor stole his directional unit. Back on Kembel, the Daleks exterminate Chen. The Doctor activates the Time Destructor which destroys the Daleks, but Sara begins aging rapidly and dies.

This was the longest *Doctor Who* story ever until *Trial of a Time Lord*. Nicholas Courtney, who plays Space Agent Bret Vyon, later appeared in a part for which he is better known, Brigadier Lethbridge-Stewart of UNIT. Two companions, Katarina and Sara, are also killed in this story.

Novelisation: *Doctor Who – Mission to the Unknown (The Daleks' Master Plan I)* by John Peel (0 426 20343 7) first published by W H Allen (now Virgin Publishing Ltd) in 1989 with cover by Alister Pearson. Target library number 141. *Doctor Who – The Mutation of Time (The Daleks' Master Plan II)* by John Peel (0 426 20344 5) first published by W H Allen (now Virgin Publishing Ltd) in 1989 with cover by Alister Pearson. Target library number 142.

Video tape: 'Counter Plot' and 'Escape Switch' included on *Daleks – The Early Years* (BBCV 4810) first released in 1992 with photomontage cover.

(W) THE MASSACRE

(4 episodes)

5 February 1966 to 26 February 1966

1. WAR OF GOD	3. PRIEST OF DEATH
2. THE SEA BEGGAR	4. BELL OF DOOM

Writer:
John Lucarotti
(episode 4 co-written with
Donald Tosh)

Director:
Paddy Russell

Regular cast: William Hartnell (the Doctor), Peter Purves (Steven Taylor), and introducing Jackie Lane (Dodo Chaplet) in the last episode.

Cast: Eric Thompson (Gaston); David Weston (Nicholas); John Tillinger (Simon); Edwin Fenn (Landlord); Christopher Tranchell (Roger); Erik Chitty (Preslin); Annette Robertson (Anne Chaplet); Clive Cazes (Captain); Reginald Jessup (Servant); William Hartnell (Abbot of Amboise); Andre Morell (Tavannes); Leonard Sachs (Admiral de Coligny); Cynthia Etherington (Old Lady); Barry Justice (Charles IX); Joan Young (Catherine de Medici); Michael Bilton (Toligny); Norman Claridge (Priest); Roy Denton, Ernest Smith, Will Stampe (Men); John Slavid (Officer); Jack Tarran, Leslic Bates (Guards); Juba Kennelly (Old Man); Hugh Cecil (Priest); George Romane (Usher).

Story: It is Paris, just before the St Bartholomew's Day Massacre in 1572, and the Catholic Queen Mother, Catherine de Medici, is planning to murder all French Protestants. The Doctor disappears to visit Charles Preslin while Steven meets some Huguenots from the Protestant Admiral de Coligny's household. Steven rescues a servant girl, Anne Chaplet, who has overheard the planning of the massacre. Later the Catholic Abbot of Amboise arrives at the Admiral's house. He is the

Doctor's double. Steven believes he is the Doctor and follows him and overhears the plan to kill de Coligny. The attempt fails and Tavannes blames the Abbot for this failure and orders his execution. The Doctor returns from his visit, and he and Steven escape Paris as the massacre begins. In the last four minutes the TARDIS stops in Wimbledon and picks up a young passenger, Dodo Chaplet.

Gerry Davis took over as Script Editor on episode 4.

Novelisation: *Doctor Who – The Massacre* by John Lucarotti (0 426 20297 X) first published by W H Allen (now Virgin Publishing Ltd) in 1987 with cover by Tony Masero. New edition in 1992 with cover by Alister Pearson. Target library number 122.

Script Editor:
Gerry Davis

(X) **THE ARK**
(4 episodes)
5 March 1966 to 26 March 1966

1. THE STEEL SKY	3. THE RETURN
2. THE PLAGUE	4. THE BOMB

Writers:
Paul Erickson,
Lesley Scott

Director:
Michael Imison

Regular cast: see W above

Cast: Eric Elliott (Commander); Inigo Jackson (Zentos); Roy Spencer (Manyak); Kate Newman (Mellium); Michael Sheard (Rhos); Ian Frost (Baccu); Edmund Coulter, Frank George (Monoids); Ralph Carrigan (Monoid Two); Terence Bayler

(Yendom); Edmund Coulter (Monoid One); Frank George (Monoid Three); John Caesar (Monoid Four); John Halstead, Roy Skelton (Monoid Voices); Stephanie Heesom, Paul Greenhalgh (Guardians); Terence Woodfield (Maharis); Brian Wright (Dassuk); Eileen Helsby (Venussa); Richard Beale (Refusian voice).

Story: The Earth is about to plunge into the Sun. All Earth life is on a huge Ark on a 700-year journey to a new planet, Refusis. Dodo has a cold, against which Steven, the Human Guardians of the Ark and the slave race called Monoids have no immunity. The Doctor eventually finds a cure, and the travellers take off. In Episodes 3 and 4 the TARDIS lands on the Ark 700 years later – at the end of the voyage to Refusis. As a result of another bout of the cold, the Monoids are strong and have made the Guardians their slaves. With the help of the invisible Refusians, the Doctor forces the Monoids and the Guardians to make peace and live together on Refusis.

Novelisation: *Doctor Who – The Ark* by Paul Erickson (0 426 20253 8) first published by W H Allen (now Virgin Publishing Ltd) in 1986 with cover by David McAllister. New edition in 1992 with cover by Alister Pearson. Target library number 114.

Producer:
Innes Lloyd

(Y) THE CELESTIAL TOYMAKER
(4 episodes)
2 April 1966 to 23 April 1966

1. THE CELESTIAL TOYROOM
2. THE HALL OF DOLLS

3. THE DANCING FLOOR
4. THE FINAL TEST

Writer:
Brian Hayles (with Gerry
Davis and Donald Tosh,
uncredited)

Director:
Bill Sellars

Regular cast: see W above

Cast: Michael Gough (Toymaker); Campbell Singer (Joey the
Clown, Sgt. Rugg, King of Hearts); Carmen Silvera (Clara the
Clown, Mrs. Wiggs, Queen of Hearts); Peter Stephens (Knave
of Hearts, Kitchen boy, Cyril); Reg Lever (Joker); Beryl
Braham, Ann Harrison, Delia Lindon (Dancing Dolls).

Story: The TARDIS materialises in the domain of the Celestial
Toymaker, an evil force who dominates a fantasy world. He is
a happy-looking mandarin character dressed in a splendid
bejewelled coat. He makes the TARDIS intangible to the
travellers and 'invites' them to play games with him. The
Doctor has to play the complex Trilogic Game while Steven
and Dodo are set a series of puzzles, which if they lose will
render them subjects of the Toymaker. They play Blind Man's
Buff – and win. Then they meet the Hearts family and play a
macabre game of Musical Chairs. Then, it's Hunt the Key in the
kitchen and, after that, they find themselves trying to reach the
end of a ballroom dodging dancing dolls. Their last opponent
is the obnoxious schoolboy, Cyril. With him, they play a death-
trap dice game across electrified triangles, but manage to reach
'home' first. The Doctor triumphs over the Toymaker by
imitating the magician's voice – and the travellers are on their
way once again.

Novelisation: *Doctor Who – The Celestial Toymaker* by Gerry
Davis and Alison Bingeman (0 426 20251 1) first published by
W H Allen (now Virgin Publishing Ltd) in 1986 with cover by
Graham Potts. New edition in 1992 with cover by Alister
Pearson. Target library number 111.

Video tape: 'The Final Test' included on *The Hartnell Years* (BBCV 4608) first released in 1991 with photomontage cover.

(Z) **THE GUNFIGHTERS**
(4 episodes)
30 April 1966 to 21 May 1966

1. A HOLIDAY FOR THE DOCTOR
2. DON'T SHOOT THE PIANIST

3. JOHNNY RINGO
4. THE OK CORRAL

Writer:
Donald Cotton

Director:
Rex Tucker

Regular cast: see W above

Cast: William Hurndell (Ike Clanton); Maurice Good (Phineas Clanton); David Cole (Billy Clanton); Sheena Marshe (Kate); Shane Rimmer (Seth Harper); David Graham (Charlie); John Alderson (Wyatt Earp); Anthony Jacobs (Doc Holliday); Richard Beale (Bat Masterson); Reed de Rouen (Pa Clanton); Laurence Payne (Johnny Ringo); Martyn Huntley (Warren Earp); Victor Carin (Virgil Earp).

Story: The Doctor, Steven and Dodo arrive in Tombstone on 25 October 1881. The Doctor has toothache and finds the local dentist is none other than the infamous gunslinger, Doc Holliday, who is feuding with the Clanton family. The Clantons' gunfighter, Harper, nearly shoots the Doctor by mistake. Marshal Wyatt Earp arrests the Doctor and rescues Steven from lynching. Pa Clanton hires gunfighter Johnny Ringo, but Earp wins the famous shoot-out at the OK corral.

This is the last story in which episodes have individual titles. *The Ballad of the Last Chance Saloon*, written by Tristram Cary and Donald Cotton, was sung by Lynda Baron.

Novelisation: *Doctor Who – The Gunfighters* by Donald

Cotton (0 426 20195 7) first published by W H Allen (now Virgin Publishing Ltd) in 1985 with cover by Andrew Skilleter. Target library number 101.

(AA) THE SAVAGES
(4 episodes)
28 May 1966 to 18 June 1966

Writer:
Ian Stuart Black

Director:
Christopher Barry

Regular cast: see W above

Cast: Ewen Solon (Chal); Patrick Godfrey (Tor); Peter Thomas (Edal); Geoffrey Frederick (Exorse); Frederick Jaeger (Jano); Robert Sidaway (Avon); Kay Patrick (Flower); Clare Jenkins (Nanina); Norman Henry (Senta); Edward Caddick (Wylda); Andrew Lodge, Christopher Denham, Tony Holland (Assistants), John Dillon, John Raven (Savages); Tim Goodman (Guard).

Story: On a distant planet live the ultra-civilised Elders and the wild primitive Savages. The TARDIS crew are escorted to the Elders' capital to meet Jano, leader of the City. Steven and Dodo are taken on a conducted tour. Inevitably the curious Dodo takes a detour, and finds herself in a strange laboratory presided over by Senta. When Dodo is back with the Doctor the truth suddenly dawns: The Elders' advanced civilisation has been formed by transferring the life force and energy of the Savages to the Elders. The Doctor finds this hard to believe but then his own life force is tranferred to Jano. This means that Jano adopts some of the Doctor's attitudes – and conscience. With a new sense of justice Jano goes out into the Savages' wilderness and recruits them to destroy the transference laboratory. The Elders and the Savages choose Steven to be their leader; Dodo and the Doctor leave him to his task.

5 1

Novelisation: *Doctor Who – The Savages* by Ian Stuart Black (0 426 20230 9) first published by W H Allen (now Virgin Publishing Ltd) in 1986 with cover by David McAllister. New edition in 1992 with cover by Alister Pearson. Target library number 109.

(BB) **THE WAR MACHINES**
(4 episodes)
25 June 1966 to 16 July 1966

Writer:
Ian Stuart Black
(with Kit Pedler and
Pat Dunlop, uncredited)

Director:
Michael Ferguson

Regular cast: William Hartnell (the Doctor); Jackie Lane (Dodo), and introducing Anneke Wills (Polly Lopez) and Michael Craze (Ben Jackson).

Cast: Alan Curtis (Major Green); John Harvey (Professor Brett); Sandra Bryant (Kitty); Ewan Proctor (Flash); William Mervyn (Sir Charles Summer); John Cater (Professor Krimpton); Ric Felgate (American Journalist); John Doye (Interviewer); Desmond Cullum-Jones (Worker); Roy Godfrey (Tramp); Gerald Taylor (War Machine Operator/Voice of WOTAN); John Rolfe (Captain); John Boyd-Brent (Sergeant); Frank Jarvis (Corporal); Robin Dawson (Soldier); Kenneth Kendall (Himself); George Cross (Minister); Edward Colliver (Mechanic); John Slavid (Man in phone box); Dwight Whylie (Announcer); Carl Conway (U.S. Correspondent); Michael Rathborne (Taxi Driver); Eddie Davis (Worker).

Story: In London's Post Office Tower the travellers find Professor Brett and his revolutionary computer called WOTAN – Will Operating Thought Analogue device – a universal problem-solver that can think for itself. Suddenly the machine reverses its process and starts to take over men, beginning with Brett. WOTAN programmes them to build War Machines, self-contained mobile computers, to prepare for the takeover of Earth. Ben, a young merchant seaman who has befriended Dodo, and Brett's secretary, Polly, are captured, but Ben escapes and warns civil servant Sir Charles Summer. Troops are powerless against the War Machines but by using a series of magnetic force fields the Doctor captures one and reprogrammes it to destroy WOTAN. Dodo decides to stay in England but Ben and Polly accompany the Doctor in the TARDIS . . .

Wotan identifies the Doctor as 'Doctor Who'.

Novelisation: *Doctor Who – The War Machines* by Ian Stuart Black (0 426 20328 3) first published by W H Allen (now Virgin Publishing Ltd) in 1989 with cover by Alister Pearson and Graeme Way. Target library number 136.

Fourth Season

Producer:
Innes Lloyd

Script Editor:
Gerry Davis

(CC) **THE SMUGGLERS**
(4 episodes)
10 September 1966 to 1 October 1966

Writer:
Brian Hayles

Director:
Julia Smith

Regular cast: William Hartnell (the Doctor); Anneke Wills (Polly); Michael Craze (Ben Jackson).

Cast: Terence de Marney (Churchwarden); George A. Cooper

(Cherub); David Blake Kelly (Jacob Kewper); Mike Lucas (Tom); Paul Whitsun-Jones (Squire); Derek Ware (Spaniard); Michael Godfrey (Pike); Elroy Josephs (Jamaica); John Ringham (Blake); Jack Bligh (Gaptooth).

Story: The TARDIS materialises on a wild and remote part of 17th-century Cornish coast. Pirates are searching for treasure, while smugglers (who include the local squire) are trying to sell contraband. The Doctor unwittingly receives a clue to the treasure's whereabouts from the churchwarden – just before a pirate murders him. The pirates try to extract the information from the TARDIS crew, who are rescued by the militia.

Novelisation: *Doctor Who – The Smugglers* by Terrance Dicks (0 426 20328 3) first published by W H Allen (now Virgin Publishing Ltd) in 1988 with cover by Alister Pearson. Target library number 133.

(DD) **THE TENTH PLANET**
(4 episodes)
8 October 1966 to 29 October 1966

Writer:
Kit Pedler
(with Pat Dunlop and
Gerry Davis, uncredited)

Director:
Derek Martinus

Regular cast: see CC above

Cast: Robert Beatty (General Cutler); Dudley Jones (Dyson); David Dodimead (Barclay); Alan White (Schultz); Earl Cameron (Williams); Shane Shelton (Tito); John Brandon (Sergeant); Steve Plytas (Wigner); Christopher Matthews (Radar technician); Ellen Cullen (Technician); Glenn Beck (Announcer); Callen Angelo (Terry Cutler); Christopher Dunham, Nicholas Edwards (R/T Technicians); Harry Brooks (Krang, Talon);

Reg Whitehead (Jarl, Krail); Gregg Palmer (Gern, Shav); Peter Hawkins, Roy Skelton (Cyberman voices); Bruce Wells, John Haines, John Knott (Cybermen); Sheila Knight (Secretary); Alec Coleman (Corporal).

Story: In the late 1980s the TARDIS lands at a South Pole Space Tracking Station, where General Cutler battles with invaders from the Tenth Planet, Mondas – Earth's missing sister planet – which is draining away Earth's energy. The planet's inhabitants, called Cybermen, are ruthless and logical; their original bodies have been replaced with plastic to make them invulnerable and immune to disease. The Cybermen take control of Earth; they plan to use the powerful Z-Bomb at the South Pole base to destroy Earth before it destroys Mondas. They want to take Earth people to Mondas to turn them into Cybermen. Ben outwits them and before the Cybermen can again infiltrate the base Mondas absorbs too much energy and is destroyed. Without energy from Mondas to sustain them the Cybermen die. Worn out by the strain of recent events the Doctor seems to grow very old and when he returns to the TARDIS he collapses on the floor and begins to change . . .

This marks the first appearance of the Cybermen, and it is also the first regeneration story.

Novelisation: *Doctor Who – The Tenth Planet* by Gerry Davis (0 426 11068 4) first published by Tandem (became W H Allen) as *Doctor Who and the Tenth Planet* in 1976 with cover by Chris Achilleos. New edition in 1993 by Virgin Publishing Ltd with cover by Alister Pearson. Target library number 62.

SECOND DOCTOR

PATRICK TROUGHTON
1966 – 1969

Fourth Season (continued)

Producer:
Innes Lloyd

Script Editor:
Gerry Davis

(EE) **THE POWER OF THE DALEKS**
(6 episodes)
5 November 1966 to 10 December 1966

Writer:
David Whitaker
(with Dennis Spooner,
uncredited)

Director:
Christopher Barry

Regular cast: Patrick Troughton (the Doctor); Anneke Wills (Polly); Michael Craze (Ben Jackson).

Cast: Martin King (Examiner); Nicholas Hawtrey (Quinn); Bernard Archard (Bragen); Robert James (Lesterson); Pamela Ann Davy (Janley); Peter Bathurst (Hensell); Edward Kelsey (Resno); Richard Kane (Valmar); Peter Forbes-Robertson (Guard); Steven Scott (Kebble); Robert Russell, Robert Luckham (Guards); Gerald Taylor, Kevin Manser, Robert Jewell, John Scott Martin (Daleks); Peter Hawkins (Dalek voice).

Story: The Doctor makes a complete recovery; a new personality seems to inhabit his totally new physical form. The

TARDIS materialises on the Earth colony Vulcan in AD 2020. In a space rocket rescued from the Mercury Swamp the Doctor finds two inanimate Daleks. Lesterson, Chief Scientist of the colony, has removed one, reactivated it, and plans to use the Daleks as servants, but rebels trying to overthrow the colony's Governor decide to use them for their own ends. In fact the colony has already been infiltrated by Daleks, who have secretly set up a reproduction plant – on a conveyor-belt system – and plan to exterminate all Humans. But the Doctor finds their power source and turns it against them.

Novelisation: *Doctor Who – The Power of the Daleks* by John Peel (0 426 20390 9) first published by Virgin Publishing Ltd in 1993 with cover by Alister Pearson. Target library number 154.

Script Book: *Doctor Who – The Power of the Daleks* by David Whitaker (1 85286 327 7) first published by Titan Books in 1993 with cover by Alister Pearson.

Audio tape: *The Power of the Daleks* (catalogue number: ZBBC 1433, ISBN: 0563 40695 X) first released in 1993 with photomontage cover.

(FF) **THE HIGHLANDERS**
(4 episodes)
17 December 1966 to 7 January 1967

Writers:
Gerry Davis, Elwyn Jones

Director:
Hugh David

Regular cast: see EE above, and introducing Frazer Hines (Jamie McCrimmon).

Cast: William Dysart (Alexander); Donald Bisset (Colin McLaren); Hannah Gordon (Kirsty); Michael Elwyn (Ffinch);

Peter Welch (Sergeant); David Garth (Gray); Sydney Arnold (Perkins); Tom Bowman (Sentry); Dallas Cavell (Trask); Barbara Bruce (Mollie); Andrew Downie (MacKay); Peter Diamond (Sailor); Guy Middleton (Attwood); Eric Mills (Wounded Highlander); Nancy Gabriel (Woman at inn); Reg Dent (English horseman).

Story: The TARDIS lands on a Scottish moor in 1746 near the battlefield of Culloden, which has just seen the English defeat of the Scots and Bonnie Prince Charlie. The Doctor and his friends come across a group of hunted Highlanders led by clan laird Colin McLaren, accompanied by his daughter Kirsty and faithful piper Jamie McCrimmon. The Highlanders and the time-travellers are captured by English Lieutenant Algernon Ffinch. At the English camp a crooked solicitor named Gray is working on a scheme to transport prisoners to slavery in the West Indies. The Doctor escapes and gets arms to the Scottish prisoners, who are being held aboard a stolen ship. Gray and the Captain are overpowered and the ship returned to its owner, who takes the Scots to safety in France. The TARDIS dematerialises with an extra passenger – Jamie!

This was the last of the purely historical *Doctor Who* stories until *Black Orchid* (6A) in 1982.

Novelisation: *Doctor Who – The Highlanders* by Gerry Davis (0 426 19676 7) first published by W H Allen (now Virgin Publishing Ltd) in 1984 with cover by Nick Spender. Target library number 90.

(GG) **THE UNDERWATER MENACE**
(4 episodes)
14 January 1967 to 4 February 1967

Writer:
Geoffrey Orme

Director:
Julia Smith

Regular cast: see FF above

Cast: Joseph Furst (Professor Zaroff); Catherine Howe (Ara);
Tom Watson (Ramo); Peter Stephens (Lolem); Colin Jeavons
(Damon); Gerald Taylor (Damon's Assistant); Graham Ashley
(Overseer); Tony Handy, Alex Donald, Tony Douglas (Guards);
Paul Anil (Jacko); P. G. Stephens (Sean); Noel Johnson (Thous);
Roma Woodnutt (Nola); Bill Burridge (Executioner Priest);
Jimmy Mack (Refugee Priest).

Story: The TARDIS lands on an extinct volcanic rock sur-
rounded by sea. On leaving the ship the Doctor and his companions are kidnapped by the primitive Atlanteans and taken below
the sea to the city of Atlantis. There its inhabitants plan to
sacrifice the travellers to their Goddess Amdo, by suspending
them over a pool of hungry sharks. They are rescued by the
scientist Zaroff, who has a plan to destroy the world by draining
the ocean into its white hot core – so the super-heated steam will
explode the planet in two. Zaroff takes the Doctor with him,
sends Ben and Jamie to the mines, and orders that Polly undergo
an operation to become a fishworker, collecting food from the
sea. The TARDIS crew escape and persuade the fishmen to
revolt but Zaroff is unperturbed; he is confident that within 12
hours the world will be destroyed. He becomes the victim of his
own scheme when the Doctor enters the generating plant and
accelerates the fission to break down the sea walls. Zaroff is
drowned by the flood waters; the others escape.

Novelisation: *Doctor Who – The Underwater Menace* by Nigel
Robinson (0 426 20326 7) first published by W H Allen (now
Virgin Publishing Ltd) in 1988 with cover by Alister Pearson.
Target library number 129.

(HH) **THE MOONBASE**
(4 episodes)
11 February 1967 to 4 March 1967

Writer:
Kit Pedler (with Gerry
Davis, uncredited)

Director:
Morris Barry

Regular cast: see FF above

Cast: Patrick Barr (Hobson); Andre Maranne (Benoit); Michael
Wolf (Nils); John Rolfe (Sam); Alan Rowe (Dr Evans; Space
Control voice); Mark Heath (Ralph); Barry Ashton, Derek
Calder, Arnold Chazen, Leon Maybank, Victor Pemberton,
Edward Phillips, Ron Pinnell, Robin Scott, Alan Wells (Crew);
John Wills, Peter Greene, Reg Whitehead, Keith Goodman,
Sonnie Willis, Ronald Lee, John Clifford, Barry Noble
(Cybermen); Peter Hawkins (Cyberman voice); Denis McCarthy
(Controller Rinberg's voice).

Story: In the year 2070 Hobson and his deputy Benoit command a weather station on the Moon. There they operate the
Gravitron, a gravity machine which has control over the weather
on Earth. When the Doctor arrives he finds that a mysterious
disease has broken out. He investigates and, to add to a number
of other problems – like strange kidnappings and the Gravitron
losing coordination – discovers that the Cybermen have landed.
They are in fact responsible for the disease, and for the
Gravitron's peculiar behaviour. They plan to take control of the
kidnapped men and force them to operate the Gravitron to
destroy Earth by drastically altering its weather. Polly fights
back by spraying the Cybermen with plastic solvents but the main
enemy force is rapidly approaching. Suddenly the Doctor realises
that the Cybermen are susceptible to gravity variations – that is
why they need humans to operate the Gravitron – so by deflecting
the machine's action onto the Moon's surface he sends the
Cybermen and their ships shooting off into distant Space.

Novelisation: *Doctor Who and the Cybermen* by Gerry Davis (0 426 11463 9) first published by Universal-Tandem in 1975 with cover by Chris Achilleos. New edition by W H Allen (now Virgin Publishing Ltd) in 1981 with cover by Bill Donahoe. Target library number 14.

Video tape: Episodes 2 and 4 included on *Cybermen – The Early Years* (BBCV 4813) first released in 1992 with photomontage cover.

(JJ) **THE MACRA TERROR**
(4 episodes)
11 March 1967 to 1 April 1967

Writer:
Ian Stuart Black

Director:
John Davies

Regular cast: see FF above

Cast: Peter Jeffrey (Pilot); Graham Armitage (Barney); Ian Fairbairn (Questa); Jane Enshawe (Sunnae); Sandra Bryant, Karol Keyes (Chicki); Maureen Lane (Majorette); Terence Lodge (Medok); Gertan Klauber (Ola); Graham Leaman (Controller); Anthony Gardner (Alvis); Denis Goacher (Control voice); Richard Beale (Broadcast voice); Robert Jewell (Macra); John Harvey (Official); John Caesar, Steve Emerson, Danny Rae (Guards); Roger Jerome, Terry Wright, Ralph Carrigan (Cheerleaders); Linda Reynolds (Pilot's secretary); Paul Phillips (Scientist); Nina Huby (Girl).

Story: The Doctor and his friends find themselves in the future on a planet run like a gigantic holiday camp. A man called Medok tells the Doctor it is being secretly infiltrated at night by crab-like creatures called Macra. The Macra are in fact in control of this 'paradise' and have conditioned the workers to quarry the deadly gas the Macra need to survive. The Doctor takes control of the gas-pumping machine and stops the Macra's vital supply. Ben clinches the victory and frees the colony by blowing up the gas pumps.

Novelisation: *Doctor Who – The Macra Terror* by Ian Stuart Black (0 426 20307 0) first published by W H Allen (now Virgin Publishing Ltd) in 1987 with cover by Tony Masero. Target library number 123.

Audio tape: *The Macra Terror* (catalogue number: ZBBC 1342, ISBN: 0563 366826) first released in 1992 with photo-montage cover.

Producers:
Innes Lloyd, Peter Bryant

(KK) THE FACELESS ONES
(6 episodes)
8 April 1967 to 13 May 1967

Writers:
David Ellis, Malcolm Hulke

Director:
Gerry Mill

Regular cast: see FF above

Cast: James Appleby (Policeman); Colin Gordon (Commandant); George Selway (Meadows); Wanda Ventham (Jean Rock); Victor Winding (Spencer); Peter Whitaker (Gascoigne); Donald Pickering (Blade); Christopher Tranchell (Jenkins); Madalena Nicol (Pinto); Bernard Kay (Crossland); Pauline Collins (Samantha Briggs); Gilly Fraser (Ann Davidson); Brigit Paul (Announcer); Barry Wilsher (Heslington); Michael Ladkin (Pilot); Leonard Trolley (Reynolds); Robin Dawson, Barry du Pre, Pat Leclere, Roy Pearce (Chameleons).

Story: It is Gatwick Airport in 1966 and the TARDIS materialises on the runway in front of an incoming jet. While Polly hides in a hangar she is witness to the murder of a detective. Then Polly and Ben are kidnapped and the Doctor discovers others have disappeared – all passengers on Chameleon Tours charter nights. The kidnappers are the Chameleons, a race from another planet who have lost their identities and faces in a nuclear explosion and are dying out. Their scientists have devised a method for taking over the identity of Humans, the transfer process taking four weeks. The Chameleons have lured onto aircraft and then miniaturised 50,000 passengers, now held on a space station hundreds of miles above the Earth. The Doctor succeeds in freeing the captives and in aiding the Chameleons to survive. Ben and Polly decide to remain in the England of 1966.

Novelisation: *Doctor Who – The Faceless Ones* by Terrance Dicks (0 426 20294 5) first published by W H Allen (now Virgin Publishing Ltd) in 1986 with cover by Tony Masero. Target library number 116.

Producer:
Innes Lloyd

Script Editors:
Gerry Davis, Peter Bryant

(LL) THE EVIL OF THE DALEKS
(7 episodes)
20 May 1967 to I July 1967

Writer:
David Whitaker

Director:
Derek Martinus

Regular cast: Patrick Troughton (the Doctor); Frazer Hines (Jamie); and introducing Deborah Watling (Victoria Waterfield).

Cast: Alec Ross (Bob Hall); Griffith Davies (Kennedy); John

Bailey (Edward Waterfield); Geoffrey Colville (Perry); Robert Jewell, Gerald Taylor, Ken Tyllson, John Scott Martin (Daleks); Murphy Grumbar (Emperor Dalek); Roy Skelton, Peter Hawkins (Dalek voices); Jo Rowbottom (Mollie Dawson); Marius Goring (Theodore Maxtible); Brigit Forsyth (Ruth Maxtible); Windsor Davies (Toby); Gary Watson (Terrall); Sonny Caldinez (Kemel).

Story: The TARDIS is stolen from Gatwick Airport and driven off in a lorry. The Doctor and Jamie follow it to a Victoriana antique shop owned by Edward Waterfield. All three are transported back 100 years to the home of scientist Theodore Maxtible, who, with Waterfield's help, has devised a method of time-travel involving mirrors, static electricity – and the Daleks! The Daleks are holding Waterfield's daughter, Victoria, hostage so he is obliged to cooperate in their plan to bring the Doctor back to 1866. The Daleks want to acquire what they call 'the Human factor' to create an army of super-Daleks. They force the Doctor to run an experiment on Jamie registering every emotion he shows in his attempts to rescue Victoria. The plan backfires as the three experimental Daleks adopt attitudes of playful friendliness instead of Human cunning. All are recalled to Skaro where the Emperor Dalek reveals the true purpose of the experiment. He now plans to inject the Doctor with the 'Dalek factor' which he will take back to Earth, and turn its inhabitants into Dalek-like creatures with the impulse to destroy. The Doctor is passed through a machine for transforming Humans into mental Daleks – but remains unaffected, for he is not Human. Instead, he manages to humanise some of the Daleks. Soon civil war erupts on Skaro between humanised Daleks and real Daleks. Maxtible, mentally turned into a Dalek-like creature, is killed; Victoria's father saves the Doctor at the cost of his own life. The travellers depart whilst the war rages on . . .

This was the last Dalek story until *Day of the Daleks* (KKK) in 1972.

Novelisation: *Doctor Who – The Evil of the Daleks* by John Peel (0 426 20389 5) first published by Virgin Publishing Ltd in 1993 with cover by Alister Pearson. Target library number 155.

Video tape: Episode 2 included on *Daleks – The Early Years* (BBCV 4810) first released in 1992 with photomontage cover.

Audio tape: *The Evil of the Daleks* (catalogue number: ZBBC 1303, ISBN: 0563 366834) first released in 1992 with photomontage cover.

Fifth Season

Producer:
Peter Bryant

Script Editor:
Victor Pemberton

(MM) THE TOMB OF THE CYBERMEN
(4 episodes)
2 September 1967 to 23 September 1967

Writers:
Kit Pedler, Gerry Davis

Director:
Morris Barry

Regular cast: Patrick Troughton (the Doctor); Frazer Hines (Jamie); Deborah Watling (Victoria Waterfield).

Cast: Roy Stewart (Toberman); Aubrey Richards (Professor Parry); Cyril Shaps (Viner); Clive Merrison (Callum); Shirley Cooklin (Kaftan); George Roubicek (Hopper); George Pastell (Klieg); Alan Johns (Rogers); Bernard Holley (Haydon); Ray Grover (Crewman); Michael Kilgarriff (Cybercontroller); Hans De Vries, Tony Harwood, John Hogan, Richard Kerley, Ronald

Lee, Charles Pemberton, Kenneth Seeger, Reg Whitehead (Cybermen); Peter Hawkins (Cybermen voices).

Story: The TARDIS rematerialises in the future on the planet Telos where the time-travellers meet an Earth archaeological expedition led by Prof. Parry but financed by Kaftan and Klieg from the Brotherhood of Logicians. They are excavating a tomb where the last Cybermen are rumoured to have been buried. The deranged Klieg, who seeks allies in his plans for world domination, revives the Cybermen. But the tombs are a trap meant to provide the Cybermen with victims to convert into Cybermen. The party escapes, but the Cybermen retaliate by sending after them Cybermats, little metallic creatures capable of homing in on brain waves. The Doctor jams the Cybermats. Kaftan and Klieg attempt to force the Cybermen to help them, but are killed. Toberman, Kaftan's giant servant whose arms have been converted, destroys the Cybercontroller, enabling the humans to escape again. The Cybermen are refrozen by the Doctor.

The events in this story and in *The Tenth Planet* (DD) were to be re-examined in *Attack of the Cybermen* (6T) in 1985.

Novelisation: *Doctor Who – The Tomb of the Cybermen* by Gerry Davis (0 426 11076 5) first published by W H Allen (now Virgin Publishing Ltd) in 1978 as *Doctor Who and the Tomb of the Cybermen* with cover by Jeff Cummins. New edition in 1992 with cover by Alister Pearson. Target library number 66.

Script book: *Doctor Who – The Tomb of the Cybermen* by Gerry Davis and Kit Pedlar* (1 85286 146 0) first published by Titan Books in 1989 with cover by Tony Clark.

Video tape: *The Tomb of the Cybermen* (BBCV 4772) first released in 1992 with cover by Alister Pearson.

* The correct spelling of this name is Pedler.

Audio tape: *The Tomb of the Cybermen* (catalogue number: ZBBC 1343, ISBN: 0563 401478) first released in 1993 with photomontage cover.

Producer:
Innes Lloyd

Script Editor:
Peter Bryant

(NN) **THE ABOMINABLE SNOWMEN**
(6 episodes)
30 September 1967 to 4 November 1967

Writers:
Mervyn Haisman,
Henry Lincoln

Director:
Gerald Blake

Regular cast: see MM above

Cast: Jack Watling (Professor Travers); Norman Jones (Khrisong); David Spenser (Thonmi); David Grey (Rinchen); Raymond Llewellyn (Sapan); Charles Morgan (Songsten); Wolfe Morris (Padmasambhava); David Baron (Ralpachan); Reg Whitehead, Tony Harwood, Richard Kerley, John Hogan (Yeti).

Story: Explorer Travers is in the Himalayas searching for the Yeti when his companion is killed. Travers accuses the Doctor, whose TARDIS rematerialised nearby, of his friend's murder. It appears, however, that the Yeti are fur-covered robots directed by the evil Great Intelligence, a cosmic entity who now possesses the body of the High Lama Padmasambhava, an old friend of the Doctor. The Doctor finds a way to immobilise the Yeti and defeats the Great Intelligence. Travers finally discovers a real Yeti – a shy and harmless creature!

Novelisation: *Doctor Who and the Abominable Snowmen* by

Terrance Dicks (0 426 11455 8) first published by Universal-Tandem in 1974 with cover by Chris Achilleos. New edition by W H Allen (now Virgin Publishing Ltd) in 1983 with cover by Andrew Skilleter. Target library number 1.

Video tape: Episode 2 included on *The Troughton Years* (BBCV 4609) first released in 1991 with photomontage cover.

(OO) THE ICE WARRIORS
(6 episodes)
11 November 1967 to 16 December 1967

Writer:
Brian Hayles

Director:
Derek Martinus

Regular cast: see MM above

Cast: Wendy Gifford (Miss Garrett); Peter Barkworth (Clent); George Waring (Arden); Malcolm Taylor (Walters); Peter Diamond (Davis); Angus Lennie (Storr); Peter Sallis (Penley); Bernard Bresslaw (Varga); Roy Skelton (Computer voice); Roger Jones (Zondal); Sonny Caldinez (Turoc); Tony Harwood (Rintan); Michael Attwell (Isbur).

Story: It is England during the Second Ice Age – AD 3000. The Doctor and his companions seek refuge in a scientific base where the ice barrier is being combated with an ioniser. Embedded in the ice they find a perfectly preserved body: Varga, leader of the Ice Warriors, inhabitants of Mars who visited Earth during its previous Ice Age in prehistoric times. Revived, Varga captures Victoria and frees the rest of his crew from the ice. Learning that Varga plans to conquer the world, the Doctor manages to save Victoria and, taking over the base, uses the ioniser at full strength to blow up the warriors' spacecraft and halt the glacier.

Novelisation: *Doctor Who and the Ice Warriors* by Brian Hayles (0 426 10866 3) first published by Tandem (now Virgin Publishing Ltd) in 1976 with cover by Chris Achilleos. Target library number 33.

(PP) **THE ENEMY OF THE WORLD**
(6 episodes)
23 December 1967 to 27 January 1968

Writer:
David Whitaker

Director:
Barry Letts

Regular cast: see MM above

Cast: Henry Stamper (Anton); Rhys McConnochie (Rod); Simon Cain (Curly); Mary Peach (Astrid); Bill Kerr (Kent); Colin Douglas (Bruce); Milton Johns (Benik); George Pravda (Denes); David Nettheim (Fedorin); Patrick Troughton (Salamander); Carmen Munroe (Fariah); Gordon Faith, Elliott Cairnes (Guard Captains); Bill Lyons (Guard); Reg Lye (Griffin); Andrew Staines (Sergeant); Christopher Burgess (Swann); Adam Verney (Colin); Margaret Hickey (Mary); Dibbs Mather, Bob Anderson, William McGuirk (Guards).

Story: Arriving on an Australian beach, the time-travellers are attacked by a hovercraft, then rescued by a helicopter girl named Astrid. Her boss, Giles Kent, explains that the Doctor is the double of a would-be world dictator, Salamander. Jamie and Victoria infiltrate Salamander's retinue and discover he is the instigator of the 'natural' volcanic disasters sweeping the world. But they are captured and, to organise their rescue, the Doctor must impersonate Salamander. He penetrates the villain's HQ to be confronted by Kent, attempting to seize Salamander's power for himself. Salamander tries to impersonate the Doctor and steal the TARDIS – but he is ejected into space.

Novelisation: *Doctor Who – The Enemy of the World* by Ian Marter (0 426 20126 4) first published by W H Allen (now Virgin Publishing Ltd) in 1981 as *Doctor Who and the Enemy of the World* with cover by Bill Donohoe. New edition in 1993 with cover by Alister Pearson. Target library number 24.

Video tape: Episode 3 included on *The Troughton Years* (BBCV 4609) first released in 1991 with photomontage cover.

Producer:
Peter Bryant

Script Editor:
Derrick Sherwin

(QQ) **THE WEB OF FEAR**
(6 episodes)
3 February 1968 to 9 March 1968

Writers:
Mervyn Haisman,
Henry Lincoln

Director:
Douglas Camfield

Regular cast: see MM above

Guest star: Nicholas Courtney (Colonel Lethbridge-Stewart).

Cast: Jack Watling (Professor Travers); Tina Packer (Anne Travers); Frederick Schrecker (Julius Silverstein); Rod Beacham (Lane); Ralph Watson (Knight); Richardson Morgan (Blake); Jon Rollason (Chorley); Jack Woolgar (Arnold); Stephen Whittaker (Weams); Bernard G. High, Joseph O'Connell (Soldiers); John Levene, John Lord, Gordon Stothard, Colin Warman, Jeremy King, Roger Jacombs (Yeti); Derek Pollitt (Evans); Bert Sims (Newspaper seller).

Story: The TARDIS is immobilised by a mysterious cobweb substance but the time-travellers escape and find themselves on a deserted present-day London underground station. They meet an old friend, Professor Travers, who confesses he has reactivated a Yeti. This in turn has brought the return of the Great Intelligence. Yeti are at large in the underground, which is being invaded by the same cosmic cobweb which enveloped the TARDIS. The Doctor meets the man in charge of the Army's operations, Colonel Lethbridge-Stewart. Unfortunately, the Intelligence controls the mind of Staff Sergeant Arnold. The Doctor is forced to give himself up as the Intelligence now holds Travers and Victoria hostage. A brain-draining helmet is placed on his head. But the Doctor has reversed the polarities and attempts to drain the Intelligence, and almost succeeds – until he is 'rescued' by his friends, leaving the Intelligence free again. After their departure, according to the novel of the story, Lethbridge-Stewart plans the creation of an international task force to fight alien invasion.

This is the UNIT seed story.

Novelisation: *Doctor Who – The Web of Fear* by Terrance Dicks (0 426 11084 6) first published by Wyndham Publications as *Doctor Who and the Web of Fear* in 1976 with cover by Chris Achilleos. New edition by W H Allen (now Virgin Publishing Ltd) in 1983 with cover by Andrew Skilleter. New edition in 1993 with cover by Alister Pearson. Target library number 72.

(RR) **FURY FROM THE DEEP**
(6 episodes)
16 March 1968 to 20 April 1968

Writer:
Victor Pemberton

Director:
Hugh David

Regular cast: see MM above

Cast: Victor Maddern (Robson); Roy Spencer (Harris); Graham

Leaman (Price); Peter Ducrow (Guard); June Murphy (Maggie Harris); John Garvin (Carney); Hubert Rees (Chief Engineer); John Abineri (Van Lutyens); Richard Mayes (Baxter); Bill Burridge (Quill); John Gill (Oak); Margaret John (Megan Jones); Brian Cullingford (Perkins).

Story: The Doctor and his companions are suspected of sabotage at a North Sea gas refinery off the east coast of England. The refinery boss, Robson, blames them for the disappearance of rig crews, and leaks and pressure build-ups in the pipelines. The Doctor reports strange 'heartbeats' from the pipelines but Robson refuses to halt the gas flow. The noises come from a form of parasitic seaweed, which absorbs Human brains and transforms men into Weed creatures. The Weed, exhaling toxic gases, launches an attack on the refinery, but after Victoria's screaming kills one, the Doctor realises that the creatures can be destroyed by high-frequency sound waves. After having killed all the creatures, the Doctor is ready to go on but Victoria decides to remain at the refinery and is adopted by the Harrises.

Novelisation: *Doctor Who – Fury from the Deep* by Victor Pemberton (0 426 20259 7) first published by W H Allen (now Virgin Publishing Ltd) in 1986 with cover by David McAllister. Also published in *The Doctor Who Omnibus* by Book Club Associates in 1977. Target library number 110.

Audio tape: *Fury from the Deep* (catalogue number: ZBBC 1434, ISBN: 0563 401079) first released in 1993 with photomontage cover.

(SS) THE WHEEL IN SPACE
(6 episodes)
27 April 1968 to 1 June 1968

Writer:
David Whitaker
(from a story by Kit Pedler)

Director:
Tristan de Vere Cole

Regular cast: Patrick Troughton (the Doctor); Frazer Hines (Jamie), and introducing Wendy Padbury (Zoe Heriot).

Cast: Deborah Watling (Victoria Waterfield – beginning of episode 1 only); Freddie Foote (Servo-Robot); Eric Flynn (Ryan); Anne Ridler (Dr Corwyn); Clare Jenkins (Tanya Lernov); Michael Turner (Bennett); Donald Sumpter (Enrico Casali); Kenneth Watson (Duggan); Michael Goldie (Laleham); Derrick Gilbert (Vallance); Kevork Malikyan (Rudkin); Peter Laird (Chang); James Mellor (Flannigan); Jerry Holmes, Gordon Stothard (Cybermen); Peter Hawkins, Roy Skelton (Cybermen voices).

Story: The TARDIS rematerialises inside a drifting rocket in which lurks a hostile Servo-Robot. The rocket itself is in the orbit of the Wheel in Space, a giant space station, where there have been reports of space rodents. The Doctor and Jamie are taken aboard the Wheel and find that the so-called rodents are Cybermats, a creation of the Cybermen, who are again planning an Earth invasion. With the help of a young astrophysicist with an eidetic memory, Zoe, who joins the TARDIS crew, the Doctor succeeds in saving the Wheel from a meteorite storm engineered by the Cybermen, then destroys the Cyber-Ship with the Wheel's boosted laser cannon.

Novelisation: *Doctor Who – The Wheel in Space* by Terrance Dicks (0 426 20321 6) first published by W H Allen (now Virgin Publishing Ltd) in 1988 with cover by Ian Burgess. Target library number 130.

Video tape: Episodes 3 and 6 included on *Cybermen – The Early Years* (BBCV 4813) first released in 1992 with photo-montage cover.

Sixth Season

Producer:
Peter Bryant

Script Editor:
Derrick Sherwin

(TT) THE DOMINATORS
(5 episodes)
10 August 1968 to 7 September 1968

Writer:
Norman Ashby
(Mervyn Haisman and
Henry Lincoln)

Director:
Morris Barry

Regular cast: Patrick Troughton (the Doctor); Frazer Hines (Jamie); Wendy Padbury (Zoe Heriot).

Cast: Ronald Allen (Rago); Kenneth Ives (Toba); Arthur Cox (Cully); Philip Voss (Wahed); Malcolm Terris (Etnin); Nicolette Pendrell (Tolata); Felicity Gibson (Kando); Giles Block (Teel); Johnson Bayly (Balan); Walter Fitzgerald (Senex); Ronald Mansell, John Cross, Malcolm Watson, Aubrey Danvers Walker (Council Members); Alan Gerrard (Bovem); Brian Cant (Tensa); John Hicks, Gary Smith, Freddie Wilson (Quarks); Sheila Grant (Quark voices).

Story: The TARDIS rematerialises on the planet Dulkis, threatened by the alien Dominators and their deadly robot servants, the Quarks, who have secretly landed on an island. The Dulcians are pacifists and cannot retaliate. They ignore the Doctor's warnings and some of them are captured. The Doctor discovers the Dominators' plan: to fire rockets down bore holes, causing an eruption of the molten core of the planet. They will then drop an atomic seed capsule down a bore hole, turning Dulkis into a radioactive mass, fuel for the Dominators' space fleet. Jamie and Cully, rebellious son of the Dulcian leader, become impatient and destroy a Quark. The Doctor and Zoe are captured by the Dominators. The Doctor intercepts the seed capsule as it is dropped and conceals it in the Dominators' flag ship, which is then destroyed in an atomic blast. The TARDIS, however, is in the path of a lava flow . . .

Novelisation: *Doctor Who – The Dominators* by Ian Marter (0 426 19553 1) first published by W H Allen (now Virgin Publishing Ltd) in 1984 with cover by Andrew Skilleter. New edition in 1991 with cover by Alister Pearson. Target library number 86.

Video tape: *The Dominators* (BBCV 4406) first released in 1990 with cover by Alister Pearson.

(UU) THE MIND ROBBER
(5 episodes)
14 September 1968 to 12 October 1968

Writer:
Peter Ling;
Derrick Sherwin (episode 1).

Director:
David Mahoney

Regular cast: see TT above

Cast: Emrys Jones (Master of the Land); John Atterbury, Ralph Carrigan, Bill Weisener, Terry Wright (White Robots); Hamish Wilson (Jamie); Philip Ryan (Redcoat); Bernard Horsfall (Gulliver); Barbara Loft, Sylvestra Le Touzel, Timothy Horton, Martin Langley, Christopher Reynolds, David Reynolds (Children); Paul Alexander, Ian Hines, Richard Ireson (Clockwork Soldiers); Christine Pirie (Rapunzel and Book Narrator); Sue Pulford (Medusa); Richard Ireson (Minotaur); Christopher Robbie (Karkus); David Cannon (Cyrano); John Greenwood (D'Artagnan and Lancelot); Gerry Wain (Blackbeard).

Story: To escape the lava flow caused by the atomic explosion in the previous story the TARDIS jumps out of Space and Time, and arrives in the Land of Fiction, a huge white void where fiction appears as reality. The travellers are hunted by White Robots and encounter mechanical soldiers and fictional characters such as Lemuel Gulliver. Jamie gains entrance to the Citadel of the Master, an aged gentleman who wants to retire and insists that the Doctor takes his place. The Doctor refuses, so the White Robots capture Jamie and Zoe. In the following battle of wits the Doctor calls up champions from famous Earth fictions to defeat the Master. Meanwhile, Zoe finds the true Master of the Land: a giant computer. They manage to overload the machine and escape.

Novelisation: *Doctor Who – The Mind Robber* by Peter Ling (0 426 20286 4) first published by W H Allen (now Virgin Publishing Ltd) in 1986 with cover by David McAllister. New edition in 1990 with cover by Alister Pearson. Target library number 115.

Video tape: *The Mind Robber* (BBCV 4352) first released in 1990 with cover by Alister Pearson.

Script Editor:
Terrance Dicks

(VV) **THE INVASION**
(8 episodes)
2 November 1968 to 21 December 1968

Writer:
Derrick Sherwin
(from a story by Kit Pedler)

Director:
Douglas Camfield

Regular cast: see TT above

Guest stars: Nicholas Courtney (Brigadier Lethbridge-Stewart); John Levene (Benton).

Cast: Murray Evans (Lorry Driver); Walter Randall (Patrolman); Sally Faulkner (Isobel Watkins); Geoffrey Cheshire (Tracy); Kevin Stoney (Tobias Vaughn); Peter Halliday (Packer); Edward Burnham (Professor Watkins); Ian Fairbairn (Gregory); James Thornhill (Sergeant Walters); Robert Sidaway (Captain Turner); Sheila Dunn (Operator); Edward Dentith (Rutlidge); Peter Thompson (Workman); Dominic Allan (Policeman); Stacy Davies (Perkins); Clifford Earl (Branwell); Norman Hartley (Peters); Pat Gorman, Ralph Carrigan, Charles Finch, Richard King, John Spradbury, Peter Thornton (Cybermen); Peter Halliday (Cyber Director Voice).

Story: The Doctor, back in 20th-century London, calls at the home of his friend Professor Travers, but finds that he has let it to a computer scientist, Professor Watkins, and his niece Isobel. Watkins has disappeared – last heard of at International Electromatics, the major supplier of the world's computers. The Doctor visits the firm and distrusts the managing director, Tobias Vaughn. So does Brigadier Lethbridge-Stewart of the newly formed UNIT (United Nations Intelligence Taskforce).

Zoe and Isobel are captured by Vaughn, who is forcing Watkins to develop the Cerebration Mentor, the purpose of which is to generate emotional impulses. The Doctor discovers Vaughn is in the employ of the Cybermen – but too late. The Cybermen manage to paralyse Earth's population and launch an invasion through the sewers, in which their troops had been previously hidden by Vaughn's men. With Zoe's assistance, British missiles destroy the Cyberman invasion fleet. The Cybermen then turn on Vaughn and announce their intention of wiping out life on Earth with a megatron bomb. With the help of the Cerebration Mentor, which induces madness in the Cybermen, a now-reformed Vaughn helps the Doctor and UNIT destroy the radio beacon guiding the Cybership, but is killed in the process. The ship is finally destroyed by a Russian rocket.

This is the first UNIT story, and the last Cybermen story until *Revenge of the Cybermen* (4D) in 1975.

Novelisation: *Doctor Who – The Invasion* by Ian Marter (0 426 20169 8) first published by W H Allen (now Virgin Publishing Ltd) in 1985 with cover by Andrew Skilleter. New edition in 1993 with cover by Alister Pearson. Target library number 98.

Video tape: *The Invasion* (BBCV 4974) first released in 1993 with cover by Andrew Skilleter.

(WW) **THE KROTONS**
(4 episodes)
28 December 1968 to 18 January 1969

Writer:
Robert Holmes

Director:
David Maloney

Regular cast: see TT above

Cast: James Copeland (Selris); Gilbert Wynne (Thara); Terence

Brown (Abu); Madeleine Mills (Vana); Philip Madoc (Eelek); Richard Ireson (Axus); James Cairncross (Beta); Maurice Selwyn (Custodian); Bronson Shaw (Student); Robert La Bassiere, Miles Northover, Robert Grant (Krotons); Roy Skelton, Patrick Tull (Kroton voices).

Story: The primitive Gonds are ruled and taught by means of the Kroton Machine. The Krotons are crystalline beings awaiting in suspended animation until they have drained enough mental energy from the Gonds' brains to be reanimated. Each year the two most brilliant Gonds are received into the Kroton Machine. Zoe and the Doctor take the Teaching Machine Test and their mental power reanimates the Krotons. The Doctor discovers the Kroton life system is based on telurium and destroys them with sulphuric acid.

Novelisation: *Doctor Who – The Krotons* by Terrance Dicks (0 426 20189 2) first published by W H Allen (now Virgin Publishing Ltd) in 1985 with cover by Andrew Skilleter. New edition in 1991 with cover by Alister Pearson. Target library number 99.

Video tape: *The Krotons* (BBCV 4452) first released in 1991 with cover by Alister Pearson.

(XX) **THE SEEDS OF DEATH**
(6 episodes)
25 January 1969 to 1 March 1969

Writer:
Brian Hayles
(with Terrance Dicks,
uncredited)

Director:
Michael Ferguson

Regular cast: see TT above

Cast: Alan Bennion (Slaar); Steve Peters, Tony Harwood, Sonny Caldinez (Ice Warriors); Philip Ray (Eldred); Louise Pajo (Gia Kelly); John Witty (Computer voice); Ric Felgate (Brent); Harry Towb (Osgood); Ronald Leigh-Hunt (Radnor); Terry Scully (Fewsham); Christopher Coll (Phipps); Martin Cort (Locke); Derrick Slater (Guard); Graham Leaman (Marshal); Hugh Morton (Sir James Gregson); Peter Whittaker (Weather station operator).

Story: Earth in the 21st century enjoys the T-Mat, a form of instantaneous travel directed from a Moon relay station. The machine breaks down and the Doctor investigates. He finds the Moon overrun by Ice Warriors, who are preparing to launch an invasion against Earth. To weaken Earth's resistance they are using the T-Mat to send Martian Seed Pods, which emit a lethal fungus, over Earth's winter zones. The Doctor manages to use the T-Mat to return to a chaotic Earth, where Ice Warriors have taken control of the weather. The Doctor finds that the only thing that can destroy the fungus is heavy rains and warmth, which he provokes after regaining control of the weather station. A solar heat gun takes care of the Ice Warriors.

Novelisation: *Doctor Who – The Seeds of Death* by Terrance Dicks (0 426 20252 X) first published by W H Allen (now Virgin Publishing Ltd) in 1986 with cover by Tony Masero. Target library number 112.

Video tape: *The Seeds of Death* (BBCV 2019/4072) first released in 1985 with photomontage cover.

Script Editor:
Derrick Sherwin

(YY) **THE SPACE PIRATES**
(6 episodes)
8 March 1969 to 12 April 1969

Writer: **Director:**
Robert Holmes   Michael Hart

Regular cast: see TT above

Cast: Brian Peck (Dervish); Dudley Foster (Caven); Jack May (Hermack); Donald Gee (Warne); George Layton (Penn); Nik Zaran (Sorba); Anthony Donovan (Guard); Gordon Gostelow (Clancey); Lisa Daniely (Madeleine); Steve Peters (Guard); Esmond Knight (Dom Issigri).

Story: The TARDIS materialises on a navigation beacon far out in space. A group of space pirates, using explosives, breaks up the beacon into its constituent parts in an attempt to steal it. The Doctor and his companions are separated from the TARDIS, which is on a part of the beacon the pirates manage to steal. The International Space Corps is convinced that the thief is an innocent yet eccentric space mining pioneer named Milo Clancey. Milo joins forces with the Doctor, and the TARDIS crew hide him on the planet Ta. Here dwells Caven, a notorious space criminal in league with space pirates, and responsible for the theft. He is assisted by Madeleine, daughter of his ex-partner Dom Issigri, who is now Caven's captive. Madeleine sees the error of her ways and Caven is arrested.

Novelisation: *Doctor Who – The Space Pirates* by Terrance Dicks (0 426 20346 1) first published by W H Allen (now Virgin Publishing Ltd) in 1990 with cover by Tony Clark. Target library number 147.

Video tape: Episode 2 included on *The Troughton Years* (BBCV 4609) first released in 1991 with photomontage cover.

Producer:
Derrick Sherwin

Script Editor:
Terrance Dicks

(ZZ) THE WAR GAMES
(10 episodes)
19 April 1969 to 21 June 1969

Writers:
Malcolm Hulke,
Terrance Dicks

Director:
David Maloney

Regular cast: see TT above

Cast: Jane Sherwin (Lady Buckingham); David Savile (Carstairs); John Livesey, Bernard Davies (German Soldiers); Terence Bayler (Barrington); Brian Forster (Willis); Noel Coleman (General Smythe); Hubert Rees (Captain Ransom); Esmond Webb (Burns); Richard Steele (Gorton); Peter Stanton (Chauffeur); Pat Gorman (Policeman); Tony McEwan (Redcoat); David Valla (Crane); Gregg Palmer (Lucke); David Garfield (Von Weich); Edward Brayshaw (War Chief); Philip Madoc (War Lord); James Bree (Security Chief); Bill Hutchinson (Thompson); Terry Adams (Riley); Leslie Schofield (Leroy); Vernon Dobtcheff (Scientist), Rudolph Walker (Harper); John Atterbury, Charles Pemberton (Aliens); Michael Lynch (Spencer); Graham Weston (Russell); David Troughton (Moor); Peter Craze (Du Pont); Michael Napier-Brown (Villar); Stephen Hubay (Petrov); Bernard Horsfall, Trevor Martin, Clyde Pollitt (Time Lords); Clare Jenkins (Tanya); Freddie Wilson (Quark); John Levene (Yeti); Tony Harwood (Ice Warrior); Roy Pearce (Cyberman); Robert Jewell (Dalek).

Story: The TARDIS materialises in what appears to be no-man's-land on a First World War battlefront in France. When the Doctor and his companions emerge from a cloud of mist they find that they are really on another planet. It is split into time zones and a fierce war is being waged in each one. The wars are controlled by aliens, who have gathered soldiers from many periods of history, brainwashed them and put them to battle with the aim of forming an invincible army from the survivors to take over the Galaxy. The Doctor is identified by the War Chief, assistant to the leader of the aliens, the War Lord, but he manage to seize the alien HQ with the help of soldiers no longer under the aliens' control, and calls on the Time Lords for help.

The Time Lords are a nearly omnipotent race, with the ability to control Time and Space. Both the Doctor and the War Chief are renegade Time Lords who each stole a TARDIS and escaped. The Doctor fled to explore the Universe (Time Lord policy is one of strict non-intervention) whilst the War Chief gave Time Lord technology to the War Lords – in particular the SIDRATs, an inferior kind of TARDIS – which enabled him to start the war games. The Time Lords intervene, capture and execute the War Lord, return all the soldiers to their proper time zones on Earth and, finally, try the Doctor. They find him guilty of intervention and exile him to Earth after having changed his appearance. Jamie and Zoe are returned to their respective eras a moment in time before they met the Doctor, thus erasing all their memories of their adventures with him.

This is the first story introducing the Time Lords – and explaining the Doctor's origins.

Novelisation: *Doctor Who – The War Games* by Malcolm Hulke (0 426 20082 9) first published by W H Allen (now Virgin Publishing Ltd) in 1979 as *Doctor Who and the War Games* with cover by John Geary. New edition in 1990 with cover by Alister Pearson. Target library number 70.

Video tape: *The War Games* (BBCV 4310) first released in 1990 with cover by Alister Pearson.

THIRD DOCTOR

JON PERTWEE
1970 – 1974

Seventh Season

Producer:
Derrick Sherwin

Script Editor:
Terrance Dicks

(AAA) SPEARHEAD FROM SPACE
(4 episodes)
3 January 1970 to 24 January 1970

Writer:
Robert Holmes

Director:
Derek Martinus

Regular cast: Jon Pertwee (the Doctor), Caroline John (Liz Shaw).

Guest star: Nicholas Courtney (Brigadier Lethbridge-Stewart).

Cast: Hugh Burden (Channing); Neil Wilson (Seeley); John Breslin (Captain Munro); Antony Webb (Dr Henderson); Helen Dorward (Nurse); Talfryn Thomas (Mullins); George Lee (Corporal Forbes); Iain Smith, Tessa Shaw, Ellis Jones (UNIT personnel); Allan Mitchell (Wagstaffe); Prentis Hancock (Reporter); Derek Smee (Ransome); John Woodnutt (Hibbert); Betty Bowden (Meg Seeley); Hamilton Dyce (Scobie); Henry McCarthy (Dr Beavis); Clifford Cox (Soldier); Edmund Bailey (Waxworks Attendant); Ellis Jones (voice of Dr Lomax).

Story: A shower of meteorites falls on Essex and the Brigadier and his newly recruited scientist Liz Shaw, from Cambridge, enlist the aid of a physically changed Doctor to investigate the phenomenon. Factory boss Channing is a Nestene – a member of an alien collective intelligence which colonises planets by copying native life forms. Nestenes have a special ability to control plastic; Channing is making Autons, plastic manne-quins able to fight and kill, controlled by the Nestene Con-sciousness. He has also been making plastic facsimiles of Cabinet members to enable him to gain world domination. The Doctor manages to defeat the Nestene as the Autons start on a killing rampage. He agrees to work for UNIT as scientific advisor in return for facilities to repair the TARDIS, grounded by the Time Lords on 20th-century Earth, and a sprightly yellow roadster later known as Bessie.

Novelisation: *Doctor Who – The Auton Invasion* by Terrance Dicks (0 426 11295 4) first published as *Doctor Who and the Auton Invasion* by Universal-Tandem in 1974 with cover by Chris Achilleos. New edition by W H Allen (now Virgin Publishing Ltd) in 1982 with cover by Andrew Skilleter. New edition in 1991 with cover by Alister Pearson. Target library number 6.

Video tape: *Spearhead from Space* (BBCV 4107) first released in 1988 with photomontage cover.

Producer:
Barry Letts

(BBB) **THE SILURIANS**
(7 episodes)
31 January 1970 to 14 March 1970

Writer:
Malcolm Hulke

Director:
Timothy Combe

Regular cast: see AAA above

Guest star: see AAA above

Cast: John Newman (Spencer); Bill Matthews (Davis); Peter Miles (Dr Lawrence); Norman Jones (Baker); Thomasine Heiner (Miss Dawson); Fulton Mackay (Dr Quinn); Roy Branigan (Roberts); Ian Cunningham (Dr Meredith); Paul Darrow (Hawkins); Pat Gorman (Silurian Scientist); Dave Carter (Old Silurian); Nigel Johns (Young Silurian); Paul Barton, Simon Cain, John Churchill (Silurians); Peter Halliday (Silurian voice); Nancie Jackson (Doris Squire); Gordon Richardson (Squire); Richard Steele (Hart); Ian Talbot (Travis); Geoffrey Palmer (Masters); Harry Swift (Robins); Brendan Barry (Doctor); Derek Pollitt (Wright); Alan Mason (Corporal Nutting).

Story: On Wenley Moor, a secret Derbyshire atomic research centre where a reactor converting nuclear energy to electrical power is being developed, work is being held up by inexplicable power losses and breakdowns among staff. The Doctor traces the trouble to underground caves where prehistoric monsters live with a nest of highly intelligent man-like reptiles, the Silurians. They went into hibernation millions of years ago but have been resuscitated by accidental electric discharges from the research centre. They now claim back 'their' Earth. The Doctor strives for harmony between Man and Silurian and at first seems to succeed with the Old Silurian. But then the rebellious and intolerant Young Silurian releases a terrible disease that will wipe out Humans. The Doctor finds an antidote. The Silurians take over the research centre and plan to destroy the Van Allen Belt, which shields Earth from the Sun. The reptiles are tricked into returning to their caves by the threat of radiation and the Brigadier – to the Doctor's disgust – blows them up.

This story was actually entitled *Doctor Who and the Silurians*.

Novelisation: *Doctor Who – The Silurians* by Malcolm Hulke (0 426 11471 X) first published as *Doctor Who and the Cave-Monsters* by Universal-Tandem (became W H Allen) in 1974 with cover by Chris Achilleos. New edition in 1992 by Virgin Publishing Ltd with cover by Alister Pearson. Target library number 9.

Video tape: *Doctor Who and the Silurians* (BBCV 4990) first released in 1993 with cover by Andrew Skilleter.

(CCC) THE AMBASSADORS OF DEATH
(7 episodes)
21 March 1970 to 2 May 1970

Writer:	**Director:**
David Whitaker	Michael Ferguson
(with Malcolm Hulke,	
uncredited)	

Regular cast: see AAA above

Guest stars: see AAA above, and John Levene (Sergeant Benton).

Cast: Robert Cawdron (Taltalian); Ric Felgate (Van Lyden); Ronald Allen (Ralph Cornish); Michael Wisher (John

Wakefield); Cheryl Molineaux (Miss Rutherford); John Abineri (Carrington); Ray Armstrong (Grey); Robert Robertson (Collinson); Juan Moreno (Dobson); James Haswell (Champion); Bernard Martin (Control Room Assistant); Dallas Cavell (Quinlan); Steve Peters, Neville Simons (Astronauts); Gordon Sterne (Heldorf); William Dysart (Reegan); Cyril Shaps (Lennox); John Lord (Masters); Max Faulkner (Soldier); Joanna Ross (First Assistant); Carl Conway (Second Assistant); Ric Felgate (Astronaut); James Clayton (Parker); Peter Noel Cook (Alien); Peter Halliday (Alien voice); Neville Simons (Michaels); Steve Peters (Lefee); Geoffrey Beevers (Johnson); Roy Scammell (Peterson); Tony Harwood (Flynn).

Story: Seven months after leaving Mars the *Probe 7* ship has still not returned to Earth and a *Recovery 7* rocket is despatched to investigate. *Recovery 7* returns to Earth but, after landing, the astronauts are kidnapped by men masquerading as UNIT forces. Liz Shaw notices the ship's Geiger counter is at maximum; the crew would normally have been killed by radiation. The Doctor is convinced the crew are not Human. He makes a solo space mission and finds the real astronauts held aboard a large alien spaceship. The captain of the alien ship asks for the return of his 'ambassadors' or he will destroy the planet. The three recaptured aliens are exchanged.

Novelisation: *Doctor Who – The Ambassadors of Death* by Terrance Dicks (0 426 20305 4) first published by W H Allen (now Virgin Publishing Ltd) in 1987 with cover by Tony Masero. New edition in 1991 with cover by Alister Pearson. Target library number 121.

(DDD) **INFERNO**
(7 episodes)
9 May 1970 to 20 June 1970

Writer:
Don Houghton

Directors:
Douglas Camfield
Barry Letts

Regular cast: see AAA above

Guest stars: see CCC above

Cast: Olaf Pooley (Stahlman); Christopher Benjamin (Sir Gold); Ian Fairbairn (Bromley); Walter Randall (Slocum); Sheila Dunn (Petra Williams); Derek Newark (Greg Sutton); David Simeon (Latimer); Derek Ware (Wyatt); Roy Scammell (Sentry); Keith James (Patterson); Dave Carter, Pat Gorman, Philip Ryan, Peter Thompson, Walter Henry (Primords).

Story: A crisis develops on a top-secret drilling project – Inferno – which aims to penetrate the Earth's crust and releases a new energy source to be called Stahlman's Gas, named after Professor Stahlman, in charge of Inferno. The drilling pipes are leaking a green liquid which, on contact with Human skin, transforms its victims into vicious primeval ape-like creatures called Primords. The Doctor is transported by accident into a parallel world, where England is ruled by a military dictatorship and Inferno is about to destroy the planet. Thwarted by his friends' counterparts on this parallel world, the Doctor is powerless to stop the destruction of the planet but manages to escape and return to Earth. There, he overcomes the power-crazed Professor Stahlman, who has become a Primord and threatens to unleash the full forces of the Earth's core. Inferno is stopped in time and Earth is saved.

This was the last story to feature the original TARDIS console as introduced in 1963.

Novelisation: *Doctor Who – Inferno* by Terrance Dicks (0 426 19617 1) first published by W H Allen (now Virgin Publishing Ltd) in 1984 with cover by Nick Spender. Target library number 89.

Video tape: *Inferno* (BBCV 5269) first released in 1994 with a cover by Colin Howard.

Eighth Season

Producer:
Barry Letts

Script Editor:
Terrance Dicks

(EEE) TERROR OF THE AUTONS
(4 episodes)
2 January 1971 to 23 January 1971

Writer:
Robert Holmes

Director:
Barry Letts

Regular cast: Jon Pertwee (the Doctor); Katy Manning (Jo Grant).

Guest stars: Nicholas Courtney (Brigadier Lethbridge-Stewart); Roger Delgado (the Master); John Levene (Sergeant Benton); Richard Franklin (Captain Mike Yates).

Cast: John Baskcomb (Rossini); Dave Carter (Museum Attendant); Christopher Burgess (Professor Phillips); Andrew Staines (Goodge); Frank Mills (Radiotelescope Director); David Garth (Time Lord); Michael Wisher (Rex Farrel); Harry Towb (McDermott); Barbara Leake (Mrs Farrel); Stephen Jack (Farrel Sr); Roy Stewart (Strong Man); Terry Walsh, Pat Gorman

(Autons); Haydn Jones (Auton voice); Dermot Tuohy (Brownrose); Norman Stanley (Telephone Man); Tommy Reynolds (Troll Doll); Les Conrad (Soldier); Les Clark, Bob Blaine, Ian Elliott, Charles Pickess, Mike Stevens, Nick Hobbs, Tom O'Leary (Daffodil Men/Autons).

Story: The Master, another renegade Time Lord, materialises in his TARDIS disguised as a horse-box at Rossini's Circus. Warned of his presence by another Time Lord, the Doctor and his new assistant, Jo Grant, realise that, with the Master's help, the Nestenes are planning a new invasion, using the Autons. The Doctor thwarts all the plans of the Nestenes, including the lethal use, under Nestene control, of a plastic flower. The Master, to save his own life, helps the Doctor prevent the materialisation of the Nestene Monster. He then escapes to fight another day.

This is the first story in which the Master appears.

Novelisation: *Doctor Who and the Terror of the Autons* by Terrance Dicks (0 426 11500 7) first published by Universal-Tandem in 1975 with cover by Peter Brookes. New edition by W H Allen (now Virgin Publishing Ltd) in 1979 with cover by Alun Hood. Target library number 63.

Video tape: *Terror of the Autons* (BBCV 4957) first released in 1993 with cover by Alister Pearson.

(FFF) **THE MIND OF EVIL**
(6 episodes)
30 January 1971 to 6 March 1971

Writer:
Don Houghton

Director:
Timothy Combe

Regular Cast: see EEE above

Guest stars: see EEE above

Cast: Eric Mason (Green); Roy Purcell (Powers); Raymond Westwell (Governor); Simon Lack (Professor Kettering); Michael Sheard (Dr Summers); Bill Matthews, Barry Wade Dave Carter, Martin Gordon, Leslie Weekes, Tony Jenkins, Les Conrad, Les Clark, Gordon Stothard, Richard Atherton (Officers); Neil McCarthy (Barnham); Clive Scott (Linwood); Fernanda Marlowe (Corporal Bell); Pik-Sen Lim (Chin Lee) Kristopher Kum (Fu Peng); Haydn Jones (Vosper); William Marlowe (Mailer); Tommy Duggan (Alcott); David Calderisi (Charlie); Patrick Godfrey (Cosworth); Johnny Barrs (Fuller); Matthew Walters (Prisoner); Paul Blomley (Police Superintendant); Maureen Race (Student); Nick Hobbs (American aide); Billy Horrigan (UNIT corporal); Peter Roy (Policeman); Michael Ely (UNIT chauffeur); Francis Williams (African delegate/Master's chauffeur); Laurence Harrington (Voices); Paul Tann (Chinese aide); Jim Delaney (Passer-by); Charles Saynor (Commissionaire); Basil Tang (Chinese chauffeur); Richard Atherton (Police Inspector).

Story: The Doctor believes there is an alien Mind Parasite in the Keller Machine, which extracts evil from criminals' minds. In London the Chinese delegate dies at the World Peace Conference. Meanwhile, UNIT is charged with the mission of dumping a banned Thunderbolt nerve gas missile at sea. Professor Keller is really the Master, who captures the Doctor and Jo by inciting a riot at Stangmoor Prison. He uses the convicts to hijack the nerve gas missile, which will enable him to destroy the Peace Conference. The Doctor traps the Master by using the Mind Parasite, then explodes it with the nerve gas. But the Master escapes again.

Novelisation: *Doctor Who – The Mind of Evil* by Terrance Dicks (0 426 20166 3) first published by W H Allen (now Virgin Publishing Ltd) in 1985 with cover by Andrew Skilleter. Target library number 96.

(GGG) THE CLAWS OF AXOS
(4 episodes)
13 March 1971 to 3 April 1971

Writers:
Bob Baker
Dave Martin

Director:
Michael Ferguson

Regular cast: see EEE above

Guest stars: see EEE above

Cast: Peter Bathurst (Chinn); Michael Walker, David G. March (Radar Operators); Paul Grist (Bill Filer); Fernanda Marlowe (Corporal Bell); Derek Ware (Pigbin Josh); Donald Hewlett (Sir George Hardiman); David Savile (Winser); Bernard Holley (Axon Man, voice of Axos); Kenneth Benda (Minister); Tim Pigott-Smith (Harker); Nick Hobbs (Driver); Royston Farrell (Technician); Patricia Gordino (Axon woman); John Hicks (Axon boy); Debbie Lee London (Axon girl); Roger Minnice, Geoff Righty, Steve King, David Aldridge (Humanoid Axons); Douglas Roe, Clinton Morris, Clive Roger, Eden Fox, Stuart Myers (Axon globs); Gloria Walker (Secretary/Nurse); Clinton Morris (Corporal); Peter Holmes, Steve Smart, Marc Boyle (Axon monsters).

Story: An alien spaceship contains the Axons: humanoid, beautiful, and friendly. They ask for hospitality on Earth as their planet has been crippled by a solar flare. But the Doctor is suspicious, and discovers that the Axons, their ship and a substance they brought to Earth called Axonite are all part of a single, collective parasite – Axos – brought by the Master to absorb all living energy on Earth. The Doctor forces Axos into a time loop, exiling it forever in the time vortex.

Novelisation: *Doctor Who and the Claws of Axos* by Terrance Dicks (0 426 11703 4) first published by Wyndham Publica-

tions in 1977 with cover by Chris Achilleos. New edition by W
H Allen (now Virgin Publishing Ltd) in 1979 with cover by
John Geary. Target library number 10.

Video tape: *The Claws of Axos* (BBCV 4742) first released in
1992 with cover by Andrew Skilleter.

(HHH) **COLONY IN SPACE**
(6 episodes)
10 April 1971 to 15 May 1971

Writer: **Director:**
Malcolm Hulke   Michael Briant

Regular cast: see EEE above

Guest stars: Roger Delgado (the Master); Nicholas Courtney
(Brigadier Lethbridge-Stewart).

Cast: Peter Forbes-Robertson, John Baker, Graham Leaman
(Time Lords); John Scott Martin (Robot); David Webb (Leeson);
Sheila Grant (Jane); John Line (Martin); John Ringham (Ashe);
Mitzi Webster (Mrs Martin); Nicholas Pennell (Winton); Helen
Worth (Mary Ashe); Roy Skelton (Norton); Pat Gorman (Primi-
tive/Long); Bernard Kay (Caldwell); Morris Perry (Dent);
Tony Caunter (Morgan); John Herrington (Holden); Stanley
McGeagh (Allen); John Tordoff (Leeson); Norman Atkyns
(Guardian); Roy Heymann, Stanley Mason, Antonia Moss
(Alien priests).

Story: The Time Lords permit the TARDIS to make its first
voyage through Space and Time for more than a year. The
Master has stolen the Doomsday Machine file and it must be
retrieved. The Time Lords despatch the Doctor and Jo to a bleak
Earth-type planet in the year 2472, where they meet the Colonists, farmers who left Earth because of overcrowding. Since

their arrival the Colonists have faced inexplicable crop failures. There are two other groups on the planet: the Primitives, the original savage inhabitants, who steal the TARDIS and imprison Jo in their underground city, and Earthmen from the Interplanetary Mining Corporation, who have come to exploit the rich mineral deposits. If successful, they would make the planet uninhabitable. The IMC have been demoralising the Colonists with attacks by robot lizards. An adjudicator from Earth, brought in to judge between the relative merits of mining and farming, is impersonated by the Master, whose single aim is to acquire the Doomsday Machine, guarded in a nearby ruined city by alien priests. The Doctor and Jo prevent the exile of the Colonists by exposing the IMC. They also stop the Master from seizing the Machine by convincing its guardian – the sole survivor of the race that built the Machine – to set it to self-destruct. The Master escapes.

Novelisation: *Doctor Who and the Doomsday Weapon* by Malcolm Hulke (0 426 10372 6) first published by Universal-Tandem in 1974 with cover by Chris Achilleos. New edition by W H Allen (now Virgin Publishing Ltd) in 1979 with cover by Jeff Cummins. Target library number 23.

(JJJ) **THE DAEMONS**
(5 episodes)
22 May 1971 to 19 June 1971

Writer:
Guy Leopold
(Barry Letts and
Robert Sloman)

Director:
Christopher Barry

Regular cast: see EEE above

Guest stars: see EEE above

Cast: Damaris Hayman (Miss Hawthorne); Eric Hillyard (Dr Reeves); David Simeon (Alastair Fergus); James Snell (Harry); Robin Wentworth (Professor Horner); Rollo Gamble (Winstanley); Don McKillop (Bert); John Croft (Tom Girton); Christopher Wray (Groom); John Joyce (Garvin); Gerald Taylor (Baker's Man); Stanley Mason (Bok); Alec Linstead (Osgood); John Owens (Thorpe); Stephen Thorne (Azal); Matthew Corbett (Jones); Robin Squire (TV cameraman); Patrick Milner (Corporal); The Headington Quarry Men (Morris dancers).

Story: Against the advice of a local white witch, a prehistoric barrow at Devil's End is cut open. A mysterious force erupts, killing the professor responsible for the excavation and concussing the Doctor. When he recovers he finds that the village has been cut off by a heat barrier. The Master – posing as the new vicar – has used psionic science to release the power of a Daemon named Azal. The Daemons are outer space creatures who came on Earth a long time ago and contributed to the shaping of Human history. Azal, last of the Daemons on Earth, has remained to offer his power to a worthy Human – or to destroy Earth as a flawed experiment! The Doctor shows the Brigadier how to make a tunnel through the heat barrier. The Doctor is attacked by the villagers, under the Master's control, then he meets Azal, who offers him his power. The Doctor refuses and is about to be destroyed when Jo interposes herself. Azal, confused by this act of self-sacrifice, destroys himself. The Master is finally captured.

Novelisation: *Doctor Who – The Daemons* by Barry Letts (0 426 11332 2) first published by Universal-Tandem in 1974 as *Doctor Who and the Daemons* with cover by Chris Achilleos. New edition by W H Allen (now Virgin Publishing Ltd) in 1980 with cover by Andrew Skilleter. New edition in 1993 with cover by Alister Pearson. Target library number 15.

Script book: *Doctor Who – The Daemons* by Robert Sloman and Barry Letts (1 85286 324 2) first published by Titan Books in 1992 with cover by Alister Pearson.

Video tape: *The Daemons* (BBCV 4950) first released in 1993 with cover by Alister Pearson.

Ninth Season

Producer:
Barry Letts

Script Editor:
Terrance Dicks

(KKK) DAY OF THE DALEKS
(4 episodes)
1 January 1972 to 22 January 1972

Writer:
Louis Marks

Director:
Paul Bernard

Regular cast: Jon Pertwee (the Doctor); Katy Manning (Jo Grant).

Guest stars: Nicholas Courtney (Brigadier Lethbridge-Stewart); John Levene (Sergeant Benton); Richard Franklin (Captain Yates).

Cast: Jean McFarlane (Miss Paget); Wilfrid Carter (Sir Reginald Styles); Tim Condren (Guerilla); John Scott Martin (Chief Dalek); Oliver Gilbert, Peter Messaline (Dalek voices); Aubrey Woods (Controller); Deborah Brayshaw (Technician); Gypsie Kemp (Radio Operator); Anna Barry (Anat); Jimmy Winston (Shura); Scott Fredericks (Boaz); Valentine Palmer (Monia); Andrew Carr (Guard); Peter Hill (Manager); George Raistrick (Guard); Alex MacIntosh (TV Reporter); Rick Lester, Maurice Bush, Frank Menzies, Bruce Wells, Geoffrey Todd, David

Joyce (Ogrons); Ricky Newby, Murphy Grumbar (Daleks); Leon Maybank, Barbara Chambers (UNIT personnel); Desmond Verini (Styles' aide); David Melbourne (UNIT guard).

Story: The peace diplomat Sir Reginald Styles is attacked by guerillas, who escape to their 22nd-century world taking Jo Grant with them. The Doctor follows and discovers the future is ruled by the Daleks and their ape-like slaves, the Ogrons. The guerillas say they are after Styles because in the 20th century he murdered world leaders, starting a world war which enabled the Daleks to conquer the Earth. They want to prevent this. The Doctor realises that the real murderer, however, was a guerilla sent to kill Styles! The Doctor escapes from the Daleks and hurries back to the 20th century, where he has Styles' house evacuated. The guerilla, Shura, destroys only the Daleks and the Ogrons, who were pursuing the Doctor, with a Dalekenium Bomb. The future is saved.

Novelisation: *Doctor Who – The Day of the Daleks* by Terrance Dicks (0 426 10380 7) first published by Universal-Tandem as *Doctor Who and the Day of the Daleks* in 1974 with cover by Chris Achilleos. New edition by W H Allen (now Virgin Publishing Ltd) in 1985 with cover by Andrew Skilleter. New edition in 1991 with cover by Alister Pearson. Also published in *Doctor Who – The Dalek Omnibus* by Terrance Dicks first published by W H Allen in 1983 with cover by Andrew Skilleter. Target library number 18.

Video tape: *Day of the Daleks* (BBCV 2036/4109) first released in 1986 with photomontage cover. Uncut edition (BBCV 5219) released in 1994.

(MMM) THE CURSE OF PELADON
(4 episodes)
29 January 1972 to 19 February 1972

Writer:
Brian Hayles

Director:
Lennie Mayne

Regular cast: see KKK above

Cast: Henry Gilbert (Torbis); David Troughton (Peladon); Geoffrey Toone (Hepesh); Gordon StClair (Grun); Nick Hobbs (Aggedor); Stuart Fell (Alpha Centauri); Ysanne Churchman (voice of Alpha Centauri); Murphy Grumbar (Arcturus); Terry Bale (voice of Arcturus); Sonny Caldinez (Ssorg); Alan Bennion (Izlyr); George Giles (Captain); Wendy Danvers (Amazonia).

Story: The Time Lords send the Doctor and Jo to the planet Peladon, which has just applied for membership of the Galactic Federation. King Peladon and Chancellor Torbis favour the union; High Priest Hepesh does not. Torbis is murdered and Aggedor, a semi-mythical sacred monster, is blamed. The Doctor arrives and is taken for the Earth's delegate. Other delegates have arrived: Alpha Centauri, Arcturus, and Izlyr of the Ice Warriors. The Doctor finds that Hepesh and Arcturus are behind the murders. With the help of the Ice Warriors the Doctor defeats Arcturus and exposes Hepesh. The Priest orders Aggedor to kill the King but the Doctor has tamed the Monster and it is Hepesh who dies instead. The Doctor leaves as the true delegate from Earth arrives.

Novelisation: *Doctor Who – The Curse of Peladon* by Brian Hayles (0 426 11498 1) first published by Universal-Tandem in 1974 as *Doctor Who and the Curse of Peladon* with cover by Chris Achilleos. New edition by W H Allen (now Virgin Publishing Ltd) in 1980 with cover by Bill Donohoe. New edition in 1992 with cover by Alister Pearson. Target library number 13.

Video tape: *The Curse of Peladon* (BBCV 498) first released in 1993 with cover by Andrew Skilleter.

(LLL) **THE SEA DEVILS**
(6 episodes)
26 February 1972 to 1 April 1972

Writer:
Malcolm Hulke

Director:
Michael Briant

Regular cast: see KKK above

Guest star: Roger Delgado (the Master).

Cast: Clive Morton (Trenchard); Royston Tickner (Robbins); Edwin Richfield (Hart); Alec Wallis (Bowman); Neil Seiler (Radio Operator); Terry Walsh (Barclay); Brian Justice (Wilson); June Murphy (Jane Blythe); Hugh Futcher (Hickman); Declan Mulholland (Clark); Pat Gorman, Brian Nolan, Steven Ismay, Frank Seton, Jeff Witherick (Sea Devils); Eric Mason (Smedley); Donald Sumpter (Ridgway); Stanley McGeagh (Drew); David Griffin (Mitchell); Christopher Wray (Lovell); Colin Bell (Summers); Brian Vaughan (Watts); Martin Boddey (Walker); Norman Atkyns (Rear Admiral); Rex Rowland (Girton); John Caesar (Myers); Peter Forbes-Robertson (Chief Sea Devil).

Story: The Doctor and Jo visit the Master, held in captivity on a small island. The Governor, Colonel Trenchard, tells them that ships have been mysteriously disappearing. They investigate and the Doctor is attacked by an underwater Silurian, a man-like lizard called a Sea Devil. The Doctor discovers that the Master, assisted by a misguided Trenchard, is stealing electrical equipment from a naval base to build a machine that will control the Sea Devils – and then enable him to conquer the world. The Doctor enters the Sea Devils' base and tries to

100

encourage peace. But his efforts are frustrated by a depth charge attack ordered by a ruthless politician, Walker. The Doctor persuades Walker to allow him a final attempt at negotiating peace but in the meantime the Sea Devils capture the naval base. The evil Master then forces the Doctor to help finish his machine, which will revive Sea Devil colonies all over the world. The Sea Devils want to kill the Master, now useless to them, but the Doctor sabotages the machine and escapes with the Master. The Sea Devils are blown up.

Novelisation: *Doctor Who and the Sea-Devils* by Malcolm Hulke (0 426 11308 X) first published by Universal-Tandem in 1974 with cover by Chris Achilleos. New edition by W H Allen (now Virgin Publishing Ltd) in 1981 with cover by John Geary. Target library number 54.

(NNN) **THE MUTANTS**
(6 episodes)
8 April 1972 to 13 May 1972

Writers:
Bob Baker
Dave Martin

Director:
Christopher Barry

Regular cast: see KKK above

Cast: Paul Whitsun-Jones (Marshal); Geoffrey Palmer (Administrator); Christopher Coll (Stubbs); Rick James (Cotton); James Mellor (Varan); Jonathan Sherwood (Varan's Son); Garrick Hagon (Ky); George Pravda (Jaeger); John Hollis (Sondergaard); Sidney Johnson, David J. Graham (Old Men); Roy Pearce (Solos Guard); David Arlen (Guard Warrior); Damon Sanders, Martin Taylor (Guards); Peter Howell (Investigator); John Scott Martin, Mike Torres, Eddie Sommer, Laurie Goode, Nick Thompson Hill, Mike Mungarvan, Ricky Newby, Bill Gosling (Mutts); Steve Ismay (Bodyguard); Terry

Walsh (Overlord guard); Joe Santo (Exit guard).

Story: The Time Lords send the Doctor and Jo to the planet Solos to deliver a mysterious message to an unknown party. Solos is about to become independent from Earth, to the chagrin of its sadistic Marshal, whose hobby is to hunt Solonian Mutants. He commissions a Solonian to murder the Earth Administrator and plans to oxygenise Solos's atmosphere. Ky, a Solonian unjustly accused of the murder, takes Jo with him to the planet's surface. The Doctor escapes from the Marshal and tries to find them. On the surface he meets Sondergaard, a doctor who is searching for a cure for the mutating disease which threatens the Solonians. The Doctor, recaptured, is forced to perfect the Marshal's oxygenising machine. Sondergaard gives Ky a crystal which turns him first into a Mutant, then into a super-being. The crystal – found in a cave indicated on the Time Lords' message – enables Ky to kill the Marshal, present his case to the newly arrived Earth Investigator, and help the rest of the Solonians to evolve into super-beings too, part of a century-long evolution process.

Novelisation: *Doctor Who and the Mutants* by Terrance Dicks (0 426 11690 9) first published by Wyndham Publications (now Virgin Publishing Ltd) in 1977 with cover by Jeff Cummins. Target library number 44.

(OOO) **THE TIME MONSTER**
(6 episodes)
20 May 1972 to 24 June 1972

Writer:	**Director:**
Robert Sloman	Paul Bernard
(with Barry Letts, uncredited)	

Regular cast: see KKK above

Guest stars: Nicholas Courtney (Brigadier Lethbridge-Stewart); Roger Delgado (the Master); John Levene (Sergeant Benton); Richard Franklin (Captain Yates).

Cast: Wanda Moore (Dr Ingram), Ian Collier (Stuart Hyde); John Wyse (Dr Percival); Terry Walsh (Window-cleaner); Neville Barber (Dr Cook), Barry Ashton (Proctor); Donald Eccles (Krasis); Keith Dalton (Neophite); Aidan Murphy (Hippias); Marc Boyle (Kronos); George Cormack (Dalios); Gregory Powell (Knight); Simon Legree (Sergeant); Dave Carter (Officer); George Lee (Farmworker); Ingrid Pitt (Galleia); Susan Penhaligon (Lakis); Michael Walker (Miseus); Derek Murcott (Crito); Dave Prowse; Terry Walsh (Minotaur); Melville Jones (Guard); Ingrid Bower (Face of Kronos); Darren Plant (Baby Benton).

Story: The Master, disguised as Professor Thascales, is working on TOM-TIT – Transmission of Matter through Interstitial Time – a device which would enable him to go through Time to Atlantis and steal the Crystal of Kronos, thus giving him control over Kronos, an entity that lives and feeds on Time itself. The Master fails to control the Kronavore in the 20th century and decides to go back in Time to Atlantis. The Doctor follows him but fails to prevent him from using the Queen of Atlantis to gain access to the Great Crystal. Betrayed by the Queen, the Master unleashes Kronos and orders him to destroy Atlantis. The two Time Lords fight again in the time vortex. Their two TARDISes collide – but they are saved by a grateful Kronos. The Doctor pleads for the Master and obtains his freedom.

Novelisation: *Doctor Who – The Time Monster* by Terrance Dicks (0 426 20221 X) first published by W H Allen (now Virgin Publishing Ltd) in 1985 with cover by Andrew Skilleter. Target library number 101.

Tenth Season

Producer:
Barry Letts

Script Editor:
Terrance Dicks

(RRR) **THE THREE DOCTORS**
(4 episodes)
30 December 1972 to 20 January 1973

Writers:
Bob Baker,
Dave Martin

Director:
Lennie Mayne

Regular cast: Jon Pertwee (the Doctor); Katy Manning (Jo Grant).

Guest stars: William Hartnell (First Doctor); Patrick Troughton (Second Doctor); Nicholas Courtney (Brigadier Lethbridge-Stewart); John Levene (Sergeant Benton).

Cast: Stephen Thorne (Omega); Graham Leaman, Tony Lang, Lincoln Wright, Richard Orme, Peter Evans (Time Lords); Clyde Pollitt (Chancellor); Roy Purcell (President); Laurie Webb (Ollis); Patricia Prior (Mrs Ollis); Rex Robinson (Dr Tyler); Denys Palmer (Palmer); Alan Chuntz (Omega's champion); Cy Town, Ricky Newby, John Scott Martin, Murphy Grumbar (Gell guards).

Story: The energy of the Time Lords is being drained by a black hole. A Cosmic Ray Research Balloon brings back a blob of animated energy which dematerialises things on contact. It expands and besieges the Doctor and Jo in the TARDIS. The only way the Time Lords can help is by sending the Doctor's previous selves. The three Doctors discover the incidents are caused by Omega, a bitter Solar Engineer trapped behind the black hole in a universe of anti-matter for thousands of years while the rest of his race went on to become Time Lords. Omega wants the Doctor to take his place in his universe so he can return to ours. But it is too late – anti-matter radiation has already destroyed the body of Omega, only his will remains and controls his world. Omega wants to destroy the Universe, but the Doctors offer him a positive-matter artefact, thus turning him into a supernova, whose energy will replenish the Time Lords' reserves. The three Doctors return to their rightful places. The Time Lords lift their exile sentence. The Doctor is free again to roam Time and Space.

William Hartnell was ill during filming, and therefore the First Doctor appears only as an image on video screens.

Novelisation: *Doctor Who – The Three Doctors* by Terrance Dicks (0 426 11578 3) first published by Tandem in 1975 with cover by Chris Achilleos. New edition by W H Allen (now Virgin Publishing Ltd) in 1978 published as *Doctor Who and the Three Doctors*. New edition in 1991 with cover by Alister Pearson. Target library number 64.

Video tape: *The Three Doctors* (BBCV 4650) first released in 1991 with cover by Alister Pearson.

(PPP) **CARNIVAL OF MONSTERS**
(4 episodes)
27 January 1973 to 17 February 1973

Writer: **Director:**
Robert Holmes   Barry Letts

Regular cast: see RRR above

Cast: Stuart Fell (Functionary); Michael Wisher (Kalik); Terence Lodge (Orum); Cheryl Hall (Shirna); Leslie Dwyer (Vorg); Tenniel Evans (Major Daly); Andrew Staines (Captain); Ian Marter (Andrews); Jenny McCracken (Claire Daly); Peter Halliday (Pletrac).

Story: Free to travel in Time and Space again, the Doctor promises Jo a trip to Metebelis 3, the famous blue planet of the Actian Group. But instead he materialises the TARDIS on a cargo ship crossing the Indian Ocean in 1926. Or is it? The Doctor discovers that not only are they an alien planet trapped in a time loop but they are captives of a showman, Vorg, and his Scope – a miniaturised peepshow of Galaxy life forms. The Doctor tries to escape by entering another section of the Scope – a swamp – where he is confronted by the Drashigs, huge underwater dragons. Finally the Doctor breaks out of the Scope and materialises to full size. He becomes involved in the intrigues of the two natives Kalik and Orum, who plan to overthrow their superior by allowing the Drashigs to escape. Vorg destroys the Drashigs and the Doctor breaks the time link by contriving to link the TARDIS to the Scope and returning the unwilling participants (Cybermen, Ogrons, etc) to their rightful times and places.

Novelisation: *Doctor Who – The Carnival of Monsters* by Terrance Dicks (0 426 11025 0) first published by Tandem/ Wyndham Publications as *Doctor Who and the Carnival of Monsters* in 1977 with cover by Chris Achilleos. New edition in 1993 by Virgin Publishing Ltd with cover by Alister Pearson. Target library number 8.

(QQQ) FRONTIER IN SPACE
(6 episodes)
24 February 1973 to 31 March 1973

Writer:
Malcolm Hulke

Director:
Paul Bernard

Regular cast: see RRR above

Guest star: Roger Delgado (the Master).

Cast: John Rees (Hardy); James Culliford (Stewart); Roy Pattison (Draconian Pilot); Peter Birrel (Draconian Prince); Vera Fusek (President); Michael Hawkins (Williams); Louis Mahoney (Newscaster); Karol Hagar (Secretary); Ray Lonnen (Gardiner); Barry Ashton (Kemp); Lawrence Davidson (Draconian First Secretary); Timothy Craven (Guard); Luan Peters (Sheila); Caroline Hunt (Technician); Madhav Sharma (Patel); Richard Shaw (Cross); Dennis Bowen (Governor); Harold Goldblatt (Professor Dale); Laurence Harrington (Guard); Bill Wilde (Draconian Captain); Stephen Thorne, Michael Kilgarriff, Rick Lester (Ogrons); John Woodnutt (Emperor); Ian Frost (Draconian Messenger); Clifford Elkin (Earth Cruiser Captain); Bill Mitchell (Newcaster); Ramsay Williams (Brook); Stanley Price (Pilot); John Scott Martin, Cy Town, Murphy Grumbar (Daleks); Michael Wisher (Dalek voice).

Story: To avoid a head-on collision in Space the Doctor and Jo materialise in the hold of a future Earth spaceship. Almost immediately the ship is attacked. They emerge from the hold and the crew 'see' them as their enemies, the Draconians, an alien humanoid race rivalling Earth for the control of the Galaxy. The Doctor and Jo, however, see the true face of the attackers: Ogrons! A rescue ship takes them all to Earth where they are accused of being Draconian spies. The Doctor is sent to the Moon but he and Jo are freed by the Master, whose plot is to provoke a space war between Earth and Draconia, using the Ogrons and a hypnotic device. The Doctor escapes and is captured by the Draconians, who believe him to be an *agent provocateur* from Earth. The Doctor succeeds in convincing the Draconians of the truth. Jo is recaptured by the Master and taken to the bleak terrifying Ogron planet. The Doctor follows to rescue her. There he discovers the true masterminds behind the whole plot: the Daleks! The Doctor wins the day but the Master escapes. The Daleks flee after the Doctor has been severely wounded by an Ogron.

107

Because of the death of Roger Delgado in June 1973 this is the last story to feature the Master until *The Deadly Assassin* (4P) in 1976.

Novelisation: *Doctor Who and the Space War* by Malcolm Hulke (0 426 11033 1) first published by Wyndham Publications (now Virgin Publishing Ltd) in 1976 with cover by Chris Achilleos. Also published in *The Doctor Who Omnibus* published by Book Club Associates in 1977. Target library number 57.

Video tape: Episode 6 on *The Pertwee Years* (BBCV 4756) first released in 1992 with photomontage cover.

(SSS) **PLANET OF THE DALEKS**
(6 episodes)
7 April 1973 to 12 May 1973

Writer:
Terry Nation

Director:
David Maloney

Regular cast: see RRR above

Cast: Bernard Horsfall (Taron), Prentis Hancock (Vaber); Tim Preece (Codal); Roy Skelton (Wester); Jane How (Rebec); Hilary Minster (Marat); Alan Tucker (Latep); Tony Starr (Dalek Supreme); John Scott Martin, Murphy Grumbar, Cy Town (Daleks); Michael Wisher, Roy Skelton (Dalek voices).

Story: Escaping from the Daleks, the TARDIS materialises on the planet Spiridon. The Doctor has not yet recovered and Jo does not know of his recuperative powers. She sets out alone to find help and meets old allies of the Time Lord, the Thals, who are on a suicide mission to destroy the Daleks. Jo contracts a fungus disease and is cured by a friendly but invisible native. The Thals tell the Doctor, now recovered, that there are thousands of Daleks on Spiridon, immobilised by cold but ready to become an army and conquer the Galaxy with the unwilling help of the Spiridons, who retain the secret of invisibility. The Doctor finds the whereabouts of the Dalek army and succeeds in reactivating an ice volcano, which refreezes the entire Dalek army.

Novelisation: *Doctor Who – Planet of the Daleks* by Terrance Dicks (0 426 11252 0) first published by Wyndham Publications (now Virgin Publishing Ltd) as *Doctor Who and the Planet of the Daleks* in 1976 with cover by Chris Achilleos. New edition by Virgin Publishing Ltd in 1992 with cover by Alister Pearson. Also published in *Doctor Who – The Dalek Omnibus* by Terrance Dicks first published by W H Allen in 1983 with cover by Andrew Skilleter. Target library number 46.

(TTT) **THE GREEN DEATH**
(6 episodes)
19 May 1973 to 23 June 1973

Writer:
Robert Sloman
(with Barry Letts, uncredited)

Director:
Michael Briant

Regular cast: see RRR above

Guest stars: Nicholas Courtney (Brigadier Lethbridge-Stewart); John Levene (Sergeant Benton); Richard Franklin (Captain Yates).

Cast: Stewart Bevan (Professor Clifford Jones); Jerome Willis (Stevens); John Scott Martin (Hughes); Ben Howard (Hinks); Tony Adams (Elgin); Mostyn Evans (Dai Evans); Ray Handy (Milkman); Talfryn Thomas (Dave); Roy Evans (Bert); John Dearth (voice of BOSS); John Rolfe (Fell); Terry Walsh, Billie

Horrigan, Brian Justice, Alan Chuntz (Guards); Mitzi McKenzie (Nancy); Jean Burgess (Cleaner); Roy Skelton (James); Richard Beale (Minister of Ecology).

Story: The villagers of Llanfairfach in Wales are delighted when the local Global Chemicals unit gets a Government grant to build a full-scale refinery. But the project is fiercely opposed by ecologist Professor Clifford Jones. He has set up a commune in the valley dubbed Nuthutch by the locals. Professor Jones feels that the refinery is a threat to the environment. A strange death in some disused mines brings UNIT to the scene. The Doctor, who has managed to get to Metebelis 3 and has found it very hostile, discovers a swarm of giant green maggots and green slime – both fatal to touch – which have come from waste pumped from the refinery. The director, Stevens, refuses to discuss this with UNIT because he has been taken over by BOSS, the giant computer behind Global Chemicals that has a will of its own. The Doctor uses the only souvenir he brought back from Metebelis 3 – a Blue Crystal – to successfully counteract the hypnotic powers of BOSS. He finally succeeds in stopping both the maggots and the maniac computer. Jo Grant falls in love with Professor Jones and leaves UNIT to marry him. The Doctor gives her the Blue Crystal.

Novelisation: *Doctor Who and the Green Death* by Malcolm Hulke (0 426 11543 0) first published by Tandem in 1975 with cover by Peter Brookes. New edition in 1979 by W H Allen (now Virgin Publishing Ltd) with cover by Alun Hood. Target library number 29.

Eleventh Season

Producer:
Barry Letts

Script Editor:
Terrance Dicks

(UUU) **THE TIME WARRIOR**
(4 episodes)
15 December 1973 to 5 January 1974

Writer:
Robert Holmes

Director:
Alan Bromly

Regular cast: Jon Pertwee (the Doctor); Elisabeth Sladen (Sarah Jane Smith).

Guest star: Nicholas Courtney (Brigadier Lethbridge-Stewart).

Cast: Kevin Lindsay (Linx); David Daker (Irongron); John J. Carney (Bloodaxe); Sheila Fay (Meg); Donald Pelmear (Professor Rubeish); June Brown (Lady Eleanor); Alan Rowe (Edward of Wessex); Gordon Pitt (Eric); Jeremy Bulloch (Hal); Steve Brunswick (Sentry); Jacqueline Stanbury (Mary).

Story: Linx, an alien Commander of the Sontaran race, lands his starship, cripped by the Rutans, in medieval times outside a castle belonging to the robber chief Irongron. Irongron offers shelter in exchange for modern weapons, including firearms and a robot knight. Linx uses a crude time machine to reach the 20th century to steal scientists and equipment to repair his starship. The Doctor, accompanied by a stowaway, journalist Sarah Jane Smith, who is investigating the disappearances, uses tracking instruments to find Irongron's castle. The Doctor is captured and interrogated by Linx, who discovers he is a Time Lord. The Doctor escapes and allies himself with the neighbouring people of Wessex Castle. Later, Sarah drugs

111

Irongron's men while the Doctor shows the scientists how to return to their own time. But Linx's ship is now ready to leave. During the final assault, Irongron finds Linx fighting with the Doctor. Irongron is killed by Linx, who is himself shot in the probic vent by Hal, a Wessex archer. Linx's ship blows up, destroying Irongron's castle.

This is the first time we learn of the name of the Time Lords' planet: Gallifrey.

Novelisation: *Doctor Who – The Time Warrior* by Terrance Dicks (0 426 20023 3) first published as *Doctor Who and the Time Warrior* by W H Allen (now Virgin Publishing Ltd) in 1978 with cover by Roy Knipe. New edition in 1993 with cover by Alister Pearson. Target library number 65.

Video tape: *The Time Warrior* (BBCV 4245) first released in 1989 with photomontage cover.

(WWW) **INVASION OF THE DINOSAURS**
(6 episodes)
12 January 1974 to 16 February 1974

Writer:
Malcolm Hulke

Director:
Paddy Russell

Regular cast: see UUU above

Guest stars: see UUU above, and John Levene (Sergeant Benton); Richard Franklin (Captain Yates).

Cast: Noel Johnson (Charles Grover); Peter Miles (Professor Whitaker); Martin Jarvis (Butler); Pat Gorman (UNIT Corporal); James Marcus (Peasant); Ben Aris (Shears); John Caesar (Soldier); Gordon Reid (Phillips); George Bryson (Ogden);

Terry Walsh (Looter); John Bennett (General Finch); Martin Taylor (Corporal Norton); Dave Carter (Duffy); Terence Wilton (Mark); Brian Badcoe (Adam); Carmen Silvera (Ruth); Colin Bell (Bryson); Timothy Craven (Robinson); Trevor Lawrence (Lodge).

Story: London is evacuated after prehistoric monsters suddenly appear out of nowhere. The Doctor and Sarah return to find London deserted and under martial law. At first they are arrested as looters but once back with the Brigadier they discover an incredible plot to alter Time. A group of misguided idealists, led by Charles Grover MP, wants to reverse Time, wiping out all Earth's previous history and returning it to a golden age before technological pollution. Captain Yates has been converted to their cause and is working against UNIT. Thanks to his powers as a Time Lord, the Doctor is able to foil the scheme.

Episode 1 of this story was broadcast under the title *Invasion*.

Novelisation: *Doctor Who – The Invasion of the Dinosaurs* by Malcolm Hulke (0 426 10874 4) first published by Tandem as *Doctor Who and the Dinosaur Invasion* in 1976 with cover by Chris Achilleos. New edition by W H Allen (now Virgin Publishing Ltd) in 1978 with cover by Jeff Cummins. New edition in 1993 with cover by Alister Pearson. Target library number 22.

(XXX) **DEATH TO THE DALEKS**
(4 episodes)
23 February 1974 to 16 March 1974

Writer:
Terry Nation

Director:
Michael Briant

Regular cast: see UUU above

Cast: Arnold Yarrow (Bellal); Roy Heymann (Gotal); Duncan Lamont (Galloway); John Abineri (Railton); Julian Fox (Hamilton); Joy Harrison (Jill Tarrant); Neil Seiler (Stewart); Mostyn Evans (High Priest); Terry Walsh (Spaceman); Steven Ismay, Terry Walsh (Zombies); John Scott Martin, Murphy Grumbar, Cy Town (Daleks); Michael Wisher (Dalek voices).

Story: A space plague attacks all creatures in the Galaxy. The antidote can only be found on the planet Exxilon, home of a now savagely hostile and degenerate race. The Exxilons have rejected all technology since their perfect, automated City expelled them. The Doctor's TARDIS is grounded on Exxilon, drained of its power by the City. The Doctor and Sarah find themselves caught up in a struggle between Humans and Daleks for possession of the vital antidote. Helped by Bellal, a friendly Exxilon who is a member of a breakaway group that no longer worships the City, the Doctor, followed by the Daleks, manages to get into the City, passes its tests and destroys it. It is discovered that the Daleks are the cause of the plague. One of the Humans sacrifices his life to blow up the Dalek spaceship, saving the precious antidote for Humanity.

Novelisation: *Doctor Who – Death to the Daleks* by Terrance Dicks (0 426 20042 X) first published by Wyndham Publications in 1978 with cover by Roy Knipe. New edition by Virgin Publishing Ltd in 1991 with cover by Alister Pearson. Target library number 19.

Video tape: *Death to the Daleks* (BBCV 4073) first released in 1987 with photomontage cover.

(YYY) THE MONSTER OF PELADON
(6 episodes)
23 March 1974 to 27 April 1974

Writer:
Brian Hayles

Director:
Lennie Mayne

Regular cast: see UUU above

Cast: Ralph Watson (Ettis); Donald Gee (Eckersley); Gerald Taylor (Vega Nexos); Nina Thomas (Queen Thalira); Frank Gatliff (Ortron); Michael Crane (Blor); Stuart Fell (Alpha Centauri); Ysanne Churchman (Voice of Alpha Centauri); Terry Walsh (Captain); Rex Robinson (Gebek); Graeme Eton (Preba); Nick Hobbs (Aggedor); Roy Evans (Rima); Sonny Caldinez (Sskel); Alan Bennion (Azaxyr); Max Faulkner (Miner).

Story: The Doctor returns to Peladon fifty years after his last visit and finds that the spirit of the sacred monster Aggedor is again spreading terror and death. While helping Queen Thalira (King Peladon's daughter), the Doctor finds that some renegade Ice Warriors are behind a plot to seize the mineral wealth of the planet to help an invading enemy – Galaxy 5. The Federation Ambassador, Alpha Centauri, calls upon Federation troops to settle the troubles on Peladon, but the trisilicate mines are occupied by the Ice Warriors and a Human traitor, Eckersley. The Doctor uses the monster-producing machine of his enemies to despatch the Ice Warriors. Eckersley is killed by the real Aggedor creature.

Novelisation: *Doctor Who – The Monster of Peladon* by Terrance Dicks (0 426 20132 9) first published by W H Allen (now Virgin Publishing Ltd) in 1980 as *Doctor Who and the Monster of Peladon* with cover by Steve Kyte. New edition in 1992 with cover by Alister Pearson. Target library number 43.

(ZZZ) **PLANET OF THE SPIDERS**
(6 episodes)
4 May 1974 to 8 June 1974

Writer:
Robert Sloman
(with Barry Letts, uncredited)

Director:
Barry Letts

Regular cast: see UUU above

Guest stars: Nicholas Courtney (Brigadier Lethbridge-Stewart); John Levene (Sergeant Benton); Richard Franklin (Mike Yates).

Cast: John Dearth (Lupton); Terence Lodge (Moss); Andrew Staines (Keaver); Christopher Burgess (Barnes); Carl Forgione (Land); Cyril Shaps (Professor Clegg); Kevin Lindsay (Cho-Je); John Kane (Tommy); Pat Gorman (Soldier); Chubby Oates (Policeman); Terry Walsh (Man with Boat); Michael Pinder (Hopkins); Stuart Fell (Tramp); Ysanne Churchman, Kismet Delgado, Maureen Morris (Spider voices); Ralph Arliss (Tuar); Geoffrey Morris (Sabor); Joanna Monro (Rega); Gareth Hunt (Arak); Jenny Laird (Neska); Walter Randall (Captain); Max Faulkner (Second Captain); Maureen Morris (Great One); George Cormack (K'Anpo).

Story: The Blue Crystal which the Doctor found on the planet Metebelis 3 and gave to Jo Grant as a wedding present is vitally important to the giant spiders who rule the planet. Both Humans and Spiders came to Metebelis 3 in a colonist ship but the local conditions helped the Spiders to dominate the Humans. The Spiders send an emissary to recover the Crystal. The Doctor and Sarah, alerted by the ex-UNIT Captain Yates, are transported to Metebelis 3 and the Doctor leads a revolt of the planet's Human slaves against their Spider rulers. But he finds that meanwhile the Spiders have started their invasion of Earth. The Doctor defeats them again there and returns to Metebelis 3 to confront the Great One – a gigantic mutated

116

spider – with the Crystal of Power. The stone destroys the Spider but the Doctor's body suffers irreparable damage. The Doctor returns to Earth, dying. However, the Tibetan monk Cho-Je, a new incarnation of the Time Lord K'Anpo, accelerates the regeneration process. The Doctor begins to change . . .

Novelisation: *Doctor Who – Planet of the Spiders* by Terrance Dicks (0 426 10655 5) first published by Tandem as *Doctor Who and the Planet of the Spiders* in 1975 with cover by Peter Brookes. New edition by W H Allen (now Virgin Publishing Ltd) in 1979 with cover by Alun Hood. New edition in 1991 with cover by Alister Pearson. Target library number 48.

Video tape: *Planet of the Spiders* (BBCV 4491) first released in 1991 with cover by Andrew Skilleter.

FOURTH DOCTOR

TOM BAKER
1974 – 1981

Twelfth Season

Producer:
Barry Letts

Script Editor:
Robert Holmes

(4A) **ROBOT**
(4 episodes)
28 December 1974 to 18 January 1975

Writer:
Terrance Dicks

Director:
Christopher Barry

Regular cast: Tom Baker (the Doctor); Elisabeth Sladen (Sarah Jane Smith); Ian Marter (Harry Sullivan).

Guest stars: Nicholas Courtney (Brigadier Lethbridge-Stewart); John Levene (RSM Benton).

Cast: Edward Burnham (Professor Kettlewell); Alec Linstead (Jellicoe); Patricia Maynard (Miss Winters); Michael Kilgarriff (Robot); John Scott Martin (Guard); Timothy Craven (Short); Walter Goodman (Chambers).

Story: The Doctor is recovering from the effects of his latest body change. Meanwhile, a robot breaks into a top-secret government establishment and steals the plans of a new Disintegrator Gun. The Doctor investigates and traces the crime to a group of dissident scientists known as Think Tank who, led by the formidable Miss Winters, are planning to take over the world. To do this they are using a robot designed by Professor Kettlewell, who pretends to oppose them but is really on their side. The Think Tank steals a Destructor Code which will enable them to launch a nuclear missile attack and start the Third World War. UNIT attacks the bunker where they are fortified. In an attempt to protect its masters the robot kills Kettlewell and goes berserk. An infusion of energy provided by the Disintegrator Gun makes it grow to enormous size. The Doctor arrives in time with a metal virus which destroys the robot. Harry Sullivan joins the Doctor and Sarah as they leave in the TARDIS.

Novelisation: *Doctor Who – Robot* by Terrance Dicks (0 426 11279 2) first published by Universal-Tandem as *Doctor Who and the Giant Robot* in 1975 with cover by Peter Brookes. New edition by W H Allen (now Virgin Publishing Ltd) in 1978 with cover by Jeff Cummins. New edition in 1992 with cover by Alister Pearson. Target library number 28.

Video tape: *Robot* (BBCV 4714) first released in 1992 with cover by Alister Pearson.

Producer:
Philip Hinchcliffe

(4C) **THE ARK IN SPACE**
(4 episodes)
25 January 1975 to 15 February 1975

Writer:	**Director:**
Robert Holmes	Rodney Bennett
(based on a story by	
John Lucarotti)	

Regular cast: see 4A above

Cast: Wendy Williams (Vira); Kenton Moore (Noah); Christopher Masters (Libri); John Gregg (Lycett); Richardson Morgan (Rogin); Stuart Fell, Nick Hobbs (Wirrn); Gladys Spencer, Peter Tuddenham (voices); Brian Jacobs (Dune).

Story: The TARDIS materialises on a fully automated space station, which appears to be empty and deserted. In reality it contains the whole future population of Earth stored away in deepfreeze until the planet – ravaged by solar flares – is again habitable. Due to a fault in the machinery they have failed to awaken on schedule. The Doctor discovers that the station has been invaded by the Wirrn, giant insect-like creatures, who had laid their eggs in one of the Humans and who plan to take over Earth. They have taken over the body of Noah, leader of the Ark. Expelled from the Ark, Noah sacrifices himself and blows up the Wirrn. The Doctor, Sarah and Harry beam down to Earth to check the planet's condition for the arrival of the Humans from the space station.

Novelisation: *Doctor Who – The Ark in Space* by Ian Marter (0 426 11631 3) first published by Wyndham Publications as *Doctor Who and the Ark in Space* in 1977 with cover by Chris Achilleos. New edition by Virgin Publishing Ltd in 1991 with cover by Alister Pearson. Target library number 4.

Video tape: *The Ark in Space* (BBCV 4244) first released in 1989 with photomontage cover. Uncut edition (BBCV 5218) released in 1994.

(4B) **THE SONTARAN EXPERIMENT**
(2 episodes)
22 February 1975 to 1 March 1975

Writers:
Bob Baker
Dave Martin

Director:
Rodney Bennett

Regular cast: see 4A above

Cast: Kevin Lindsay (Styre/Marshal); Peter Walshe (Erak); Terry Walsh (Zake); Glyn Jones (Krans); Peter Rutherford (Roth); Donald Douglas (Vural); Brian Ellis (Prisoner).

Story: On Earth the Doctor discovers that Styre, a Sontaran field-major, is conducting cruel experiments on Human captives – people from one of Earth's colonies, stranded on Earth since their ship was vaporised after answering a fake mayday signal. Styre is there in order to discover the strength of Human resistance to a planned invasion of the Galaxy. The Doctor challenges Styre to physical combat to enable Harry to remove the terrulian diode bypass transformer from the Sontaran ship. When Styre attempts to repower, he finds himself drained of energy. Earth is safe for resettlement by the Human race.

Novelisation: *Doctor Who and the Sontaran Experiment* by Ian Marter (0 426 20049 7) first published by W H Allen (now Virgin Publishing Ltd) in 1978 with cover by Roy Knipe. Target library number 56.

Video tape: *The Sontaran Experiment/Genesis of the Daleks* (BBCV 4643) first released in 1991 with cover by Andrew Skilleter.

(4E) **GENESIS OF THE DALEKS**
(6 episodes)
8 March 1975 to 12 April 1975

Writer:
Terry Nation

Director:
David Maloney

Regular cast: see 4A above

Cast: Michael Wisher (Davros); John Scott Martin, Max Faulkner, Keith Ashley, Cy Town (Daleks); Roy Skelton (Dalek voices); Peter Miles (Nyder), Guy Siner (Ravon), Dennis Chinnery (Gharman); Richard Reeves (Kaled Leader); John Franklyn-Robbins (Time Lord); Stephen Yardley (Sevrin); James Garbutt (Ronson); Drew Wood (Tane); Jeremy Chandler (Gerrill); Pat Gorman, Hilary Minster, John Gleeson (Thal Soldiers); Andrew Johns (Kravos); Peter Mantle (Kaled Guard); Harriet Philpin (Bettan); Max Faulkner (Thal Guard); Michael Lynch (Thal Politician); Ivor Roberts (Mogran), Tom Georgeson (Kavell).

Story: The Time Lords send the Doctor, Sarah and Harry to the planet Skaro at a time when the war between Thals and Kaleds is reaching its final stage. The Doctor's mission is to prevent the birth of the dreaded Daleks who evolved out of this war. Hunted by both sides in a war-torn world, the Doctor eventually becomes the prisoner of Davros, the brilliant crippled Kaled scientist. Davros has invented a travel machine to house the creature into which the Kaleds, genetically mutated by centuries of warfare, will eventually evolve. But Davros is obsessed by his own creation and is giving it destructive powers and a ruthless intelligence which were not part of the original design. These travel machines are destined to become the Daleks! The Doctor helps to lead a revolt of Kaled scientists, horrified by what Davros is doing. But Davros in his determination to preserve the Daleks, helps the Thals to destroy his own people with a super-missile. Then he uses the Daleks, now fully operational, first to wipe out the Thal City, then to destroy those remaining Kaleds who oppose him. Some Thals survive. The Doctor manages to entomb Davros in the fortified bunker which has become his final refuge. Here the Daleks turn on Davros, destroying their creator. The Doctor refuses to destroy the Daleks when he has the chance on the grounds that it would be genocide; he says that even from the Daleks a greater good will eventually emerge. Whisked away from Skaro by the Time Lords, the travellers disappear.

The Doctor and his Companions travel to Skaro and back using a Time Ring provided by the Time Lords.

Novelisation: *Doctor Who – Genesis of the Daleks* by Terrance Dicks (0 426 11260 1) first published by Tandem as *Doctor Who and the Genesis of the Daleks* in 1976 with cover by Chris Achilleos. New edition by Virgin Publishing Ltd in 1991 with cover by Alister Pearson. Target library number 27.

Video tape: *The Sontaran Experiment/Genesis of the Daleks* (BBCV 4643) first released in 1991 with cover by Andrew Skilleter.

Audio tape: *Genesis of the Daleks/Slipback* (catalogue number: ZBBC 1494, ISBN: 0563 401761) first released in 1988 with photomontage cover.

(4D) **REVENGE OF THE CYBERMEN**
(4 episodes)
19 April 1975 to 10 May 1975

Writer:
Gerry Davis
(with Robert Holmes,
uncredited)

Director:
Michael E. Briant

Regular cast: see 4A above

Cast: Alec Wallis (Warner); Ronald Leigh-Hunt (Stevenson); Jeremy Wilkin (Kellman); William Marlowe (Lester); David Collings (Vorus); Michael Wisher (Magrik/Colville/Voices); Christopher Robbie (Cyberleader); Melville Jones (Cyberman); Kevin Stoney (Tyrum); Brian Grellis (Sheprah); Tony Lord, Pat Gorman (Cybermen); Michael E. Briant (Monitor voice).

Story: The Doctor, Sarah and Harry return to the space station only to find that they are in a completely different time period. The station, known as Nerva, is now fulfilling its original function as a space beacon, in orbit around a mysterious planetoid. It is in the grip of a strange plague which has reduced the crew to a mere handful. The Doctor discovers that the plague is carried by Cybermats – deadly machines built by the Cybermen – introduced to the station by a traitor, Kellman. The planetoid is all that is left of Voga, the planet of gold, which was instrumental in the defeat of the Cybermen by the Humans in the Cyberwars centuries ago (gold is deadly to Cybermen). The Vogans have bribed Kellman to attract the remaining Cybermen to Nerva, where they can be blasted out of existence by a Vogan missile, thus freeing the Vogans from a life in hiding. But the Cybermen have other plans. They capture the Doctor and the station crew and, after having attached bombs to them, send them on a deadly errand to the core of Voga. The Doctor eventually helps the Vogans defeat the Cybermen by the use of gold dust. The rest of the Cybermen are destroyed by the Vogan

124

missile. The Doctor prevents Nerva from crashing down on Voga. The TARDIS arrives and the Doctor finds an SOS from the Brigadier.

Novelisation: *Doctor Who – Revenge of the Cybermen* by Terrance Dicks (0 426 10997 X) first published by Tandem as *Doctor Who and the Revenge of the Cybermen* in 1976 with cover by Chris Achilleos. New edition by Virgin Publishing Ltd in 1991 with cover by Alister Pearson. Also published in *The Doctor Who Omnibus* first published by Book Club Associates in 1977. Target library number 51.

Video tape: *Revenge of the Cybermen* (BBCV 2003/4013) first released in 1983 with photomontage cover.

Thirteenth Season

Producer:
Philip Hinchcliffe

Script Editor:
Robert Holmes

(4F) TERROR OF THE ZYGONS
(4 episodes)
30 August 1975 to 20 September 1975

Writer:
Robert Banks Stewart

Director:
Douglas Camfield

Regular cast: Tom Baker (the Doctor); Elisabeth Sladen (Sarah Jane Smith).

Guest stars: Ian Marter (Harry Sullivan); Nicholas Courtney (Brigadier Lethbridge-Stewart); John Levene (RSM Benton).

Cast: John Woodnutt (Duke of Forgill/Broton); Hugh Martin

(Munro); Tony Sibbald (Huckle); Angus Lennie (Angus McRanald); Robert Russell (The Caber); Bruce Wightman (Radio Operator); Lillias Walker (Sister Lamont); Bernard G. High (Corporal); Peter Symonds (Soldier); Keith Ashley, Ronald Gough (Zygons).

Story: Summoned back to Earth by the Brigadier, the Doctor investigates a series of mysterious attacks on North Sea oil rigs. Centre of the attacks is the village of Tullock, very close to Loch Ness. The Doctor discovers that the cause of these attacks is the Loch Ness Monster, in reality a Skarasen, a creature half-animal, half-machine, created by the Zygons, an alien race whose crippled spaceship has rested on the bottom of the Loch for centuries. Unable to return home (their planet was destroyed), the Zygons plan to take over Earth and turn it into a new home planet for their race. Able to change form and take on the physical appearance of Humans, the Zygons have infiltrated the village. The Doctor exposes the Zygons and frees their captives, including the local Duke. The Brigadier blows up the Zygon ship but Broton, leader of the Zygons, now in London, threatens to destroy a World Energy Conference. He is stopped by the Doctor. The Skarasen survives to swim happily back to Loch Ness.

Novelisation: *Doctor Who – Terror of the Zygons* by Terrance Dicks (0 426 11041 2) first published by Tandem as *Doctor Who and the Loch Ness Monster* in 1976 with cover by Chris Achilleos. New edition by Virgin Publishing Ltd in 1993 with cover by Alister Pearson. Target library number 40.

Video tape: *Terror of the Zygons* (BBCV 4186) first released in 1988 with photomontage cover.

(4H) **PLANET OF EVIL**
(4 episodes)
27 September 1975 to 18 October 1975

Writer:
Louis Marks

Director:
David Maloney

Regular cast: see 4F above

Cast: Terence Brook (Braun); Tony McEwan (Baldwin); Frederick Jaeger (Sorenson); Ewen Solon (Vishinsky); Prentis Hancock (Salamar); Michael Wisher (Morelli/Voice of Ranjit); Graham Weston (De Haan); Louis Mahoney (Ponti); Hadyn Wood (O'Hara); Melvyn Bedford (Reig); Mike Lee Lane (Monster); Ray Knight, Douglas Stark (Sorenson monsters).

Story: Answering a mayday call, the Doctor and Sarah arrive on Zeta Minor, a planet far out on the edge of the known Universe. A geological expedition from the planet Morestra has run into trouble. Only its leader, Professor Sorenson, is still alive, all the other crew members having been killed by an invisible entity. A military party from Morestra, led by the young Controller Salamar, arrives to investigate. The Doctor and Sarah come under suspicion but when the whole party is attacked by the entity they are released. Zeta Minor is a gate to a universe of Anti-matter, from which the entity originates. They all leave the planet but Sorenson, disregarding the Doctor's advice, has taken some Anti-matter on board. Sorenson turns into an Anti-matter monster and the ship is dragged back to the planet. The Doctor manages to collect all the Anti-matter and captures Sorenson. After the substance is returned to the Anti-matter universe the ship is freed and Sorenson cured.

Novelisation: *Doctor Who and the Planet of Evil* by Terrance Dicks (0 426 11682 8) first published by W H Allen (now Virgin Publishing Ltd) in 1977 with cover by Mike Little. New edition in 1982 with cover by Andrew Skilleter. Target library number 47.

Video tape: *Planet of Evil* (BBCV 5180) first released in 1994 with cover by Colin Howard.

(4G) **PYRAMIDS OF MARS**
(4 episodes)
25 October 1975 to 15 November 1975

Writer:
Stephen Harris
(Lewis Griefer and
Robert Holmes)

Director:
Paddy Russell

Regular cast: see 4F above

Cast: Bernard Archard (Professor Marcus Scarman); Vik Tablian (Ahmed); Peter Mayock (Namin); Michael Bilton (Collins); Peter Copley (Dr Warlock); Michael Sheard (Laurence Scarman); George Tovey (Ernie Clements); Gabriel Woolf (Sutekh/Voice of Horus); Nick Burnell, Melvyn Bedford, Kevin Selway (Mummies); Tony Alless, Oscar Charles (Egyptian labourers).

Story: The Doctor and Sarah are returning to UNIT HQ on Earth when the TARDIS is caught up by a mysterious force. Sarah sees an evil face materialise which terrifies her. Egyptologist Marcus Scarman has inadvertently broken into the pyramid prison of Sutekh, last of the Osirians. Sutekh is a creature with god-like powers and his only ambition is to destroy all life in the Cosmos. Defeated by his brother Horus and the other Osirians, Sutekh has lain prisoner for centuries in his pyramid. The Doctor and Sarah arrive in Professor Scarman's house in England (which will later become the site of UNIT's HQ) just as Scarman, possessed by the spirit of Sutekh, returns to build a rocket to go to the Pyramids of Mars; they contain the

Eye of Horus, the key to Sutekh's prison. Scarman's robots – dressed as Egyptian mummies – kill Scarman's brother but the Doctor manages, by distracting Sutekh, to blow up the rocket. Sutekh forces the Doctor to take Scarman to Mars in the TARDIS. Scarman destroys the Eye of Horus, but the Doctor returns to Earth in time to prevent Sutekh from leaving the Space/Time tunnel which is the only exit from his prison. Controlling the time factor of the tunnel, the Doctor sends Sutekh to the ends of time.

Novelisation: *Doctor Who - Pyramids of Mars* by Terrance Dicks (0 426 11666 6) first published by Wyndham Publications as *Doctor Who and the Pyramids of Mars* in 1976 with cover by Chris Achilleos. New edition by W H Allen (now Virgin Publishing Ltd) in 1982 with cover by Andrew Skilleter. New edition in 1993 with cover by Alister Pearson. Target library number 50.

Video tape: *Pyramids of Mars* (BBCV 2014/4055) first released in 1985 with photomontage cover.

(4J) THE ANDROID INVASION
(4 episodes)
22 November 1975 to 13 December 1975

Writer:
Terry Nation

Director:
Barry Letts

Regular cast: see 4F above

Guest stars: Ian Marter (Harry Sullivan); John Levene (RSM Benton).

Cast: Martin Friend (Styggron); Roy Skelton (Chedaki); Max Faulkner (Adams); Peter Welch (Morgan); Milton Johns (Guy Crayford); Stuart Fell (Kraal); Patrick Newell (Faraday); Dave

129

Carter (Grierson); Heather Emmanuel (Tessa); Hugh Lund (Matthews).

Story: The TARDIS lands near what appears to be a peaceful English village. But the inhabitants are strange and unfriendly, responding like robots to mysterious signals. Mechanics with gun-like hands appear from nowhere. The Doctor discovers that they are not on Earth at all but in a replica village built on their own planet by the Kraals, an alien race bent on the conquest of Earth with the aid of Androids. The Doctor and Sarah return to Earth in the Kraal ship in time to foil the Kraal invasion. Some of the UNIT's leaders have already been replaced. The Doctor reprogrammes an Android copy of himself to prevent Styggron, the Kraal scientist, from destroying Earth's population with a super-virus.

This is the last UNIT story until *Battlefield* (7N) in 1989.

Novelisation: *Doctor Who and the Android Invasion* by Terrance Dicks (0 426 20037 3) first published by W H Allen (now Virgin Publishing Ltd) in 1978 with cover by Roy Knipe. Target library number 2.

(4K) **THE BRAIN OF MORBIUS**
(4 episodes)
3 January 1976 to 24 January 1976

Writer:
Robin Bland
(Terrance Dicks and
Robert Holmes)

Director:
Christopher Barry

Regular cast: see 4F above

Cast: Philip Madoc (Solon); Colin Fay (Condo); Gilly Brown (Ohica); Cynthia Grenville (Maren); Michael Spice (voice of Morbius); Stuart Fell (Morbius Monster); John Scott Martin

(Kriz); Sue Bishop, Janie Kells, Gabrielle Mowbray, Veronica Ridge (Sisters); Alan Crisp (Headless monster).

Story: The TARDIS lands on Karn, a bleak and stormy planet, where Solon, a disreputable galactic surgeon, is carrying out strange experiments. The planet is also the home of the Sisterhood, witch-like guardians of the mysterious Sacred Flame, from which is prepared the Elixir of Life, an immortality drug shared by the Sisters with the Time Lords. The Flame is dying and the High Priestess, Maren, believes the Doctor is a spy sent by the Time Lords to steal the few precious remaining drops of the Elixir. Meanwhile, the Doctor discovers that Solon is concealing the still-living brain of Morbius, a high-ranking renegade Time Lord and cosmic villain, supposed to have been executed some centuries ago. Solon is making a monstrous new body in which Morbius will live again to lead his followers in the conquest of the Galaxy. The Doctor and Sarah have to battle with Morbius, revived and on the rampage, and with the suspicious Sisterhood. The Doctor defeats Morbius in mental battle, and the body is destroyed by the Sisters, convinced of the Doctor's good faith after he restored the Flame to its former brilliance. Some of the Elixir is used to save the Doctor's life.

Novelisation: *Doctor Who – The Brain of Morbius* by Terrance Dicks (0 426 11674 7) first published by W H Allen (now Virgin Publishing Ltd) as *Doctor Who and the Brain of Morbius* in 1977 with cover by Mike Little. New edition in 1991 with cover by Alister Pearson. Target library number 7.

Video tape: *The Brain of Morbius* (BBCV 2012) first released in 1984 with photomontage cover. New edition (BBCV 4388) in 1990 with cover by Alister Pearson.

(4L) **THE SEEDS OF DOOM**
(6 episodes)
31 January 1976 to 6 March 1976

Writer:
Robert Banks Stewart

Director:
Douglas Camfield

Regular cast: see 4F above

Cast: Tony Beckley (Harrison Chase); John Challis (Scorby); John Gleeson (Charles Winlett/Krynoid humanoid); Michael McStay (Derek Moberley); Hubert Rees (John Stevenson); Kenneth Gilbert (Dunbar); Seymour Green (Hargreaves); Michael Barrington (Sir Colin Thackeray); Mark Jones (Arnold Keeler); Ian Fairbairn (Dr Chester); Alan Chuntz (Chauffeur); Sylvia Coleridge (Amelia Ducat); David Masterman, Harry Fielder, Ian Elliott (Guards); John Acheson (Major Beresford); Ray Barron (Sergeant Henderson); Mark Jones (Krynoid's voice); Keith Ashley (Secretary); Ronald Gough, Keith Ashley (Krynoid monster).

Story: Deep in the permafrost of the Antarctic, scientists discover two vegetable pods. The Doctor identifies them as Krynoids, an alien species of plant, hostile to all animal life. One of the pods opens and a Krynoid takes over a scientist's body. In England Harrison Chase, a rich and eccentric botanist, sends two men to steal the remaining pod. They succeed but in the ensuing battle the base and the first Krynoid monster are destroyed. Back in England the second pod opens and takes over Keeler, one of Chase's scientists. He soon evolves into a giant Krynoid monster which threatens to turn the native plants of Earth against Humanity. The Doctor and his allies at the World Ecology Bureau manage to infiltrate Chase's residence, but it is too late to stop the demented millionaire – or the Krynoid. The RAF bombs the Krynoid, now larger than Chase's house, before it germinates.

Novelisation: *Doctor Who and the Seeds of Doom* by Philip Hinchcliffe (0 426 11658 5) first published by Tandem/ Wyndham Publications (now Virgin Publishing Ltd) in 1977 with cover by Chris Achilleos. Target library number 55.

Fourteenth Season

Producer:
Philip Hinchcliffe

Script Editor:
Robert Holmes

(4M) MASQUE OF MANDRAGORA
(4 episodes)
4 September 1976 to 25 September 1976

Writer:
Louis Marks

Director:
Rodney Bennett

Regular cast: Tom Baker (the Doctor); Elisabeth Sladen (Sarah Jane Smith).

Cast: Jon Laurimore (Count Federico); Gareth Armstrong (Giuliano); Tim Pigott-Smith (Marco); Norman Jones (Hieronymous); Antony Carrick (Captain Rossini); Robert James (High Priest); Pat Gorman, James Appleby, John Clamp (Guards); Peter Walshe, Jay Neill (Pikemen); Brian Ellis (Brother); Peter Tuddenham (Mandragora's voice); Peggy Dixon, Jack Edwards, Alistair Fullarton, Michael Reid, Kathy Wolff (Dancers); Stuart Fell (Entertainer).

Story: The TARDIS is drawn off course by the Mandragora Helix, a powerful alien energy complex. Unknown to the Doctor, a portion of Mandragora conceals itself inside the TARDIS, which subsequently lands on Earth. The Doctor and

Sarah find themselves in the Dukedom of San Martino in Italy in the 15th century. The evil Count Federico is planning to usurp the rule of his nephew, Giuliano. He is aided by Hieronymous, the Court Astrologer and secret leader of the Brothers of Demnos, a cult of star-worshippers. Mandragora takes over Hieronymous, seeking to form a bridgehead so that it can kill the great minds of the Renaissance and plunge Earth back into the Dark Ages. Federico is murdered by Hieronymous now transformed into an energy creature. The Doctor defeats the Helix by draining its energies.

A new TARDIS control room was introduced in this story.

Novelisation: *Doctor Who – The Masque of Mandragora* by Philip Hinchcliffe (0 426 11893 6) first published by W H Allen (now Virgin Publishing Ltd) as *Doctor Who and the Masque of Mandragora* in 1977 with cover by Mike Little. New edition in 1991 with cover by Alister Pearson. Target library number 42.

Video tape: *The Masque of Mandragora* (BBCV 4642) first released in 1991 with cover by Alister Pearson.

(4N) **THE HAND OF FEAR**
(4 episodes)
2 October 1976 to 23 October 1976

Writers:
Bob Baker,
Dave Martin

Director:
Lennie Mayne

Regular cast: see 4M above

Cast: Roy Pattison (Zazzka); Roy Skelton (Rokon); David Purcell (Abbott); Renu Setna (Intern); Rex Robinson (Dr Carter); Robin Hargrave (Guard); Glyn Houston (Professor Watson); Frances Pidgeon (Miss Jackson); Roy Boyd (Driscoll); John Cannon (Elgin); Judith Paris, Stephen Thorne (Eldrad);

Libby Ritchie (Hospital Nurse); Derek Suthern, John Delieu (Technicians); Barry Summerford, Michael Dewild (Security Guards); Peter Roy (Frozen Kastrian).

Story: Back on 20th-century Earth Sarah finds a fossilised hand. It is in fact the hand of Eldrad, a Kastrian criminal executed by his own race. Eldrad's hand forces Sarah to go inside a nuclear research station, where it regenerates itself by absorbing the energy released in an explosion. To save Earth from Eldrad's powers, the Doctor is forced to take him back to Kastria. But in the 150-million-year interval since Eldrad's execution Kastria's civilisation has ended. Eldrad attempts to regenerate his race – but fails because of the measures taken centuries ago by King Rokon as a precaution against Eldrad's possible return. The Doctor and Sarah leave Kastria, abandoning Eldrad to his solitary fate. The Doctor receives a telepathic summons from Gallifrey and – much to her dismay – has to say goodbye to Sarah.

Novelisation: *Doctor Who and the Hand of Fear* by Terrance Dicks (0 426 20033 0) first published by W H Allen (now Virgin Publishing Ltd) in 1979 with cover by Roy Knipe. Target library number 30.

(4P) **THE DEADLY ASSASSIN**
(4 episodes)
30 October 1976 to 20 November 1976

Writer:
Robert Holmes

Director:
David Maloney

Regular cast: Tom Baker (the Doctor)

Cast: Peter Pratt (the Master); Llewellyn Rees (President); Angus Mackay (Cardinal Borusa); Bernard Horsfall (Chancellor Goth); George Pravda (Castellan Spandrell); Derek Seaton (Commander Hilred); Eric Chitty (Coordinator Engin); Hugh Walters (Commentator Runcible); John Dawson, Michael Bilton (Time Lords); Maurice Quick (Gold Usher); Peter Mayock (Solis); Helen Blatch (Voice).

Story: Having seen the assassination of the President of the Council of Time in a vision, the Doctor returns to his home world, Gallifrey. There he is pursued by the Chancellery Guards but manages to avoid capture and breaks into the Panopticon, where he actually watches the President being murdered. The Doctor is arrested and convicted for the murder. To escape execution he proposes himself as candidate for the presidency. Having convinced Castellan Spandrell that he is innocent, the Doctor discovers that his old enemy the Master is behind the plot. To find out who has been aiding the Master the Doctor has to fight for his life in the fantasy world of the Amplified Panatropic Computer, also known as the Matrix, where he defeats the real murderer, Chancellor Goth. The Master, whose body has reached the end of his regenerations, seizes the instruments of the presidency to tap the power needed to start a new cycle of lives. But if he releases the power of the Black Hole kept captive under the Panopticon, Gallifrey will be destroyed. The Doctor succeeds in defeating the Master, who escapes.

This is the first story featuring the Master since *Frontier in Space* (QQQ), and the last until *The Keeper of Traken* (5T).

Novelisation: *Doctor Who and the Deadly Assassin* by Terrance Dicks (0 426 11965 7) first published by Wyndham Publications (now Virgin Publishing Ltd) in 1977 with cover by Mike Little. Target library number 20.

Video tape: *The Deadly Assassin* (BBCV 4645) first released in 1991 with cover by Andrew Skilleter.

(4Q) THE FACE OF EVIL
(4 episodes)
1 January 1977 to 22 January 1977

Writer:
Chris Boucher

Director:
Pennant Roberts

Regular cast: Tom Baker (the Doctor), and introducing Louise Jameson (Leela).

Cast: Leslie Schofield (Calib); Victor Lucas (Andor); Brendan Price (Tomas); Colin Thomas (Sole); David Garfield (Neeva); Lloyd McGuire (Lugo); Tom Kelly, Brett Forrest (Guards); Leon Eagles (Jabel); Mike Elles (Gentek); Peter Baldock (Acolyte); Tom Baker, Rob Edwards, Pamela Salem, Anthony Frieze, Roy Herrick (voices of Xoanon); Alan Charles (Crowd voices); David Nichol, Harry Fielder (Assassins).

Story: The Doctor lands on a planet where he is captured by a tribe which calls itself the Sevateem. The Doctor survives the Test of the Horda. He discovers that the god Xoanon revered by the Sevateem is a giant computer which has developed a split personality after having been reprogrammed long ago by the Doctor – with his own brain patterns. To correct his mistake the Doctor and a group of warriors from the Sevateem invade the sanctuary of Xoanon and encounter another tribe, the Tesh, who have developed destructive psychic powers. The Doctor succeeds in removing his brain patterns from Xoanon and in reconciling the two warring tribes. Leela, a Sevateem warrior who befriends the Doctor, slips into the TARDIS and follows the Doctor in pursuit of adventure .

Novelisation: *Doctor Who – The Face of Evil* by Terrance Dicks (0 426 20006 3) first published by W H Allen (now Virgin Publishing Ltd) as *Doctor Who and the Face of Evil* in 1978 with cover by Jeff Cummins. New edition in 1993 with cover by Alister Pearson. Target library number 25.

(4R) **THE ROBOTS OF DEATH**

(4 episodes)

29 January 1977 to 19 February 1977

Writer:
Chris Boucher

Director:
Michael E. Briant

Regular cast: see 4Q above

Cast: Russell Hunter (Commander Uvanov); Pamela Salem (Toos); David Bailie (Dask); Rob Edwards (Chub); Brian Croucher (Borg); Tariq Yunus (Cass); David Collings (Poul); Tania Rogers (Zilda); Miles Fothergill (SV7); Gregory de Polnay (D84); Mark Blackwell Baker, John Bleasdale, Mark Cooper, Peter Langtry, Jeremy Ranchev, Richard Seager (Robots).

Story: The Doctor and Leela arrive aboard a huge Sandminer, a mobile factory which mines metal ores from the surface of a deserted planet. The Sandminer has only a token force of Humans, the rest of the crew being robots divided into three classes: Dums, Vocs and one supervising Super Voc, SV7. Mysteriously, a member of the crew is murdered and when the Doctor and Leela are discovered they become suspects. Leela discovers that a crew member and a robot, D84, are in reality investigators despatched by the company which chartered the Sandminer. There is a sabotage attempt on the ship but the craft is saved by the Doctor. Dask, a member of the crew, is found to be the killer: he is actually Taren Capel, a scientist who has been raised by robots and thinks of them as his brothers. He wants the robots to take control over Mankind and has programmed them to kill. The Doctor, Leela, Commander Uvanov and his aide Toos escape. The Time Lord releases helium into the atmosphere, changing Dask's voice. The robots, now unable to identify him, destroy him.

Novelisation: *Doctor Who – The Robots of Death* by Terrance

138

Dicks (0 426 20061 6) first published by W H Allen (now Virgin Publishing Ltd) as *Doctor Who and the Robots of Death* in 1979 with cover by John Geary. New edition in 1994 with cover by Alister Pearson. Target library number 53.

Video tape: *The Robots of Death* (BBCV 2030/4108) first released in 1986 with photomontage cover.

(4S) **THE TALONS OF WENG-CHIANG**
(6 episodes)
26 February 1977 to 2 April 1977

Writer:
Robert Holmes
(based on an idea by
Robert Banks Stewart)

Director:
David Maloney

Regular cast: see 4Q above

Cast: John Bennett (Li H'sen Chang); Deep Roy (Mr Sin); Michael Spice (Weng-Chiang/Greel); Trevor Baxter (Professor Litefoot); Christopher Benjamin (Henry Gordon Jago); Tony Then (Lee); Alan Butler (Buller); Chris Gannon (Casey); John Wu (Coolie); Conrad Asquith (PC Quick); David McKail (Sergeant Kyle); Patsy Smart (Ghoul); Judith Lloyd (Teresa); Vaune Craig-Raymond (Cleaning Woman); Penny Lister (Singer); Vincent Wong (Ho); Stuart Fell (Giant rat).

Story: The TARDIS materialises in Victorian London, where a series of murders are committed by the Chinese Tong of the Black Scorpion, led by Weng-Chiang. Weng-Chiang is in reality Magnus Greel, a war criminal from the future, whose time experiments backfire and whose body needs the energy of others to survive. Victims are provided by Greel's servant, Li H'sen Chang, who performs as a magician in a local theatre managed by the boisterous Henry Gordon Jago. The Doctor finds Weng-Chiang's lair in the sewers under the theatre but is chased away by a rat mutated to giant size by Greel. Meanwhile, Li H'sen Chang's men have located the long-lost time cabinet of Weng-Chiang – in the hands of one of the Doctor's friends, Professor Litefoot. Li H'sen Chang fails in his mission to kill the Doctor and recover the Cabinet and is dismissed by Greel. With the help of his Homunculus, Mr Sin, Weng-Chiang recaptures the cabinet, and the Doctor's friends with it. A dying Li H'sen Chang (he was attacked by Greel's giant rat) gives the address of Weng Chiang's new refuge to the Doctor. Greel dies a victim of his own life-absorbing equipment and Mr Sin is disconnected by the Doctor.

Novelisation: *Doctor Who – The Talons of Weng-Chiang* by Terrance Dicks (0 426 11973 8) first published by W H Allen (now Virgin Publishing Ltd) as *Doctor Who and the Talons of Weng-Chiang* in 1977 with cover by Jeff Cummins. New edition in 1994 with cover by Alister Pearson. Target library number 61.

Script book: *Doctor Who – The Talons of Weng-Chiang* by Robert Holmes (1 85286 144 4) first published by Titan Books in 1989 with cover by Duncan Fegredo. New edition in 1994 with cover by Alister Pearson.

Video tape: *The Talons of Weng-Chiang* (BBCV 4187) first released in 1988 with photomontage cover.

Fifteenth Season

Producer:
Graham Williams

Script Editor:
Robert Holmes

(4V) **HORROR OF FANG ROCK**
(4 episodes)
3 September 1977 to 24 September 1977

Writer:
Terrance Dicks

Director:
Paddy Russell

Regular cast: Tom Baker (the Doctor); Louise Jameson (Leela).

Cast: Colin Douglas (Reuben/Voice of the Rutan); John Abbott (Vince); Ralph Watson (Ben); Alan Rowe (Colonel Skinsale); Sean Caffrey (Lord Palmerdale); Annette Woollett (Adelaide); Rio Fanning (Harker).

Story: The TARDIS materialises at the turn of the century on the lone island of Fang Rock. A few hours earlier Vince, the youngest of the three lighthouse-men who are the only inhabitants of the island, watched as a streak of light came down from the sky and landed in the ocean. Not long after, an eerie fog rises and the electrical engineer is mysteriously killed. The Doctor and Leela are suspected of the crime. Meanwhile a passing clipper runs aground. The survivors are rescued and made comfortable. The Doctor tries to convince them to help him against what he now believes to be an alien menace that feeds on electricity. By the time the Doctor realises that the alien has taken the form of Reuben, the old lighthouse keeper, more members of the small group have died. The alien reveals itself as a Rutan, a blob-like race which is at war with the Sontaran Empire. The Doctor constructs a crude laser cannon and destroys the Rutan and its mother ship.

The laser blast is used to explain the change in Louise Jameson's eye colour. Until now, her blue eyes had been covered by brown contact lenses.

Novelisation: *Doctor Who and the Horror of Fang Rock* by Terrance Dicks (0 426 20009 8) first published by W H Allen (now Virgin Publishing Ltd) in 1978 with cover by Jeff Cummins. Target library number 32.

(4T) THE INVISIBLE ENEMY
(4 episodes)
1 October 1977 to 22 October 1977

Writers:
Bob Baker,
Dave Martin

Director:
Derrick Goodwin

Regular cast: see 4V above, and introducing John Leeson (voice of K9).

Cast: Michael Sheard (Lowe); Frederick Jaeger (Professor Marius); Brian Grellis (Safran); Jay Neill (Silvey); Edmund Pegge (Meeker); Anthony Rowlands (Crewman); John Leeson (Nucleus voice); John Scott Martin (Nucleus Operator); Nell Curran (Nurse); Jim McManus (Ophthalmologist); Roderick Smith (Cruikshank); Kenneth Waller (Hedges); Elizabeth Norman (Marius' Nurse); Roy Herrick (Parsons); Pat Gorman (Medic).

Story: A space virus infiltrates an Earth shuttlecraft *en route* to the Titan base. The TARDIS is also attacked by the virus which goes through its flight system and into the Doctor, who is unaware of its presence. When they land on Titan the time-travellers are threatened by the shuttlecraft crew. The Doctor discovers that he is carrying the virus nucleus and that incubation tanks are being prepared. He and Leela manage to escape and seek medical assistance at the Bi-Al Foundation, where Professor Marius and his dog-like mobile computer, K9, become their allies. To remove the nucleus from the Doctor's body Marius sends miniaturised clone copies of the Time Lord and Leela into the Doctor's brain. Released and enlarged to Human-size, the nucleus is taken by the possessed crewmen, led by Lowe, who intend to return it to Titan for incubation. To prevent this, the Doctor sets up an explosion which destroys the base.

Novelisation: *Doctor Who and the Invisible Enemy* by Terrance Dicks (0 426 20054 3) first published by W H Allen (now Virgin Publishing Ltd) in 1979 with cover by Roy Knipe. Target library number 36.

(4X) IMAGE OF THE FENDAHL
(4 episodes)
29 October 1977 to 19 November 1977

Writer:
Chris Boucher

Director:
George Spenton-Foster

Regular cast: see 4V above

Cast: Wanda Ventham (Thea Ransome/Fendahl Core); Denis Lill (Dr Fendelman); Edward Arthur (Colby); Scott Fredericks (Stael); Edward Evans (Moss); Derek Martin (Mitchell); Daphne Heard (Martha Tyler); Graham Simpson (Hiker); Geoffrey Hinsliff (Jack Tyler); David Elliott, Roy Pearce (Security Guards).

Story: Dr Fendelman and his assistants, Thea Ransome and Maximilian Stael, through their experiments with a sonic Time Scanner, are in danger of bringing to life the powerful forces that lie dormant in a 12-million-year-old skull. Thea is unaware that she is a medium and that through her the Fendahl, an entity

143

which feeds on life itself, will materialise on Earth. Drawn by the Time Scanner, the TARDIS appears nearby and the Doctor attempts to persuade Fendelman of the hazardous nature of his experiments. The Doctor discovers that the Fendahl originated on the Fifth Planet, which was time-looped by the Time Lords. Thea becomes the Fendahl Core and Stael, a practitioner of the black arts, pays for his folly with his life. Using mystical defences the Doctor steals the skull and then uses the Time Scanner to cause a gigantic explosion which destroys the Fendahl. He and Leela take the skull to be jettisoned near a supernova.

Novelisation: *Doctor Who and the Image of the Fendahl* by Terrance Dicks (0 426 20077 2) first published by W H Allen (now Virgin Publishing Ltd) in 1979 with cover by John Geary. Target library number 34.

Video tape: *Image of the Fendahl* (BBCV 4941) first released in 1993 with cover by Andrew Skilleter.

(4W) **THE SUNMAKERS**
(4 episodes)
26 November 1977 to 17 December 1977

Writer:
Robert Holmes

Director:
Pennant Roberts

Regular cast: see 4T above

Cast: Roy Macready (Cordo); Richard Leech (Gatherer Hade); Jonina Scott (Marn); Michael Keating (Goudry); William Simons (Mandrel); Adrienne Burgess (Veet); Henry Woolf (Collector); David Rowlands (Bisham); Colin McCormack (Commander); Derek Crewe (Synge); Carole Hopkin (Nurse); Tom Kelly (Guard); John Leeson (Computer voice).

Story: The TARDIS lands on Pluto. The Doctor is surprised to find a colony of Humans living there under the light of several small artificial suns. The time-travellers prevent Cordo from committing suicide because of his inability to pay the heavy and unjust taxes requested by the Company, the entity which made the suns around Pluto. Cordo flees the arrival of the Gatherer and leads the Doctor and Leela to the underground city where they meet members of a resistance movement. To convince its hostile leader, Mandrel, that he is not a spy the Doctor attempts to defraud a bank but is captured by the Gatherer, who releases him and places him under surveillance. Joining forces with the rebels the Doctor leads them to capture the PCM production complex where a gas is manufactured and released into the atmosphere to keep the citizens under control. Leela is captured and condemned to be steamed alive. The Doctor saves her. When the PCM gas no longer affects them the citizens rebel and kill the Gatherer. The Doctor confronts the Collector and learns that he is a member of the Usurian race. Unable to deal with the inflation that the Doctor has introduced into his computer, the Usurian shrinks back to its original form and is bottled by the Doctor.

Novelisation: *Doctor Who and the Sunmakers* by Terrance Dicks (0 426 20059 4) first published by W H Allen (now Virgin Publishing Ltd) in 1982 with cover by Andrew Skilleter. Target library number 60.

Script Editor:
Anthony Read

(4Y) **UNDERWORLD**
(4 episodes)
7 January 1978 to 28 January 1978

Writers:
Bob Baker,
Dave Martin

Director:
Norman Stewart

Regular cast: see 4T above

Cast: James Maxwell (Jackson); Alan Lake (Herrick); Imogen Bickford-Smith (Tala); Jonathan Newth (Orfe); Jimmy Gardner (Idmon); Norman Tipton (Idas); Godfrey James (Tarn); James Marcus (Rask); Jay Neill (Klimt); Frank Jarvis (Ankh); Richard Shaw (Lakh); Stacey Tendeter (Naia); Christine Pollon (voice of the Oracle).

Story: At the edge of the universe, where planets are born from cosmic debris, the TARDIS rematerialises on a Minyan ship. To the Minyans Time Lords are gods who helped them build an advanced civilisation. Destroyed by internecine warfare, Minyos is dead; a few Minyans have escaped to found Minyos 2. Jackson and his crew have spent an eternity on the Quest, looking for the long-lost vessel *P7E*, which carried all of Minyos's Race Banks. The Doctor helps Jackson locate the *P7E*, now the core of a planet composed of space debris. The Minyans discover that the *P7E*'s original purpose has been forgotten and that the crew now serve the ship's computer, the Oracle. A hierarchy has formed with the half-man, half-robot Seers tending the Oracle and ruling the Trogs, descendants of the original Minyans. The Doctor and Jackson's crew fight their way to the Oracle's Citadel and manage to steal the two cylinders containing the Race Banks. The Oracle is destroyed by an explosion of its own making. The Minyans blast away, carrying the Trogs to Minyos 2.

Novelisation: *Doctor Who and the Underworld* by Terrance Dicks (0 426 20068 3) first published by W H Allen (now Virgin Publishing Ltd) in 1980 with cover by Bill Donahoe. Target library number 67.

(4Z) **THE INVASION OF TIME**
(6 episodes)
4 February 1978 to 11 March 1978

Writer:
David Agnew
(Anthony Read and
Graham Williams)

Director:
Gerald Blake

Regular cast: see 4T above

Cast: Milton Johns (Kelner); John Arnatt (Borusa); Stan McGowan (Vardan Leader); Chris Tranchell (Andred); Dennis Edwards (Gomer); Tom Kelly (Vardan); Reginald Jessup (Savar); Charles Morgan (Gold Usher); Hilary Ryan (Rodan); Max Faulkner (Nesbin); Christopher Christou (Chancery Guard); Michael Harley (Bodyguard); Ray Callaghan (Ablif); Gai Smith (Presta); Michael Mundell (Jasko); Eric Danot (Guard); Derek Deadman (Stor); Stuart Fell (Sontaran).

Story: The Doctor returns to Gallifrey after meeting mysterious aliens in space. Immediately after arriving he demands to see Cardinal Borusa and invokes his right to the presidency. The inauguration plans are monitored by the aliens, identified as Vardans, creatures that have the ability to travel along any wavelength (including thought) and materialise at the end. The Vardans have invaded the Matrix via the Time Lords' own scan beams for watching over the Universe. As President the Doctor

147

exiles Leela from the Capitol because he is afraid the Vardans will be able to read her mind, and tries to neutralise the Vardan threat by finding their planet of origin. In order to do that, however, the Vardans must materialise completely. To gain their trust the Doctor and K9 destroy the transduction barriers that protect Gallifrey. Meanwhile Leela, who has met the young female trainee Time Lord Rodan, encounters the Shobogans, ex-Time Lords now living like savages. They join together to organise a resistance movement. The Vardans finally material-ise and the Doctor forces them and their home world into a time loop. As everyone is celebrating a new danger appears: the Sontarans have used the Vardans to gain access to Gallifrey. The Castellan Kelner, who betrayed the Doctor to the Vardans helps the Sontarans to take control of the Capitol. The Doctor forces Borusa to reveal the location of the Great Key of Time. The Doctor uses the power of the Key to build the supreme weapon, the Demat Gun, which he uses to destroy the Sontarans. In the ensuing explosion the Doctor loses his memory of recent events. Leela chooses to stay on Gallifrey to marry Andred, Commander of the Guards, and K9 stays with its mistress. As the TARDIS heads toward its next destination the Doctor reveals a K9 Mark 2!

Novelisation: *Doctor Who and the Invasion of Time* by Terrance Dicks (0 426 20093 4) first published by W H Allen (now Virgin Publishing Ltd) in 1980 with cover by Andrew Skilleter. Target library number 35.

Producer:
Graham Williams

Script Editor:
Anthony Read

(5A) THE RIBOS OPERATION
(4 episodes)
2 September 1978 to 23 September 1978

Writer:
Robert Holmes

Director:
George Spenton-Foster

Regular cast: Tom Baker (the Doctor); Mary Tamm (Romana); John Leeson (voice of K9).

Cast: Iain Cuthbertson (Garron); Nigel Plaskitt (Unstoffe); Paul Seed (Graff Vynda-K); Robert Keegan (Sholakh); Prentis Hancock (Captain); Timothy Bateson (Binro); Ann Tirard (Seeker); Cyril Luckham (White Guardian); Oliver Maguire, John Hamill, Barry Summerford, David Young, Roy Brent, Yuri Gridneff (Shrieves); Nick Wilkinson, Stuart Fell (Shrivenzales).

Story: The Doctor is chosen by the White Guardian to assemble the all-powerful Key to Time, which is split into many segments throughout the Cosmos. Joining the Doctor on his quest is a female Time Lord, Romanadvoratrelundar (Romana for short) and the new K9 Mark 2. The first stop in the search for the Key's first segment takes them to the world of Ribos, currently in its 32-year long Ice Time season. Also on Ribos are the two Earth con-men Garron and Unstoffe, out to sell the planet to a deposed tyrant, the Graff Vynda-K. An important part of their scheme is a lump of Jethrik, one of the most valuable minerals in the Galaxy, which is in reality the first segment of the Key to Time. The Doctor and Romana become involved in Garron's plans, which backfire when the Graff realises he has been cheated. Hunted by the Ribans and by the Graff's men, all seek refuge in catacombs inhabited by ferocious beasts, the Shrivenzales. The Graff calls on a local witch, the Seeker, to locate the Doctor and Garron. In the ensuing hunt the Graff dies in an explosion of his own making. Garron is free to leave Ribos with the Graff's ship, which is full of riches. The Doctor and Romana leave with the first segment.

Novelisation: *Doctor Who and the Ribos Operation* by Ian Marter (0 426 20092 6) first published by W H Allen (now Virgin Publishing Ltd) in 1979 with cover by John Geary. Target library number 52.

(5B) **THE PIRATE PLANET**
(4 episodes)
30 September 1978 to 21 October 1978

Writer: **Director:**
Douglas Adams   Pennant Roberts

Regular cast: see 5A above

Cast: Bruce Purchase (Captain); Andrew Robertson (Mr Fibuli); Rosalind Lloyd (Nurse); David Sibley (Pralix); Bernard Finch (Mentiad); Ralph Michael (Balaton); Primi Townsend (Mula); David Warwick (Kimus); Clive Bennett (Citizen); Adam Kurakin (Guard); Vi Delmar (Queen Xanxia).

Story: The TARDIS heads for the planet Calufrax, where the second segment of the Key is located, but instead lands on Zanak. Zanak is a hollow world equipped with massive transmat engines which enable it to jump through the space vortex and rematerialise around another world, draining it of its matter and energy. Romana is captured by guards and taken to the Bridge to the Captain, half-man, half-machine, but the Doctor rescues her. He realises that the planet is in the process of absorbing Calufrax. The Time Lords find unusual allies in the Mentiads, a race of telepaths who have recently appeared on Zanak. The Doctor organises an attack on the Bridge but is captured. He finds that the true master of Zanak is not the Captain but its original ruler, Queen Xanxia, who has been using the pillaged energies to keep her original body alive. The Doctor and the Mentiads try to stop the planet's next jump through the space vortex, which would take Zanak to Earth. During the fighting the Captain attempts to revolt and is killed by Xanxia. Cut off from her much needed energy sources, Xanxia is shot by a rebel. The Doctor discovers that Calufrax, now reduced to a football-sized husk, is the second segment of the Key to Time. The Time Lords leave after the citizens of Zanak have destroyed the Bridge.

(5C) **THE STONES OF BLOOD**
(4 episodes)
28 October 1978 to 18 November 1978

Writer:
David Fisher

Director:
Darrol Blake

Regular cast: see 5A above

Cast: Susan Engel (Vivien Fay); Beatrix Lehmann (Professor Rumford); Nicholas McArdle (De Vries); Elaine Ives-Cameron (Martha); Gerald Cross, David McAlister (Megara voices); James Murray, Shirin Taylor (Campers); Gerald Cross (Voice of the Guardian); James Muir, Ian Munroe, Margaret Pilleau, Judy Cowne, Decima Delaney, Mike Mungarvan (Druids).

Story: The TARDIS rematerialises on Earth. The Doctor and Romana follow the trace of the third segment of the Key to Time to an ancient Druidic circle where they meet Professor Emelia Rumford and her friend Vivien Fay. The Doctor suspects he might find a clue as to the location of the segment from the local Druidic priest – but he is nearly sacrificed to a pagan goddess, the Cailleach. Rescued by Professor Rumford, the Doctor finds that the priest has been killed by the Ogri, stone creatures that feed on blood. The Ogri serve the Cailleach and normally look like part of the stone circle. The Doctor finds that the Cailleach is in reality Vivien Fay, who has been living on Earth for about 4,000 years. Before he can alert Romana, Vivien Fay, using some of the properties of the third segment of the Key, sends her to a spaceship orbiting in hyperspace above the circle. The Doctor manages to follow and by accident frees the Megara, justice machines sent with the ship to judge an alien criminal, Cessair of Diplos. The Megara threaten to execute the Doctor but the Time Lords trick them into probing the mind of Vivien Fay. When they realise that she is in fact Cessair the justice machines turn her into a stone megalith. The Doctor manages to capture the third segment (Vivien's necklace) and banishes the Megara.

This was the 100th *Doctor Who* story.

Novelisation: *Doctor Who and the Stones of Blood* by Terrance Dicks (0 426 20099 3) first published by W H Allen (now Virgin Publishing Ltd) in 1980 with cover by Andrew Skilleter. Target library number 59.

(5D) **THE ANDROIDS OF TARA**
(4 episodes)
25 November 1978 to 16 December 1978

Writer:
David Fisher

Director:
Michael Hayes

Regular cast: see 5A above

Cast: Peter Jeffrey (Count Grendel); Neville Jason (Prince Reynart); Simon Lack (Zadek); Paul Lavers (Farrah); Lois Baxter (Madame Lamia); Declan Mulholland (Till); Martin Matthews (Kurster); Cyril Shaps (Archimandrite); Mary Tamm (Strella).

Story: The Doctor and Romana land on Tara, a peaceful planet where science is the domain of the commoners while the rulers enjoy a life patterned after chivalric models. The Doctor decides to take a fishing holiday and sends Romana looking for the fourth segment of the Key to Time – which she locates in the shape of a local statue. She is captured by the evil Count Grendel who takes her to be an Android of Princess Strella, her exact double, whom he keeps prisoner in the hope that eventually by marrying her he will become King of Tara. Meanwhile, the Doctor is approached by the rightful pretender to the Taran throne, Prince Reynart, who asks him to repair his Android double, which he plans to use to avoid assassination during the coronation ceremony. Reynart is kidnapped by Grendel and the Doctor uses the Android in his place, foiling the plans of the Count. Grendel attempts to kill the Doctor, who succeeds in freeing Romana. The Count manages to destroy Reynart's Android and recaptures Romana. He now plans to marry Reynart to Romana (posing as the captive Princess Strella), and then kill Reynart and marry Romana himself. The Doctor arrives in time to rescue the Prince and defeat the Count.

Novelisation: *Doctor Who and the Androids of Tara* by Terrance Dicks (0 426 20108 6) first published by W H Allen (now Virgin Publishing Ltd) in 1980 with cover by Andrew Skilleter. Target library number 3.

(5E) **THE POWER OF KROLL**
(4 episodes)
23 December 1978 to 13 January 1979

Writer:
Robert Holmes

Director:
Norman Stewart

Regular cast: see 5A above

Cast: Neil McCarthy (Thawn); Philip Madoc (Fenner); Grahame Mallard (Harg); Glyn Owen (Rohm-Dutt); John Leeson (Dugeen); Terry Walsh (Mensch); Carl Rigg (Varlik); John Abineri (Ranquin); Frank Jarvis (Skart).

Story: The Doctor and Romana land on Delta Magna's third moon, which is mostly swamps and marshes. They are caught up in a feud between the Swampies and a group of Human technicians. The Swampies are green humanoids, original descendants of the Delta Magnans who were given the moon as a sort of reservation by the Human colonists of Delta Magna. They resent the intrusion of the technicians, who have set up a plant to collect methane from the swamps and convert it into protein, to be shipped by rocket back to Delta Magna. Romana is captured by the Swampies and the Doctor by the refinery people. Both are highly suspicious of the newcomers and the Swampies offer Romana as a sacrifice to their god Kroll. The Doctor rescues her and they escape, along with Rohm-Dutt, a gun smuggler. They discover that he has been paid by Thawn, the refinery Controller, to give the Swampies non-functional guns, thus justifying his extermination policies. Rohm-Dutt is killed by Kroll, a squid-like creature of titanic size. The monster attacks the refinery. Thawn plans to blast the creature with a rocket, thus threatening the entire population of the moon. He is stopped by Varlik, a native who has now realised that Kroll is not a god. The Doctor finds that Kroll's gigantic size was caused by his swallowing a holy relic of the Swampies – the fifth segment of the Key to Time – and removes it, thus causing

154

the monster to be split into many smaller entities.
K9 does not appear in this story.

Novelisation: *Doctor Who and the Power of Kroll* by Terrance Dicks (0 426 20101 9) first published by W H Allen (now Virgin Publishing Ltd) in 1980 with cover by Andrew Skilleter. Target library number 49.

(5F) **THE ARMAGEDDON FACTOR**
(6 episodes)
20 January 1979 to 24 February 1979

Writers:
Bob Baker,
Dave Martin

Director:
Michael Hayes

Regular cast: see 5A above

Cast: Lalla Ward (Princess Astra); John Woodvine (Marshal); William Squire (The Shadow); Ian Saynor (Merak); Davyd Harries (Shapp); Valentine Dyall (Black Guardian); Barry Jackson (Drax); Ian Liston (Hero); Susan Skipper (Heroine); John Cannon, Harry Fielder (Guards); Iain Armstrong (Technician); Pat Gorman (Pilot); Stephen Calcutt (Mute).

Story: The search for the final segment to the Key to Time takes the Doctor, Romana and K9 to the twin planets of Atrios and Zeos. A full-scale nuclear war is raging between the twin worlds. The Marshal, who commands the Atrian defence, is intent on pursuing the war to its ultimate conclusion. The Doctor suspects that the Marshal is being controlled from elsewhere. The final segment of the Key seems to have some connection with the Atrian Royal Princess, Astra, who has been kidnapped by the evil Shadow, a servant of the Black Guardian. The Doctor, Romana and K9 go in search of her and find themselves trapped on Zeos, a planet that appears deserted but

155

for Mentalis, a giant computer which has been waging the war on Atrios. Lured on by the Shadow, the Marshal threatens a final assault on Zeos, ignorant of the fact that this will trigger Mentalis to destroy itself and both planets. To stop the oncoming armageddon the Doctor is forced to use the incomplete Key to time-loop the Marshal. The Doctor goes to the lair of the Shadow, a third planet in orbit between Zeos and Atrios, where his friends are now under the control of the Shadow. He manages to ally himself with Drax, an itinerant Time Lord and the builder of Mentalis. The Doctor discovers that the last segment of the Key is Princess Astra herself, who ceases to exist as she completes the Key. The Time Lords manage to recapture the Key and escape with it. Mentalis is disconnected by Drax and the Marshal's nuclear attack is directed by the Doctor to the Shadow's planet, which is destroyed. The Doctor now faces the Black Guardian himself, disguised as the White Guardian. Deciding that the Key is too powerful for anyone to hold, the Doctor splits it and scatters it again throughout the Cosmos, thus restoring the Princess to her original form. To escape the wrath of the Black Guardian, the Doctor equips the TARDIS with a randomiser.

The first episode of this story marks the 500th episode of *Doctor Who*.

Novelisation: *Doctor Who and the Armageddon Factor* by Terrance Dicks (0 426 20104 3) first published by W H Allen (now Virgin Publishing Ltd) in 1980 with cover by Bill Donohoe. Target library number 3.

Seventeenth Season

Producer:
Graham Williams

Script Editor:
Douglas Adams

(5J) DESTINY OF THE DALEKS
(4 episodes)
1 September 1979 to 22 September 1979

Writer:
Terry Nation

Director:
Ken Grieve

Regular cast: Tom Baker (the Doctor); Lalla Ward (Romana).

Cast: Tim Barlow (Tyssan); Peter Straker (Commander Sharrel); Suzanne Danielle (Agella); Tony Osoba (Lan); David Gooderson (Davros); Roy Skelton, David Gooderson (Dalek voices); Cy Town, Mike Mungarvan, Toby Byrne, Tony Starr (Daleks); Penny Casdagli (Jall); David Yip (Veldan); Cassandra (Movellan Guard); Maggy Armitage, Yvonne Gallagher, Lee Richards (Romanas).

Story: Romana's body regenerates and she adopts the likeness of Princess Astra of Atrios. The two Time Lords land on a desolate planet. They are intrigued by evidence of drilling operations deep underground. While investigating, the Doctor is trapped in a collapsed building and is rescued by the Movellans, a race of beautiful humanoids led by Commander Sharrel. The Doctor discovers that he is once again on Skaro, home planet of the Daleks. Meanwhile Romana has been captured by the Daleks and put to work with the other enslaved Humans working on Skaro for some unknown purpose of the Daleks. An escaped prisoner, Tyssan, leads the Doctor and the Movellans underground, where the Doctor finds Romana, who has escaped the Daleks by pretending to be dead. They discover what the Daleks were seeking all the time: Davros. They take him prisoner and return to the Movellan ship. The Movellans turn out to be a merciless, logical, robotic race which has been fighting the Daleks for centuries, but a stalemate has been reached. The Daleks need Davros to gain an advantage and the Movellans plan to use the Doctor. With the help of Tyssan the Doctor prevents the Movellans from destroying Skaro and succeeds in defeating the Daleks. The two Time Lords leave and Tyssan takes Davros prisoner back to Earth.

Novelisation: *Doctor Who – Destiny of the Daleks* by Terrance Dicks (0 426 20096 9) first published by W H Allen (now Virgin Publishing Ltd) as *Doctor Who and the Destiny of the Daleks* in 1979 with cover by Andrew Skilleter. New edition in 1992 with cover by Alister Pearson. Target library number 21.

(5H) **CITY OF DEATH**
(4 episodes)
29 September 1979 to 20 October 1979

Writer: **Director:**
David Agnew   Michael Hayes
(Douglas Adams and
Graham Williams, based on a
story by David Fisher)

Regular cast: see 5J above

Cast: Julian Glover (Scaroth/Count Scarlioni/Captain Tancredi); Catherine Schell (Countess Scarlioni); Tom Chadbon (Duggan); David Graham (Professor Kerensky); Kevin Flood (Hermann); Peter Halliday (Soldier); Pamela Stirling (Louvre Guide); John Cleese, Eleanor Bron (Gallery visitors); Peter Halliday, Tom Chadbon (Jagaroth voices); Walter Henry (Cafe Patron); James Charlton (artist); Jane Bough (Maid).

Story: A crippled Jagaroth spaceship piloted by Scaroth explodes on takeoff in 400 million BC on Earth. In 1979, Paris, the Doctor and Romana meet a British detective named Duggan. They uncover a plan by Count and Countess Scarlioni to steal the Mona Lisa with the aid of alien technology. The Count is selling a collection of art treasures to finance his time travel experiments, conducted by Professor Kerensky. In a room in the Count's castle which has been sealed for centuries the Doctor discovers six more apparently genuine Mona Lisas. He goes back to Renaissance Italy to find Leonardo da Vinci. There, the Time Lord is taken prisoner by Captain Tancredi, who looks exactly like the Count. Tancredi is forcing Leonardo to produce more Mona Lisas. The Doctor discovers that the original explosion split Scaroth into 12 segments scattered at different periods of Human history. The alien has influenced Mankind's scientific evolution so that his 20th-century self can go back in time to prevent the explosion. The Doctor returns to the 20th century to find Romana and Duggan prisoners of the Count. Scaroth, now revealed as a green scaly creature with one eye, kills Kerensky and the Countess and embarks on his journey back through time. The Doctor and his friends follow in the TARDIS. The Doctor realises that it is the explosion of the Jagaroth ship which will create life on Earth. The Doctor tries in vain to reason with Scaroth. Duggan prevents the alien from succeeding by knocking him unconscious. Dragged back through time, Scaroth perishes in the explosion of his machine.

Video tape: *City of Death* (BBCV 4492) first released in 1991 with cover by Andrew Skilleter.

(5G) THE CREATURE FROM THE PIT

(4 episodes)

27 October 1979 to 17 November 1979

Writer:
David Fisher

Director:
Christopher Barry

Regular cast: see 5J above, and David Brierley (voice of K9).

Cast: Myra Frances (Lady Adrasta); Eileen Way (Karela); Geoffrey Bayldon (Organon); David Telfer (Huntsman); John Bryans (Torvin); Edward Kelsey (Edu); Tim Munro (Ainu); Tommy Wright (Guard Master); Terry Walsh (Doran); Morris Barry (Tollund); Philip Denyer, Dave Redgrave (Guards).

Story: The Doctor and Romana arrive on Chloris, an abundantly fertile world which is extremely short of metal. They fall into the hands of Lady Adrasta, a ruler whose power derives from her monopoly of metal on the planet. She polices her people with carnivorous Wolfweeds controlled by her Huntsman. Those who displease her, she throws into the Pit, a worked-out mine which contains a terrifying creature. The Doctor finds himself in the Pit with Adrasta's Court Astrologer, Organon. There, he discovers that the creature is in reality an ambassador from Tythonus, who came to Chloris to exchange metal – which the Tythonians have in abundance – for chlorophyll, which is extremely rare on Tythonus. Frightened of losing her monopoly, Adrasta has kept Erato, the ambassador, imprisoned in the Pit for many years. Erato has not been able to communicate with the Chlorians but with the Doctor's help, he is eventually able to reveal the truth. The Huntsman turns against Adrasta and she is killed by Erato. Adrasta's treatment of the Tythonian envoy almost brings total disaster to Chloris even after her death, but with Erato's help the Doctor manages to save the planet and the ambassador returns to Tythonus.

Novelisation: *Doctor Who and the Creature from the Pit* by

160

David Fisher (0 426 20123 X) first published by W H Allen (now Virgin Publishing Ltd) in 1981 with cover by Steve Kyte. Target library number 11.

(5K) NIGHTMARE OF EDEN
(4 episodes)
24 November 1979 to 15 December 1979

Writer:
Bob Baker

Director:
Alan Bromly

Regular cast: see 5G above

Cast: David Daker (Rigg); Lewis Fiander (Tryst); Jennifer Lonsdale (Della); Geoffrey Bateman (Dymond); Barry Andrews (Stott); Stephen Jenn (Secker); Geoffrey Hinsliff (Fisk); Peter Craze (Costa); Pamela Ruddock (Computer voice); Richard Barnes, Sebastian Stride, Eden Phillips (Crewmen); Annette Peters, Lionel Sansby, Peter Roberts, Maggie Petersen (Passengers); Billy Gray (Wounded passenger); James Muir, Derek Suthern, David Korff, Jan Murzynowski, Robert Goodman (Mandrels).

Story: Two spacecraft, the luxury liner *Empress* and the *Hecate*, crash into one another while one is semi-dematerialised and ready to jump into hyperspace, with the result that they become fused. Among the passengers of the *Empress* is Tryst, a naturalist, and his assistant, Della. They have with them a Continuous Event Transmuter, a machine which allows whole areas of land to be removed from planets and to be stored on laser crystals, along with the local fauna, which continue to exist and develop while on the crystal recording. As a result of the crash, the CET becomes unstable and releases hordes of Mandrels, monsters from the planet Eden, onto the *Empress*. The Doctor also discovers that someone on board is smuggling Vraxoin, one of the most dangerous addictive drugs in the

Universe, which incapacitated the *Empress* navigator (hence the crash). Suspected of being the smugglers, the Doctor and Romana are pursued by Fisk and Costa, while simultaneously suspected of being narcotic agents by Rigg. The Time Lord discovers that the real smuggler is Tryst, and that Vraxoin is made from the very essence of the Mandrels. Tryst and the pilot of the *Hecate*, Dymond, are planning to beam the contents of the Eden crystal to the planet Azure below. The Doctor succeeds in separating the two ships and in preventing the smugglers from carrying out their plans. After Tryst's capture by customs agents the Doctor returns the Mandrels and the Eden sample to Eden.

Novelisation: *Doctor Who and the Nightmare of Eden* by Terrance Dicks (0 426 20130 2) first published by W H Allen (now Virgin Publishing Ltd) in 1980 with cover by Andrew Skilleter. Target library number 45.

(5L) **THE HORNS OF NIMON**
(4 episodes)
22 December 1979 to 12 January 1980

Writer:
Anthony Read

Director:
Kenny McBain

Regular cast: see 5G above

Cast: Simon Gipps-Kent (Seth); Janet Ellis (Teka); Graham Crowden (Soldeed); Michael Osborne (Sorak); Malcolm Terris (Co-pilot); Bob Hornery (Pilot); Clifford Norgate (Nimon voices); John Bailey (Sezom); Robin Sherringham, Bob Appleby, Trevor St John Hacker (Nimon).

Story: The TARDIS, whilst immobilised for repairs, falls into a gravity whirlpool along with a damaged ship taking a group of young men and women from the planet Aneth to the planet

Skonnos, where they are to be presented as tribute to the Nimon, a mysterious entity who lives at the centre of a huge labyrinthine complex. The Nimon has promised to return Skonnos to its former glory if the Skonnons supply young men and women and radioactive hymetusite crystals – which they have in turn exacted from the peaceful planet Aneth. The Doctor repairs the Skonnon ship but is left behind in his inoperative TARDIS by the treacherous co-pilot who flies to Skonnos, taking Romana with him. Soldeed, leader of Skonnos and servant of the Nimon, sends the Anethan sacrifices, Romana and the co-pilot into the Nimon complex. The Doctor, who has managed to repair the TARDIS, arrives on Skonnos and follows them. Inside the complex they find the Nimon, a bull-headed alien who kills the co-pilot. The Doctor discovers that the Nimon is preparing to bring the rest of his race to Skonnos through a black hole in Space fed by the hymetusite crystals. The Nimon are like a galactic plague of locusts, jumping from planet to planet after having drained them of their resources. One of them is sent ahead to promise wealth and power to unsuspecting races, and builds the huge complex which enables the rest of the Nimon to infiltrate and eventually take over the host planet. At the other end of the space tunnel Romana finds a dying planet, Crinoth. With the help of Seth, a young Anethian, the Time Lord succeeds in destroying the complex, leaving the Nimon stranded on Crinoth, where they perish. Thanks to K9, the Doctor and his friends finally escape from the complex, which is destroyed.

Novelisation: *Doctor Who and the Horns of Nimon* by Terrance Dicks (0 426 20131 0) first published by W H Allen (now Virgin Publishing Ltd) in 1980 with cover by Steve Kyte. Target library number 31.

(5M) SHADA
(6 episodes planned)
This story was not broadcast because filming was
interrupted by a strike at the BBC.

Writer:
Douglas Adams

Director:
Pennant Roberts

Regular cast: see 5G above

Cast: Denis Carey (Professor Chronotis); Daniel Hill (Chris Parsons); Victoria Burgoyne (Clare Keightley); Christopher Neame (Skagra); Gerald Campion (Porter); Derek Pollitt (Caldera); John Hallett (Constable); David Strong (Passenger); Shirley Dixon (Ship); James Coombes (voice of Krargs); Harry Fielder (Krarg Commander); Lionel Sansby, James Muir, Derek Suthern, Reg Woods (Krargs).

Story: In a remote space station called Think Tank a scientist called Skagra steals the minds of his colleagues, and escapes. Meanwhile, the Doctor and Romana visit present-day Cambridge to see Professor Chronotis, a retired Time Lord living incognito as a don. He wants them to take a book, *The Ancient Law of Gallifrey*, back to the planet of the Time Lords. Unfortunately it has accidentally been taken away by a post-graduate student, Chris Parsons. He and a colleague, Clare Keightley, are mystified by the book, which is made of no earthly substance. Skagra arrives on Earth in search of the book because it will give him directions to the Time Lord prison planet of Shada, where he believes Salyavin, the most powerful Time Lord, is imprisoned. Skagra needs access to Salyavin to learn from him the secret of projecting a print of his own mind into every sentient being in the Universe, a technique which will guarantee the success of his plan for galactic domination. The Doctor retrieves the book but Skagra sends his mind-sapping Sphere after the Doctor. On a bicycle chase through the streets of Cambridge the Doctor loses the book, which is found by

Skagra. Skagra heads for Shada in the TARDIS, having captured Romana to operate it. The Doctor takes Skagra's own spaceship and with K9 and Chris Parsons goes to Think Tank in search of Skagra and Romana. He encounters the monstrous crystalline Krargs, Skagra's servants. It transpires that Chronotis's rooms in Cambridge are the inside of his own TARDIS, which he uses to rescue the Doctor from the Krargs. Against the Professor's wishes and with the aim of rescuing Romana the Doctor follows Skagra to Shada, where Skagra has freed the criminals, including a Dalek, a Cyberman and a Zygon – but Salyavin is not there. Professor Chronotis turns out to be Salyavin. The Doctor wins a mind battle with Skagra and imprisons him in his own spaceship. Returning to Earth, the Doctor leaves the Professor in Cambridge, promising to keep his identity secret.

Video tape: *Shada* (BBCV 4814) first released in 1992 with photomontage cover (includes script book).

Eighteenth Season

Executive Producer:
Barry Letts

Producer:
John Nathan-Turner

Script Editor:
Christopher H. Bidmead

(5N) **THE LEISURE HIVE**
(4 episodes)
30 August 1980 to 20 September 1980

Writer:
David Fisher

Director:
Lovett Bickford

Regular cast: Tom Baker (the Doctor); Lalla Ward (Romana); John Leeson (voice of K9).

Cast: Adrienne Corri (Mena); David Haig (Pangol); Laurence Payne (Morix); John Collin (Brock); Nigel Lambert (Hardin); Martin Fisk (Vargos); David Allister (Stimson); Ian Talbot (Klout); Andrew Lane (Chief Foamasi); Roy Montague (Argolin Guide); Harriet Reynolds (Tannoy voice); Clifford Norgate (Generator voice); David Bulbeck, David Korff, James Muir (Foamasi); Alys Dyer (Baby).

Story: The Doctor and Romana visit the Leisure Hive on the planet Argolis, an artificial environment which is an entertainment centre for galactic travellers. The Argolins themselves are a race dying from the consequences of a war with their old enemies, the reptilian Foamasi. Accidents mysteriously happen at the Tachyon Recreation Generator – the pride of the Hive – and the Argolin leader, Mena, is pressed by her Earth agent, Brock, to sell the Hive to the Foamasi, an offer which is violently opposed by her son, Pangol. Mena believes she can be rejuvenated by Earth scientist Hardin's Tachyon experiments, but the man is a fraud. The two Time Lords are arrested on suspicion of having murdered Hardin's assistant, who discovered that the Foamasi had secretly invaded the Hive. While experimenting with Hardin's TRG machine, the Doctor ages considerably. With Mena dying, Pangol – who is revealed as a creation of the TRG – takes over the Hive and attempts to duplicate himself into an army to war against the Foamasi. Instead, a rejuvenated army of Doctors leave the machine. The Foamasi invaders reveal themselves as agents of their government and unmask Foamasi saboteurs who had been impersonating Brock and his lawyer, Klout. The army of Doctors disappears and Mena and Pangol are turned into younger versions of themselves by the TRG.

Novelisation: *Doctor Who – The Leisure Hive* by David Fisher (0 426 20147 7) first published by W H Allen (now Virgin Publishing Ltd) as *Doctor Who and the Leisure Hive* in 1982 with cover by Andrew Skilleter. New edition in 1993 with cover by Alister Pearson. Target library number 39.

(5Q) MEGLOS
(4 episodes)
27 September 1980 to 18 October 1980

Writers: **Director:**
John Flanagan   Terence Dudley
Andrew McCulloch

Regular cast: see 5N above

Cast: Edward Underdown (Zastor); Jacqueline Hill (Lexa); Crawford Logan (Deedrix); Colette Gleeson (Caris); Bill Fraser (Grugger); Frederick Treves (Brotadac); Simon Shaw (Tigellan Guard); Christopher Owen (Earthling); Tony Allef, Ranjit Nakara, Hi Ching, Bruce Callender, John Holland, James Muir

(Gaztaks); Terence Creasey, Eddie Sommer, Ray Knight, Chris Marks, Stephen Nagy, Sylvia Marriott, Lewis Hooper (Deons); Michael Brydon, David Cleeve (Guards); Stephen Kane, John Laing, David Cole, Howard Barnes (Savants); Michael Gordon Browne, Harry Fielder, Laurie Goode, Peter Gates-Fleming, Geoff Whitestone (Tigellans).

Story: Zastor, leader of the planet Tigella, has sent for the Doctor because the Dodecahedron – the crystal which powers their underground civilisation – is failing. Meanwhile, on the nearby dead planet of Zolfa-Thura, a band of Gaztak space raiders meet the cactus-like Meglos, who secures their help for his plan to steal the Dodecahedron. For that purpose, Meglos assumes the appearance of the Doctor, whom he imprisons in a Chronic Hysteresis. Having escaped, and arriving on Tigella, the Doctor is blamed for the theft and condemned by the crystal worshippers to be crushed to death. Meglos is unmasked by Caris, one of the Tigellans who believe that their planet's surface should be reclaimed from the aggressive vegetation that overruns it. Meglos is inadvertently freed by Romana after she escapes from the Gaztaks, who have captured her. The Doctor freed, the Time Lords rush to Zolfa-Thura where Meglos intends to release the power of the Dodecahedron. The Doctor now impersonates Meglos and mis-sets the crystal, which explodes, destroying the last Zolfa-Thuran and the Gaztaks. Without its power, the Tigellans are forced to begin the reclamation of their planet.

Novelisation: *Doctor Who – Meglos* by Terrance Dicks (0 426 20136 1) first published by W H Allen (now Virgin Publishing Ltd) in 1983 with cover by Andrew Skilleter. New edition in 1993 with cover by Alister Pearson. Target library number 75.

(5R) FULL CIRCLE

(4 episodes)

25 October 1980 to 15 November 1980

Writer:
Andrew Smith

Director:
Peter Grimwade

Regular cast: see 5N above, and introducing Matthew Waterhouse (Adric).

Cast: Richard Willis (Varsh); Bernard Padden (Tylos); June Page (Keara); James Bree (Nefred); Alan Rowe (Garif); Leonard Maguire (Draith); George Baker (Login); Tony Calvin (Dexeter); Norman Bacon (Marsh child); Andrew Forbes (Omril); Adrian Gibbs (Rysik); Barney Lawrence, Steve Kelly, Stephen Calcutt, Keith Guest, Graham Cole, James Jackson, Stephen Watson (Marshmen).

Story: The TARDIS goes through a Charged Vacuum Emboitement and the two Time Lords find themselves on planet Alzarius in E-Space. There, they encounter a community of Terradonians, claiming to be descendants of a starliner which crashed 40 generations earlier. The community is ruled by the Deciders who have preserved the ship and hope eventually to leave the planet with it. They warn the community of the incoming Mistfall, a time when mysterious creatures rise up from the marshes. A group of youths called Outlers, led by Varsh, refuse to believe them. However, the myth proves to be real and marsh creatures start appearing. Romana becomes their victim but is rescued by the Doctor. With the help of Adric, Varsh's brother, the Time Lord discovers that the starliner people are actually evolved marshmen who have taken over and ritually maintained the ship. The Doctor enables them to pursue their destiny by leaving Alzarius, and Adric stows away in the departing TARDIS.

Novelisation: *Doctor Who – Full Circle* by Andrew Smith

(0 426 20150 7) first published by W H Allen (now Virgin Publishing Ltd) in 1982 with cover by Andrew Skilleter. Target library number 26.

(5P) STATE OF DECAY
(4 episodes)
22 November 1980 to 13 December 1980

Writer:
Terrance Dicks

Director:
Peter Moffatt

Regular cast: see 5R above

Cast: William Lindsay (Zargo); Rachel Davies (Camilla); Emrys James (Aukon); Iain Rattray (Habris); Thane Bettany (Tarak); Arthur Hewlett (Kalmar); Stacy Davies (Veros); Clinton Greyn (Ivo); Rhoda Lewis (Marta); Dean Allen (Karl); Stuart Blake (Zoldaz); Stuart Fell (Roga); Alan Chuntz (Guard).

Story: The TARDIS lands on a medieval-like planet ruled tyrannically by King Zargo and Queen Camilla. The Doctor and Romana are captured by rebels led by the technologically minded Kalmar. Having convinced the rebels that they are on their side, the Time Lords discover that the King and the Queen are the original officers of an explorer ship which left Earth a thousand years earlier. Meanwhile Adric, who has been hiding among the peasants, is captured by the King's Councillor, Aukon. The Time Lords discover that the Tower – Zargo's castle – is in reality the lost spaceship, and that the King, the Queen and Aukon are vampires! The entity that drew them into E-Space and turned them into vampires, the Great Vampire (last survivor of a race destroyed by the Time Lords), lies in the ground beneath the Tower, ready to rise. The Doctor arranges a concerted attack on the Tower and uses one of the scout ships as a stake to kill the Great Vampire. Zargo, Camilla and Aukon crumble into dust.

170

Novelisation: *Doctor Who and the State of Decay* by Terrance Dicks (0 426 20133 7) first published by W H Allen (now Virgin Publishing Ltd) in 1981 with cover by Andrew Skilleter. Target library number 58.

(5S) **WARRIORS' GATE**
(4 episodes)
3 January 1981 to 24 January 1981

Writer:
Steve Gallagher

Director:
Paul Joyce

Regular cast: see 5R above

Cast: Clifford Rose (Rorvik); Kenneth Cope (Packard); David Weston (Biroc); Jeremy Gittins (Lazlo); Freddie Earlle (Aldo); Harry Waters (Royce); David Kincaid (Lane); Vincent Pickering (Sagan); Robert Vowles (Gundan).

Story: The TARDIS is hijacked by Biroc, a Time-sensitive Tharil, who has just escaped from the privateer ship of Captain Rorvik. Biroc steers the TARDIS into an eerie white void and leaves. The Doctor follows him to find a mirror-like gateway guarded by axe-wielding robots, the Gundans. Romana falls prisoner of Rorvik, who arrives at the gateway just as the Doctor manages to pass through to the other side of the mirror. There, the Time Lord finds Biroc and learns that the Tharils, once rulers of a vast empire and notorious slave-owners, were defeated by the Gundans, which were made by their rebellious slaves. The Tharils are now kept prisoner in the impervious dwarf star alloy hold of Rorvik's ship. Meanwhile, on the other side of the gateway, Romana has been freed by another Tharil, Lazlo. Rorvik is now determined to blast his way out of the void. The back-blast of the ship is reflected by the mirrors, shatters the hull and releases the Tharils. They return to E-Space with Romana and K9 while the Doctor and Adric are

171

blown back into N-Space.

Novelisation: *Doctor Who and Warriors' Gate* by John Lydecker (pen name of Steve Gallagher) (0 426 20146 9) first published by W H Allen (now Virgin Publishing Ltd) in 1981 with cover by Andrew Skilleter. Target library number 71.

(5T) **THE KEEPER OF TRAKEN**
(4 episodes)
31 January 1981 to 21 February 1981

Writer:
Johnny Byrne

Director:
John Black

Regular cast: Tom Baker (the Doctor); Matthew Waterhouse (Adric); and introducing Sarah Sutton (Nyssa).

Cast: Anthony Ainley (Tremas); Sheila Ruskin (Kassia); Denis Carey (the Keeper); John Woodnutt (Seron); Margot Van Der Burgh (Katura); Robin Soans (Luvic); Roland Oliver (Neman); Geoffrey Beevers (Melkur); Liam Prendergast, Philip Bloomfield (Fosters).

Story: The Union of Traken is a place of universal harmony held together by the bioelectronic Source, which is controlled by the Keeper. The current Keeper's millennium is about to end and he asks the Doctor and Adric for their help. Meanwhile, on Traken, Consul Kassia marries Consul Tremas and finds to her distress that the Keeper has chosen Tremas as his successor. A calcified, evil creature called Melkur seizes upon this fault to manipulate Kassia to have her husband, along with the Doctor and Adric, imprisoned on false charges. As Melkur becomes the new Keeper of Traken, he reveals himself to be the Master! (The statue of Melkur is in reality the Master's TARDIS.) Thanks to an almost catastrophic diversion, during which Adric and Nyssa – Tremas's daughter – nearly succeed in destroying

172

the Source, the Doctor manages to defeat his old enemy. In a last minute twist the Master seizes upon Tremas's body to effect his thirteenth regeneration.

Novelisation: *Doctor Who – The Keeper of Traken* by Terrance Dicks (0 426 20148 5) first published by W H Allen (now Virgin Publishing Ltd) as *Doctor Who and the Keeper of Traken* in 1982 with cover by Andrew Skilleter. New edition in 1993 with cover by Alister Pearson. Target library number 37.

Video tape: *The Keeper of Traken* (BBCV 4973) first released in 1993 with cover by Andrew Skilleter.

(5V) **LOGOPOLIS**
(4 episodes)
28 February 1981 to 21 March 1981

Writer:
Christopher H. Bidmead

Director:
Peter Grimwade

Regular cast: see 5T above, and introducing Janet Fielding (Tegan Jovanka) and Peter Davison (the Doctor).

Cast: Anthony Ainley (the Master); John Fraser (Monitor); Dolore Whiteman (Aunt Vanessa); Tom Georgeson (Detective Inspector); Christopher Hurst (Security Guard); Adrian Gibbs (Watcher); Ray Knight, Peter Roy, Derek Suthern (Policemen); Robin Squire (Pharos technician).

Story: The Doctor decides to repair the TARDIS's chameleon circuit and goes to England to find a real police box, thereby falling into a complex dimensional trap devised by the Master. Tegan, a young air hostess whose aunt is later murdered by the renegade Time Lord, enters the TARDIS thinking it to be a real police box. The Doctor, having been warned by the mysterious Watcher that an enormous trial lies ahead, rushes to Logopolis, a city inhabited by pure mathematicians. There, the Monitor, who is in charge of Logopolis, reveals a copy of the famous Pharos Computer Project on Earth. The Master, who has been interfering with the City in his plans to destroy the Doctor, accidentally causes it to stop functioning. The Monitor reveals that the Universe has passed the point of normal heat death and that its life has been extended only by his people's calculations. Realising the consequences of the Master's actions – the dissolution of the Universe – the two Time Lords team up and together they go to the Pharos Project on Earth, to beam the Logopolitan Program into deep Space. The Master now plans to blackmail the Cosmos into submission, and the two Time Lords begin a fight which causes the Doctor to fall to his death. The Master escapes while the Doctor's body regenerates.

Novelisation: *Doctor Who – Logopolis* by Christopher H. Bidmead (0 426 20149 3) first published by W H Allen (now Virgin Publishing Ltd) in 1983 with cover by Andrew Skilleter. New edition in 1991 with cover by Alister Pearson. Target library number 41.

Video tape: *Logopolis* (BBCV 4736) first released in 1993 with cover by Andrew Skilleter.

Producer:
John Nathan-Turner

Script Editors:
Eric Saward
Antony Root

K9 AND COMPANY
A GIRL'S BEST FRIEND
(1 50-minute episode)
28 December 1981

Writer:
Terence Dudley

Director:
John Black

Cast: Elisabeth Sladen (Sarah Jane Smith); John Leeson (Voice of K9); Bill Fraser (Commander Pollock); Ian Sears (Brendan Richards); Colin Jeavons (George Tracey); Sean Chapman (Peter Tracey); Mary Wimbush (Aunt Lavinia); Linda Polan (Juno Baker); Gillian Martell (Lily Gregson); Neville Barber (Howard Baker); John Quarmby (Henry Tobias); Nigel Gregory (Sgt. Wilson); Stephen Oxley (P.C. Carter).

Story: Sarah Jane Smith goes to Moreton Harwood where her Aunt Lavinia lives, but finds she has gone to America. Instead, Sarah meets Brendan, her Aunt's ward, retired Navy Commander Pollock, her Aunt's partner in a market garden shop, Lily Gregson, the gossipy Post Office clerk, George Tracey, whose family dates back to the Romans, and her Aunt's neighbours, the Bakers. Also, in a box sent to her by the Doctor, she finds a new K9. Because the local crops have not been doing well, Brendan is kidnapped by a cult of witches who want to sacrifice him to the goddess Hecate at the Winter Solstice. With K9's help, Sarah Jane stops the witches. Most of the locals, except the Bakers, are revealed to be members of the cult, with the High Priest and Priestess being Commander Pollock and Lily Gregson.

Novelisation: *The Companions of Doctor Who – K9 and Company* by Terence Dudley (0 426 20309 7) first published by W H Allen (now Virgin Publishing Ltd) in 1987 with cover by Peter Kelly.

FIFTH DOCTOR

PETER DAVISON
1982 – 1984

Nineteenth Season

Producer:
John Nathan-Turner

Script Editor:
Eric Saward

(5Z) CASTROVALVA
(4 episodes)
4 January 1982 to 12 January 1982

Writer:
Christopher H. Bidmead

Director:
Fiona Cumming

Regular cast: Peter Davison (the Doctor); Matthew Waterhouse (Adric); Sarah Sutton (Nyssa); Janet Fielding (Tegan Jovanka).

Cast: Anthony Ainley (the Master); Derek Waring (Shardovan); Michael Sheard (Mergrave); Frank Wylie (Ruther); Dallas Cavell (Head of Security); Souska John (Child).

Story: The Master kidnaps Adric, while the Doctor, Tegan and Nyssa escape from the Pharos Project. Weakened by his regeneration, the Doctor retreats to the Zero Room. The Master sets the TARDIS on a course towards Event One, but the Doctor averts this by jettisoning portions of the ship, including the Zero Room. Looking for another place where the Doctor can complete his regeneration, the travellers find Castrovalva, a citadel of peace and learning, where they meet Shardovan, its librarian, and the ancient Portreeve, whose strange tapestry shows scenes from the past. The Doctor soon realises Castrovalva is not what it seems; they are caught in a recursive occlusion – a space-time trap. The Portreeve is revealed to be the Master, holding Adric prisoner in an energy web behind the tapestry. Castrovalva is a Block Transfer Computation created by Adric. Shardovan dives into Adric's web, freeing the boy, but dooming Castrovalva. The Doctor and his friends escape, leaving the Master trapped in Castrovalva as it vanishes.

Novelisation: *Doctor Who – Castrovalva* by Christopher H. Bidmead (0 426 19326 1) first published by W H Allen (now Virgin Publishing Ltd) in 1983 with photomontage cover. New edition in 1991 with cover by Alister Pearson. Target library number 76.

Video tape: *Castrovalva* (BBCV 4737) first released in 1993 with cover by Andrew Skilleter.

Script Editor:
Antony Root

(5W) **FOUR TO DOOMSDAY**
(4 episodes)
18 January 1982 to 26 January 1982

Writer:
Terence Dudley

Director:
John Black

Regular cast: see 5Z above

Cast: Stratford Johns (Monarch); Philip Locke (Bigon); Paul Shelley (Persuasion); Annie Lambert (Enlightenment); Burt Kwouk (Lin Futu); Illarrio Bisi Pedro (Kurkutji); Nadia Hammam (Villagra).

Story: On a huge spacecraft, the Doctor and his companions meet the frog-like Monarch and his two ministers, Persuasion and Enlightenment, from the dead planet Urbanka. On board are also Bigon, Kurkutji, Villagra and Lin Futu, from different eras of Earth's past, who turn out to be androids with the memories of the originals. The Doctor discovers that Monarch exhausted Urbanka's resources in pursuit of his mad dream: going back to the beginning of time to meet God. The alien now plots to poison Earth's population to make room for the three billion Urbankans, whose memories have been stored on silicon chips. With the help of the human androids, the Doctor fights Monarch. The alien turns out not to be an android but still 'in the Flesh Time,' and dies, a victim of his own poison. The androids decide to look for another planet on which to settle.

Novelisation: *Doctor Who – Four to Doomsday* by Terrance Dicks (0 426 19334 2) first published by W H Allen (now Virgin Publishing Ltd) in 1983 with photomontage cover. New edition in 1991 with cover by Alister Pearson. Target library number 77.

Script Editor:
Eric Saward

(5Y) KINDA
(4 episodes)
1 February 1982 to 9 February 1982

Writer:
Christopher Bailey

Director:
Peter Grimwade

Regular cast: see 5Z above

Cast: Richard Todd (Sanders); Nerys Hughes (Todd); Mary Morris (Panna); Simon Rouse (Hindle); Adrian Mills (Aris);

179

Lee Cornes (Trickster); Sarah Prince (Karuna); Anna Wing (Anatta); Roger Milner (Anicca); Jeffrey Stewart (Dukkha).

Story: On the eden-like planet of Deva Loka, all but three members of an Earth survey team have disappeared. Deemed a suspect, the Doctor is taken prisoner by Commander Sanders and Officer Hindle. The real culprits are the Kinda, the peaceful, telepathic natives, who have been trying to get the Earthmen to mentally become one with them; instead, the two officers' minds snap. Meanwhile, Tegan is taken over by a snake-like evil entity, the Mara, who later also takes over Aris, a young Kinda. The Mara seeks to once again plunge Deva Loka into chaos, by causing the Kinda to attack the Earth Dome, thus prompting an insane Hindle to start a massive explosion. The Doctor uses a Kinda device to restore Hindle's sanity. He then defeats the Mara by trapping it inside a circle of mirrors, and banishing it. Deva Loka is classified as unsuitable for colonisation.

Novelisation: *Doctor Who – Kinda* by Terrance Dicks (0 426 19529 9) first published by W H Allen (now Virgin Publishing Ltd) in 1983 with photomontage cover. New edition in 1992 with cover by Alister Pearson. Target library number 84.

Script Editor:
Antony Root

(5X) THE VISITATION
(4 episodes)
15 February 1982 to 23 February 1982

Writer:
Eric Saward

Director:
Peter Moffatt

Regular cast: See 5Z above.

Cast: Michael Robbins (Richard Mace); Michael Melia, David Summer, Michael Leader (Terileptils), Peter Van Dissel (Android); James Charlton (Miller); John Savident (Squire John); Anthony Calf (Charles); John Baker (Ralph); Valerie Fyfer (Elizabeth); Richard Hampton (Villager); Neil West (Poacher); Eric Dodson (Headman); Jeff Wayne (Scytheman).

Story: The Doctor tries to take Tegan back to 1981 Heathrow, but instead lands in 1666, the time of the great plague. The travellers meet Richard Mace, an out-of-work actor, who tells the Doctor of the recent fall of a comet. The Doctor's suspicions of extra-terrestrial intervention are confirmed when they discover an android impersonating the Grim Reaper, and control bracelets enslaving the local villagers' minds. Behind it all are three Terileptils, alien fugitives stranded on Earth. The Terileptil leader refuses the Doctor's help; instead, he plans to depopulate Earth by releasing an army of plague-carrying rats. The Doctor and his companions pursue the Terileptil leader to London, where they destroy him and his rats, and by so doing inadvertently start the Great Fire.

Novelisation: *Doctor Who – The Visitation* by Eric Saward (0 426 20135 3) first published by W H Allen (now Virgin Publishing Ltd) as *Doctor Who and the Visitation* in 1982 with photomontage cover. New edition in 1992 with cover by Alister Pearson. Target library number 69.

Script Editor:
Eric Saward

(6A) **BLACK ORCHID**
(2 episodes)
1 March 1982 to 2 March 1982

Writer:
Terence Dudley

Director:
Ron Jones

Regular cast: see 5Z above

Cast: Sarah Sutton (Nyssa/Ann);Vanessa Paine (double for Nyssa/Ann); Barbara Murray (Lady Cranleigh); Michael Cochrane (Lord Cranleigh); Gareth Milne (George Cranleigh); Moray Watson (Sir Robert Muir); Ivor Salter (Sgt. Markham); Ahmed Khalil (Latoni); Brian Hawksley (Brewster); Andrew Tourell (Constable Cummings); Timothy Block (Tanner); James Muir (Police driver); Caron Heggie (Ann's maid); Derek Hunt (Footman); David Wilde (Digby); Jim Morris (Stationmaster).

Story: The TARDIS materialises in June, 1925, in Cranleigh Halt, where the travellers are warmly welcomed by the local gentry. After a superb performance at a cricket match, the Doctor and his companions are invited to a masked ball given by Lady Cranleigh and her son, Charles. Nyssa turns out to be a stunning look-alike of Ann, Charles' fiancee. Later, a masked man, using the same Pierrot costume as the Doctor, attacks Ann and murders a servant. The Doctor eventually discovers the true murderer: George, Charles' brother, Ann's original fiance, and an explorer believed to have died in the Amazon. Horribly disfigured by Indians, George now lives a secret existence, known only to Lady Cranleigh. But he was driven mad with jealousy and grief at the news of Ann's wedding. Exposed, George kidnaps Nyssa, but later falls to his death.

    This is the first purely historical story since *The Highlanders* (FF).

182

Novelisation: *Doctor Who – Black Orchid* by Terence Dudley (0 426 20254 6) first published by W H Allen (now Virgin Publishing Ltd) in 1986 with cover by Tony Masero. Target library number 113.

Script Editor:
Antony Root

(6B) **EARTHSHOCK**
(4 episodes)
8 March 1982 to 16 March 1982

Writer:
Eric Saward

Director:
Peter Grimwade

Regular cast: see 5Z above

Cast: Beryl Reid (Briggs); James Warwick (Scott); Clare Clifford (Kyle); June Bland (Berger); David Banks (Cyber Leader); Mark Hardy (Cyber Lieutenant); Steve Morley (Walters); Suzi Arden (Snyder); Ann Holloway (Mitchell); Anne Clements (Trooper Bane); Mark Straker (Trooper Carter); Alec Sabin (Ringway); Mark Fletcher (Crewmember Vance); Christopher Whittingham (Crewmember Carson); Carolyn Mary Simmonds, Barney Lawrence (Androids); Jeff Wayne, Steve Ismay, Peter Gates-Fleming, David Bache, Graham Cole, Norman Bradley, Michael Gordon Browne (Cybermen).

Story: In the 26th century, a party of soldiers led by Prof. Kyle and Lt. Scott, investigate the death of paleontologists murdered by mysterious androids while studying dinosaur remains in an underground cave. The Doctor discovers that the androids are protecting a bomb set up by the Cybermen and capable of destroying Earth. He disarms it and follows its radio-signal to a gigantic space freighter, under the command of Captain

Briggs. But the Cybermen take over the ship, which they plot to crash on Earth while the Galactic Congress is in session. After locking the freighter on its deadly course, the Cyber Leader forces the Doctor to take him, Tegan and Nyssa on board the TARDIS, leaving Adric behind. Scott destroys the remaining Cybermen. Adric reroutes the ship into a time spiral leading to sixty five million years ago. The Doctor destroys the Cyber Leader. Scott, Briggs and the other survivors escape the ship in the nick of time, but Adric remains on board until it crashes on Earth, causing the death of the dinosaurs.

This story features the long-awaited return of the Cybermen, and the death of Adric. This is the first death of a Companion since that of Katarina and Sara Kingdom in *The Daleks' Master Plan* (V).

Novelisation: *Doctor Who – Earthshock* by Ian Marter (0 426 19377 6) first published by W H Allen (now Virgin Publishing Ltd) in 1983 with photomontage cover. New edition in 1992 with cover by Alister Pearson. Target library number 78.

Video tape: *Earthshock* (BBCV 4840) first released in 1992 with cover by Andrew Skilleter.

Script Editor:
Eric Saward

(6C) TIME FLIGHT
(4 episodes)
22 March 1982 to 30 March 1982

Writer:
Peter Grimwade

Director:
Ron Jones

Regular cast: Peter Davison (the Doctor); Sarah Sutton (Nyssa); Janet Fielding (Tegan Jovanka).

Cast: Anthony Ainley (the Master/Kalid); Nigel Stock (Prof. Hayter); Richard Easton (Capt. Stapley); Keith Drinkel (Flight Engineer Scobie); Michael Cashman (First Officer Bilton); Peter Dahlsen (Horton); Brian McDermott (Sheard); John Flint (Capt. Urquhart); Judith Byfield (Angela Clifford/Tannoy Voice); Peter Cellier (Andrews); Hugh Hayes (Anithon); Andre Winterton (Zarak); Matthew Waterhouse, Graham Cole, Chris Bradshaw (Adric, Melkur, Terileptil illusions); Tommy Winward (Security man); Barney Lawrence (Dave Culshaw).

Story: The Doctor investigates the mysterious in-flight disappearance of a Concorde. He discovers that the plane has been taken back to the Pleistocene era through a time contour. There, he encounters Kalid, a strange Arab magician, who appears to command protoplasmic creatures bound by psychic energy, the Plasmatons. Kalid turns out to be the Master, who is trying to control the Xeraphin, an alien collective intelligence of immense mental powers, whose planet was laid waste in a galactic war. The Master gains control of the Xeraphin's evil side, but its good side helps the Doctor thwart him. The Time Lord fixes the Master's TARDIS so that the Xeraphin are sent back to their now-clean home planet, which will serve as the Master's new jail. The TARDIS departs but Tegan stays behind on twentieth-century Earth.

Novelisation: *Doctor Who – Time-Flight* by Peter Grimwade (0 426 19297 4) first published by W H Allen (now Virgin Publishing Ltd) in 1983 with photomontage cover. Target library number 74.

Twentieth Season

Producer:
John Nathan-Turner

Script Editor:
Eric Saward

(6E) ARC OF INFINITY
(4 episodes)
3 January 1983 to 12 January 1983

Writer:
Johnny Byrne

Director:
Ron Jones

Regular cast: Peter Davison (the Doctor); Sarah Sutton (Nyssa); Janet Fielding (Tegan Jovanka).

Cast: Leonard Sachs (President Borusa); Michael Gough (Hedin); Ian Collier (Omega); Colin Baker (Maxil); Paul Jerricho (Castellan); Neil Daglish (Damon); Elspet Gray (Thalia); Max Harvey (Zorac); Andrew Boxer (Robin Stuart); Alastair Cumming (Colin Frazer); John D. Collins (Talor); Maya Woolfe (Hostel receptionist); Malcolm Harvey (The Ergon); Guy Groen (2nd receptionist).

Story: A traitor in the High Council steals the Doctor's bio data extract from the Matrix and transmits it to an anti-matter alien who has crossed into our dimension through the 'Arc of Infinity,' a collapsed star. The alien must bond physically with a Time Lord to remain in our dimension, and has chosen the Doctor. The High Council decides that the Doctor must die in order to sever the bond. Meanwhile, in Amsterdam, Tegan investigates her cousin Colin's disappearance in an ancient crypt, and is eventually captured by the alien. The Doctor escapes termination, while Nyssa exposes the traitor, Councillor Hedin, who reveals the alien's identity: Omega. Omega now controls the Matrix but his use of Tegan as a hostage has revealed his location. In Amsterdam, the Doctor confronts Omega, whose body is turning into a replica of the Doctor's, but the bonding is incomplete and will cause a huge anti-matter explosion. The Doctor uses a matter converter to destroy Omega. Tegan rejoins the TARDIS' crew.

This story features the return of Omega, from *The Three Doctors* (RRR), in a new costume, and Colin Baker's *Doctor Who* debut in the role of Time Lord Security Commander Maxil.

Novelisation: *Doctor Who – Arc of Infinity* by Terrance Dicks (0 426 19342 3) first published by W H Allen (now Virgin Publishing Ltd) in 1983 with photomontage cover. New edition in 1992 with cover by Alister Pearson. Target library number 80.

Video tape: *Arc of Infinity* (BBCV 5199) first released in 1994 with cover by Pete Walbank.

(6D) SNAKEDANCE
(4 episodes)
18 January 1983 to 26 January 1983

Writer:
Christopher Bailey

Director:
Fiona Cumming

Regular cast: see 6E above

Cast: John Carson (Ambril); Colette O'Neil (Tanha); Preston Lockwood (Dojjen); Martin Clunes (Lon); Brian Miller (Dugdale); Hilary Sesta (Fortune Teller); George Ballantine (Hawker); Johnathon Morris (Chela); Barrie Smith (Puppeteer); Brian Grellis (Megaphone man); Bob Mills (Lon's bodyguard); Barney Lawrence, Chris Holmes (Attendants); Ray Lavender (Snakedancer); Derek Holt, Fred Reford (Demons).

Story: Under the Mara's control, Tegan sends the TARDIS to Manussa, once the homeworld of several galactic empires, from where the evil entity was banished five hundred years ago. There, the Mara takes over Lon, the son of the noble Lady Tanha, and uses him and Tegan to get the Great Crystal from Ambril, the Director of Historical Research. The Mara plans to use the Crystal to come into being during the ten-year Ceremony celebrating its exile. But the Doctor meets Dojjen, the last of the Snakedancers who once defeated the Mara, and from him, he learns how to destroy the Mara once and for all during the Ceremony.

Novelisation: *Doctor Who – Snakedance* by Terrance Dicks (0 426 19457 8) first published by W H Allen (now Virgin Publishing Ltd) in 1984 with cover by Andrew Skilleter. Target library number 83.

(6F) **MAWDRYN UNDEAD**
(4 episodes)
1 February 1983 to 9 February 1983

Writer:
Peter Grimwade

Director:
Peter Moffatt

Regular cast: See 6E above, and introducing Mark Strickson (Turlough).

Guest star: Nicholas Courtney (Brigadier Lethbridge-Stewart, Retd.).

Cast: Valentine Dyall (Black Guardian); David Collings (Mawdryn); Angus MacKay (Headmaster); Stephen Garlick (Ibbotson); Roger Hammond (Dr. Runciman); Sheila Gill (Matron); Peter Walmsley (1st mutant); Brian Darnley (2nd mutant); Lucy Baker (Child Nyssa); Sian Pattenden (Child Tegan).

Story: To avoid a collision, the TARDIS becomes trapped inside a huge spaceship bound on an eternal warp ellipse. To free his ship, the Doctor beams down to Earth, while Tegan and Nyssa follow him in the TARDIS. The Doctor arrives in a public school in 1983 and meets retired UNIT Brigadier Lethbridge-Stewart. He also meets Turlough, a student who is in reality a young alien recruited by the Black Guardian to kill him. Tegan and Nyssa arrive in 1977, and meet the then-Brigadier and the alien Mawdryn, who convinces them that he is a newly regenerated Doctor. Mawdryn and eight fellow scientists stole a metamorphic symbiosis regenerator from the Time Lords, and are condemned to live in a state of perpetual regeneration. The aliens want the Doctor to give them his life-force to end their suffering. When the two Brigadiers from different times meet, the energy discharge is enough to free the aliens and save the Doctor. Turlough joins the TARDIS' crew.

This story heralds the return of Brigadier Lethbridge-Stewart, last seen in *Terror of the Zygons* (4F).

Novelisation: *Doctor Who – Mawdryn Undead* by Peter Grimwade (0 426 19393 8) first published by W H Allen (now Virgin Publishing Ltd) in 1983 with photomontage cover. New edition in 1992 with cover by Alister Pearson. Target library number 82.

Video tape: *Mawdryn Undead* (BBCV 4547) first released in 1992 with cover by Andrew Skilleter.

(6G) **TERMINUS**
(4 episodes)
15 February 1983 to 23 February 1983

Writer:
Steve Gallagher

Director:
Mary Ridge

Regular cast: see 6F above

Cast: Valentine Dyall (Black Guardian); Liza Goddard (Kari); Dominic Guard (Olvir); Rachael Weaver (Inga); Martin Muncaster (Tannoy Voice); Martin Potter (Eirak); Andrew Burt (Valgard); Tim Munro (Sigurd); Peter Benson (Bor); R. J. Bell (The Garm).

Story: At the Black Guardian's behest, Turlough sabotages the TARDIS, causing it to materialise on a spaceship *en route* to Terminus, a huge alien space station located at the very centre of the Universe. Terminus is owned by the callous Terminus Inc., who use it as final home for victims of the incurable lazar disease. The Company controls Terminus through its pain-killing hydromel drug. Nyssa is infected but is saved by the ministrations of the alien Garm. Meanwhile, the Doctor discovers that it is the explosion of one of Terminus' two, unstable engines which once created the 'big bang.' He prevents a similar Universe-destroying explosion from reoccurring. Nyssa decides to stay on Terminus to help the Lazars, and plans to synthesise hydromel, thus freeing the station from Terminus Inc's grip.

Novelisation: *Doctor Who – Terminus* by John Lydecker (pen name of Steve Gallagher) (0 426 19385 7) first published by W H Allen (now Virgin Publishing Ltd) in 1983 with photomontage cover. Target library number 79.

Video tape: *Terminus* (BBCV 4890) first released in 1993 with cover by Andrew Skilleter.

(6H) ENLIGHTENMENT
(4 episodes)
1 March 1983 to 9 March 1983

Writer:
Barbara Clegg

Director:
Fiona Cumming

Regular cast: Peter Davison (the Doctor); Janet Fielding (Tegan Jovanka); Mark Strickson (Turlough).

Cast: Valentine Dyall (Black Guardian); Cyril Luckham (White Guardian); Keith Barron (Striker); Lynda Baron (Wrack); Christopher Brown (Marriner); Tony Caunter (Jackson); Clive Kneller (Collier); James McClure (1st Officer); Leee John (Mansell); John Cannon (Helmsman); Byron Sotiris (Critas).

Story: The White Guardian alerts the Doctor to a great danger. The TARDIS rematerialises on Captain Striker's Edwardian racing yacht, which turns out to be a space vessel participating in a planet-spanning race of Eternals, aliens of awesome mind powers but no imagination. The prize is 'Enlightenment' and it is fiercely coveted by Buccaneer Captain Wrack, who has been using the Black Guardian's power to destroy rival ships. The Black Guardian hopes that, with Enlightenment, the Eternals will spread chaos through time and space. Wrack uses Tegan in a plot to destroy Captain Striker's ship, but the Doctor foils her. Turlough helps the Doctor throw Wrack overboard and, together, they win the race. The two Guardians banish the remaining Eternals, and offer Enlightenment in the form of a crystal. The Doctor refuses it, and Turlough throws the crystal at the Black Guardian, thereby severing his bond with the evil entity.

This story ends the 'Black Guardian' storyline introduced in *The Ribos Operation* (5A).

Novelisation: *Doctor Who – Enlightenment* by Barbara Clegg (0 426 19537 X) first published by W H Allen (now Virgin

Publishing Ltd) in 1984 with cover by Andrew Skilleter. Target library number 85.

Video tape: *Enlightenment* (BBCV 4891) first released in 1993 with cover by Andrew Skilleter.

(6J) THE KING'S DEMONS
(2 episodes)
15 March 1983 to 16 March 1983

Writer:
Terence Dudley

Director:
Tony Virgo

Regular cast: see 6H above

Cast: Anthony Ainley (the Master/Sir Gilles Estram); Frank Windsor (Ranulf); Gerald Flood (King John/Voice of Kamelion); Isla Blair (Isabella); Christopher Villiers (Hugh); Michael J. Jackson (Sir Geoffrey); Peter Burroughs (Jester); Jakob Lindberg (Lute Player); Tony Annis (Gaoler); Chris Padmore (Kamelion).

Story: The TARDIS materialises on 4 March 1215 during a joust held in the presence of King John. The King welcomes the travellers, whom he calls his demons, but his actions towards his Barons seem unusually hostile. The Doctor discovers the King is, in reality, a shape-changing android, Kamelion, whom the Master found on Xeriphas. Disguised as Sir Gilles Estram, the King's Champion, the evil Time Lord plots to turn the Barons against the King, and prevent the signing of the Magna Carta, thereby altering history. The Doctor eventually wrests Kamelion's control from the Master, exposing his enemy's plot. The android joins the TARDIS crew.

Novelisation: *Doctor Who – The King's Demons* by Terence Dudley (0 426 20227 9) first published by W H Allen (now

Virgin Publishing Ltd) in 1986 with cover by David McAllister.
Target library number 108.

(6K) THE FIVE DOCTORS
(90-minute 20th Anniversary Special)
25 November 1983

Writer:
Terrance Dicks

Director:
Peter Moffatt

Regular cast: see 6H above

Guest stars: William Hartnell, Richard Hurndall (First Doctor); Patrick Troughton (Second Doctor); Jon Pertwee (Third Doctor); Tom Baker (Fourth Doctor); Nicholas Courtney (Brigadier Lethbridge-Stewart, Rtd.); Elisabeth Sladen (Sarah Jane Smith); John Leeson (Voice of K9); Lalla Ward (Romana); Carole Ann Ford (Susan); Richard Franklin (Mike Yates); Caroline John (Liz Shaw); Frazer Hines (Jamie McCrimmon); Wendy Padbury (Zoe Heriot).

Cast: Anthony Ainley (the Master); Philip Latham (Lord President Borusa); Dinah Sheridan (Chancellor Flavia); Paul Jerricho (Castellan); Richard Mathews (Rassilon); David Savile (Colonel Crichton); Ray Float (Sergeant); Roy Skelton (Dalek voice); John Scott Martin (Dalek operator); Stephen Meredith (Technician); David Banks (Cyber Leader); Mark Hardy (Cyber Lieutenant); William Kenton (Cyber Scout); Stuart Blake (Commander); Keith Hodiak (Raston Robot); John Tallents (Guard); Lee Woods (Yeti, Cyberman); Richard Naylor, Mark Whincup, Gilbert Gillan, Emyr Morris Jones, Myrddin Jones, Norman Bradley, Lloyd Williams, Graham Cole, Alan Riches, Ian Marshall-Fisher, Mark Bassenger (Cybermen); Johnnie Mack, Frederick Wolfe, Charles Milward (Time Lords).

Story: A mysterious Player gathers the first three incarnations of the Doctor, along with Susan, the Brigadier and Sarah Jane Smith, and dumps them inside the Death Zone on Gallifrey. However, the fourth Doctor and Romana become trapped in a time eddy, thereby endangering the existence of the Fifth Doctor, who has no choice but also to travel to the Zone, with Tegan and Turlough. Meanwhile, the High Council has become aware that the Death Zone has been reactivated, and is draining energy from the Eye of Harmony. They enlist the help of the Master to rescue the Doctor, but he too becomes a prisoner of the Game. The various Doctors encounter a Dalek, a Yeti, the Cybermen, the incredibly fast Raston Robot, and even the phantom images of other Companions, on their way to the Dark Tower, the Tomb of Rassilon, where they eventually defeat the Master. Meanwhile, the Fifth Doctor has used the Master's recall device to get to the Citadel, where he exposes the Player's identity: President Borusa, who wants the Secret of Immortality, which is locked within Rassilon's Tomb. The President and the Five Doctors eventually come face to face in the Tomb. The Spirit of Rassilon appears and offers Borusa his prize, but it is the immortality of a living statue. Rassilon then sends everyone back to his own time, and the Fifth Doctor flees rather than be made President again.

William Hartnell appears only in a clip from *The Dalek Invasion of Earth* (K). Tom Baker and Lalla Ward appear only in two clips from *Shada* (5M), the uncompleted and never broadcast story.

Novelisation: *Doctor Who – The Five Doctors* by Terrance Dicks (0 426 19510 8) first published by W H Allen (now Virgin Publishing Ltd) in 1983 with cover by Andrew Skilleter. New edition in 1991 with cover by Alister Pearson. Target library number 81.

Video tape: *The Five Doctors* (BBCV 2020) first released in 1985 with cover by Andrew Skilleter. New edition (BBCV 4387) in 1990 with cover by Alister Pearson.

Twenty-First Season

Producer:
John Nathan-Turner

Script Editor:
Eric Saward

(6L) **WARRIORS OF THE DEEP**
(4 episodes)
5 January 1984 to 13 January 1984

Writer:
Johnny Byrne

Director:
Pennant Roberts

Regular cast: Peter Davison (the Doctor); Janet Fielding (Tegan Jovanka); Mark Strickson (Turlough).

Cast: Tom Adams (Vorshak); Ingrid Pitt (Solow); Ian McCulloch (Nilson); Nigel Humphreys (Bulic); Martin Neil (Maddox); Tara Ward (Preston); Norman Comer (Icthar); Nitza Saul (Karina); Stuart Blake (Scibus); Vincent Brimble (Tarpok); Christopher Farries (Sauvix); James Coombes (Paroli); Steve Kelly, Chris Wolfe, Jules Walters, Mike Braben, Dave Ould (Sea Devils); William Perrie, John Asquith (Myrka).

Story: The TARDIS materialises on Earth in 2084 inside Sea Base Four, an undersea military base. The base is attacked by three Silurians and a squadron of Sea Devil warriors. The Silurians plan to launch the base's nuclear missiles, thereby provoking a nuclear war between the two blocs and destroying human life on Earth. The Doctor and his companions, first mistaken as enemy spies and saboteurs, help the soldiers fight off the Silurians, who later reject the Doctor's peace offerings. To save Earth, the Doctor helps the humans destroy the Silurians and Sea Devils with hexachromite, a gas deadly to reptiles, but he wishes there had been an alternative. The Doctor then successfully aborts the launch of the missiles.

This story marks the return of the Silurians and the Sea Devils, last seen in 1972.

Novelisation: *Doctor Who – Warriors of the Deep* by Terrance Dicks (0 426 19561 2) first published by W H Allen (now Virgin Publishing Ltd) in 1984 with cover by Andrew Skilleter. New edition in 1992 with cover by Alister Pearson. Target library number 87.

(6M) **THE AWAKENING**
(2 episodes)
19 January 1984 to 20 January 1984

Writer:
Eric Pringle

Director:
Michael Owen Morris

Regular cast: see 6L above

Cast: Polly James (Jane Hampden); Denis Lill (Sir George Hutchinson); Glyn Houston (Col. Wolsey); Jack Galloway (Joseph Willow); Frederick Hall (Andrew Verney); Keith Jayne (Will Chandler); Christopher Saul (Trooper).

Story: The Doctor takes Tegan to visit her grandfather, Andrew Verney, in the village of Little Hodcombe. They arrive in the middle of elaborate war games, reconstructing the English Civil War, led by Sir George Hutchinson. But the games become frighteningly real as Tegan is designated Queen of May, a human sacrifice, and Will Chandler, an actual person from 1643 appears. The Doctor identifies the source of the phenomenon as the Malus, an evil alien entity who is using psychic projections to feed on the villagers' fears. Rediscovered dormant in the local church by Verney, the Malus has been awakened by Sir George's deranged mind. The Doctor eventually finds a way to cut the Malus off from the villagers' emotions. After a last psychic attack, and Sir George's death, the Malus destroys itself and the church.

Novelisation: *Doctor Who – The Awakening* by Eric Pringle (0 426 20158 2) first published by W H Allen (now Virgin Publishing Ltd) in 1985 with cover by Andrew Skilleter. New edition in 1992 with cover by Alister Pearson. Target library number 95.

(6N) **FRONTIOS**
(4 episodes)
26 January 1984 to 3 February 1984

Writer: **Director:**
Christopher H. Bidmead   Ron Jones

Regular cast: see 6L above

Cast: John Gillett (Gravis); Peter Gilmore (Brazen); Lesley Dunlop (Norna); William Lucas (Range); Jeff Rawle (Plantagenet); Maurice O'Connell (Cockerill); Richard Ashley (Orderly); Alison Skilbeck (Deputy); Raymond Murtagh (Retrograde); George Campbell, Michael Malcolm, Stephen Speed, William Bowen, Hedi Khursandi (Tractators); Jim Dowdall (Warnsman); John Beardmore (Captain Revere).

Story: In the very far future, the TARDIS lands on Frontios, last refuge of a group of Earth survivors, led by Plantagenet. The colonists are under siege by mysterious meteorite storms. Also, an unseen force is kidnapping humans in Frontios' underground. The Doctor eventually discovers that the colony is secretly controlled by the Tractators, large worm-like aliens with gravity-controlling powers, who have been using the missing colonists as living power batteries. Their leader, the Gravis, plans to turn Frontios itself into a giant, hollow spaceship in which they can roam throughout the Universe. But the Gravis' desire for the TARDIS enables the Doctor to cut him off from the other Tractators, and thus render him and the other Tractators helpless. As the TARDIS leaves, it is caught up in a time corridor . . .

Novelisation: *Doctor Who – Frontios* by Christopher H. Bidmead (0 426 19780 1) first published by W H Allen (now Virgin Publishing Ltd) in 1984 with cover by Andrew Skilleter. Target library number 91.

(6P) **RESURRECTION OF THE DALEKS**
(2 45-minute episodes)
8 February 1984 to 15 February 1984

Writer:
Eric Saward

Director:
Matthew Robinson

Regular cast: see 6L above

Cast: Terry Molloy (Davros); Maurice Colbourne (Lytton); Rodney Bewes (Stien); Rula Lenska (Styles); Del Henney (Col. Archer); Chloe Ashcroft (Prof. Laird); Philip McGough (Sgt. Calder); Jim Findley (Mercer); Leslie Grantham (Kiston); Sneh Gupta (Osborn); Roger Davenport (Trooper); John Adam Baker, Linsey Turner (Crew members); William Sleigh (Galloway); Brian Miller, Royce Mills (Dalek voices); John Scott Martin, Cy Town, Tony Starr, Toby Byrne (Daleks); Nicholas Curry (Chemist); Michael Jeffries, Mike Braben (Policemen); Mike Mungarvan, Simon Crane (Soldiers); Pat Judge (Man with metal detector).

Story: The time corridor takes the travellers to the 20th century London docks. They meet Stien, who has escaped from a Dalek battleship in the future. There, under the command of the Black Dalek, Commander Lytton and his mercenaries have just taken over the space prison where Davros has been kept frozen for 90 years. The Daleks need his help to neutralise a deadly virus

198

created by the Movellans. But Davros plots to regain his leadership and takes control of the minds of several Daleks. Stien turns out to be a replica, genetically engineered by the Daleks, who want to create a duplicate of the Doctor to kill the Time Lords' High Council. The Doctor turns Stien round and confronts Davros, but cannot bring himself to kill him. The Black Dalek's Daleks and Davros' Daleks wage a merciless war. Davros falls victim to the Movellan virus, and Stien activates a self-destruct switch, destroying both the space prison and the Dalek ship. Back on Earth, the Doctor uses the virus to get rid of the remaining Daleks. Lytton stays in the 20th century with two Dalek-made duplicates of policemen. Tired of all the violence, Tegan leaves the TARDIS' crew.

Video tape: *Resurrection of the Daleks* (BBCV 5143) first released in 1993 with cover by Bruno Elettori.

(6Q) **PLANET OF FIRE**
(4 episodes)
23 February 1984 to 2 March 1984

Writer:
Peter Grimwade

Director:
Fiona Cumming

Regular cast: Peter Davison (the Doctor); Mark Strickson (Turlough); and introducing Nicola Bryant (Perpugilliam 'Peri' Brown).

Cast: Anthony Ainley (the Master); Peter Wyngarde (Timanov); Barbara Shelley (Sorasta); Gerald Flood (Voice of Kamelion); James Bate (Amyand); Dallas Adams (Prof. Foster); Edward Highmore (Malkon); Jonathan Caplan (Roskal); John Alkin (Lomand); Michael Bangerter (Curt); Simon Sutton (Lookout); Max Arthur (Zuko); Ray Knight (Trion).

Story: An alien beacon found by a young American girl,

Perpugilliam ('Peri') Brown, and her archaeologist step-father, Professor Foster, leads her, the Doctor, Turlough and a strangely behaving Kamelion to the planet Sarn. The natives are sharply divided over their Volcano god, which threatens to erupt and destroy them all. The Master has once again taken over Kamelion. Accidentally shrunk by his own Tissue Compression Eliminator, he needs to bathe in the volcanic numismaton flame, which will restore his size and extend his life. Sarn turns out to be a political prison for Trion, Turlough's homeworld, which banished him to Earth. Turlough eventually risks further punishment by radioing Trion to send a ship to evacuate Sarn. He then finds his exile has been rescinded and returns to his homeworld with his newly found brother, Malkon. Meanwhile, the Master becomes trapped in the flame, and is apparently vaporised.

Novelisation: *Doctor Who – Planet of Fire* by Peter Grimwade (0 426 19940 5) first published by W H Allen (now Virgin Publishing Ltd) in 1984 with cover by Andrew Skilleter. Target library number 93.

(6R) THE CAVES OF ANDROZANI
(4 episodes)
8 March 1984 to 16 March 1984

Writer:
Robert Holmes

Director:
Graeme Harper

Regular cast: Peter Davison (the Doctor); Nicola Bryant (Peri Brown); and introducing Colin Baker (the Doctor).

Guest stars: Anthony Ainley (the Master); Matthew Waterhouse (Adric); Sarah Sutton (Nyssa); Janet Fielding (Tegan); Mark Strickson (Turlough); Gerald Flood (Voice of Kamelion).

Cast: Christopher Gable (Sharaz Jek); John Normington

(Morgus); Robert Glenister (Salateen); Maurice Roeves (Stotz); Roy Holder (Krelper); Martin Cochrane (Chellak); Barbara Kinghorn (Timmin); David Neal (President); Ian Staples (Soldier); Colin Taylor (Magma creature); Keith Harvey, Andrew Smith, Stephen Smith (Androids).

Story: On Androzani Minor, the Doctor and Peri become involved in a conflict between Sharaz Jek, a disfigured scientist, hiding inside a huge network of caves, protected by his androids, and General Chellak's men from Androzani Major. Jek wants revenge against Morgus, the Chairman of the Sirius Corporation and his former partner, who betrayed him. Jek has gained control of the supply of spectrox, a precious life-giving elixir prepared from poisonous bat guano. Mistaken for gun-runners, the Doctor and Peri are rescued by Jek, who falls madly in love with the Earth girl. They later meet the real gun-runners, led by Stotz, who are in the secret employ of Morgus. The Doctor discovers that he and Peri have been poisoned by raw spectrox. Morgus eventually takes personal command of the smugglers, and is deposed by his assistant. He and Jek meet at last, and kill each other. Meanwhile, the Doctor succeeds in obtaining the bat milk antidote to Spectrox Toxoemia but accidentally spills some. He gives what's left to Peri, then regenerates.

Novelisation: *Doctor Who – The Caves of Androzani* by Terrance Dicks (0 426 19959 6) first published by W H Allen (now Virgin Publishing Ltd) in 1984 with cover by Andrew Skilleter. New edition in 1992 with cover by Andrew Skilleter. Target library number 92.

Video tape: *The Caves of Androzani* (BBCV 4713) first released in 1992 with cover by Andrew Skilleter.

SIXTH DOCTOR

COLIN BAKER
1984 – 1986

Twenty-First Season (continued)

Producer:
John Nathan-Turner

Script Editor:
Eric Saward

(6S) **THE TWIN DILEMMA**
(4 episodes)
22 March 1984 to 30 March 1984

Writer:
Anthony Steven
(with Eric Saward,
uncredited)

Director:
Peter Moffatt

Regular cast: Colin Baker (the Doctor); Nicola Bryant (Peri Brown).

Cast: Maurice Denham (Edgeworth/Azmael); Kevin McNally (Hugo Lang); Edwin Richfield (Mestor); Barry Stanton (Noma); Oliver Smith (Drak); Seymour Green (Chamberlain); Gavin Conrad (Romulus); Andrew Conrad (Remus); Dennis Chinnery (Sylvest); Helen Blatch (Fabian); Dione Inman (Elena); Roger Nott (Prisoner); John Wilson (Guard); Steve Wickham, Ridgewell Hawkes (Gastropods);

Story: The Doctor's new incarnation behaves erratically. After almost choking Peri to death, he decides to become a hermit, but instead gets involved in renegade Time Lord Azmael's plotting. Under the alias of Prof. Edgeworth, Azmael has kidnapped Romulus and Remus, two twin mathematical geniuses, at the behest of the alien Mestor, tyrant of Jaconda. Mestor's plan is to throw Jaconda into its own sun in order to create a huge explosion that will spread its eggs throughout the Universe. With the help of Intergalactic Task Force Lieutenant Hugo Lang, the Doctor foils Mestor's plan. While Azmael mentally battles Mestor, the Doctor destroys the alien's body. Azmael then destroys Mestor's mind by committing suicide through a last, fatal regeneration.

Novelisation: *Doctor Who – The Twin Dilemma* by Eric Saward (0 426 20155 8) first published by W H Allen (now Virgin Publishing Ltd) in 1985 with cover by Andrew Skilleter. New edition in 1993 with cover by Alister Pearson. Target library number 103.

Video tape: *The Twin Dilemma* (BBCV 4783) first released in 1992 with cover by Andrew Skilleter.

Twenty-Second Season

Producer:
John Nathan-Turner

Script Editor:
Eric Saward

(6T) ATTACK OF THE CYBERMEN
(2 45-minute episodes)
5 January 1985 to 12 January 1985

Writer:
Paula Moore
(with Eric Saward,
uncredited)

Director:
Matthew Robinson

Regular cast: Colin Baker (the Doctor); Nicola Bryant (Peri

Brown).

Cast: Maurice Colbourne (Lytton); Brian Glover (Griffiths); Terry Molloy (Russell); James Beckett (Payne); Jonathan David (Stratton); Michael Attwell (Bates); Sarah Berger (Rost); Esther Freud (Threst); Faith Brown (Flast); Sarah Greene (Varne); Stephen Churchett (Bill); Stephen Wale (David); Michael Kilgarriff (Cyber Controller); David Banks (Cyber Leader); Brian Orrell (Cyber Lieutenant); John Ainley, Roger Pope, Thomas Lucy, Ian Marshall-Fisher, Pat Gorman (Cybermen); Mike Braben, Michael Jeffries (Policemen); Trisha Clarke, Irela Williams, Maggie Lynton (Cryons).

Story: The Doctor is lured to 1985 Earth by Lytton's galactic distress call. Under the pretence of a jewellery heist, Lytton makes contact with the Cybermen, hiding in the London sewers. When the Doctor arrives, he is captured and taken to Telos. The Cybermen have stolen a time vessel and are planning to change history by destroying Earth before it causes the destruction of their homeworld, Mondas, in 1986. They plan to cause Halley's Comet to crash on Earth. Lytton turns out to be in the employ of Telos' natives, the Cryons, who built the huge hibernation facilities that the Cybermen have taken over. The Cryons have hired Lytton to steal the time vessel, but the mission fails in spite of the help of fellow thief Griffiths and Stratton and Bates, two men who escaped from the Cybermen. Lytton is captured and partially turned into a Cyberman. The Doctor is powerless to rescue him, but helps Lytton kill the Cyber Controller. A Cryon sacrifices herself to cause a huge explosion which totally destroys the Cyber base.

This story re-examines the themes developed in *The Tenth Planet* (DD) and *The Tomb of the Cybermen* (MM). It also sees the TARDIS' brief return to the junkyard at 76 Totters' Lane and a number of changes in its appearance, due to a temporary repair of the still somewhat erratic chameleon circuit. Lytton and two policemen make a re-appearance, having been left on 20th-century Earth in *Resurrection of the Daleks* (6P).

Novelisation: *Doctor Who – Attack of the Cybermen* by Eric Saward (0 426 20290 2) first published by W H Allen (now Virgin Publishing Ltd) in 1989 with cover by Colin Howard. New edition in 1992 with cover by Alister Pearson. Target library number 138.

(6V) **VENGEANCE ON VAROS**
(2 45-minute episodes)
19 January 1985 to 26 January 1985

Writer:
Philip Martin

Director:
Ron Jones

Regular cast: see 6T above

Cast: Martin Jarvis (Governor); Nabil Shaban (Sil); Jason Connery (Jondar); Forbes Collins (Chief Officer); Stephen Yardley (Arak); Sheila Reid (Etta); Geraldine Alexander (Areta); Owen Teale (Maldak); Graham Cull (Bax); Nicholas Chagrin (Quillam); Hugh Martin (Priest); Keith Skinner (Rondel); Bob Tarff (Executioner); Jack McGuire, Alan Troy (Madmen).

Story: The TARDIS needs Zyton-7, so the Doctor takes it to Varos, a mining planet inhabited by descendants from a colony for the criminally insane, who thrive on public torture. Varos' Governor has been trying to negotiate better prices for Zyton from Sil, the reptilian envoy from Galatron. The Doctor helps two rebels, Jondar and Areta, to escape from the Punishment Dome, but they are recaptured. Peri and Areta are almost reshaped into beast-like creatures by Quillam, the Dome's sadistic scientist, but the Doctor saves them and tells the Governor the true value of Zyton. Quillam and Varos' Chief Officer, who are in the secret employ of Sil, then attempt to kill the Doctor and the Governor, but instead, are killed by one of their own traps. Sil's plans to have Galatron invade Varos are cancelled and the company offers to buy Zyton at any price. The

Governor abolishes Varos' cruel political system.

Novelisation: *Doctor Who – Vengeance on Varos* by Philip Martin (0 426 20291 0) first published by W H Allen (now Virgin Publishing Ltd) in 1988 with cover by David McAllister. New edition in 1993 with cover by Alister Pearson. Target library number 106.

Video tape: *Vengeance on Varos* (BBCV 4962) first released in 1993 with cover by Andrew Skilleter.

(6X) **THE MARK OF THE RANI**
(2 45-minute episodes)
2 February 1985 to 9 February 1985

Writers: **Director:**
Pip and Jane Baker   Sarah Hellings

Regular cast: see 6T above

Cast: Anthony Ainley (the Master); Kate O'Mara (the Rani); Terence Alexander (Lord Ravensworth), Gawn Grainger (George Stephenson); Peter Childs (Jack Ward); Gary Cady (Luke Ward); Richard Steele (Guard); William Ilkley (Tim Bass); Hus Levent (Edwin Green); Kevin White (Sam Rudge); Martyn Whitby (Drayman); Cordelia Ditton (Older Woman); Sarah James (Young Woman); Nigel Johnson (Josh); Alan Talbot (Tom).

Story: En route to Kew Gardens, the TARDIS instead lands at the time of the Luddite uprisings. The Master has dragged the ship off course as part of his scheme to alter history by preventing the industrial revolution and using it for his own ends. But he runs afoul of the Rani, another renegade Time Lord, who has been conducting biological experiments on the local miners by extracting from their brains the chemical substance that promotes sleep, thereby increasing their aggression. The Master steals the brain fluid, forcing the Rani into an uneasy alliance with him. But the Doctor manages to outwit the two evil Time Lords, and secretly tampers with the Rani's TARDIS. She and the Master are sent spinning into the outer fringes of the Universe, at the mercy of a rapidly growing Tyrannosaurus embryo. The Doctor uses the brain fluid to restore the workers to normal.

Novelisation: *Doctor Who – The Mark of the Rani* by Pip and Jane Baker (0 426 20232 5) first published by W H Allen (now Virgin Publishing Ltd) in 1986 with cover by Andrew Skilleter. Target library number 107.

(6W) **THE TWO DOCTORS**
(3 45-minute episodes)
16 February 1985 to 2 March 1985

Writer:
Robert Holmes

Director:
Peter Moffatt

Regular cast: see 6T above

Guest stars: Patrick Troughton (Second Doctor); Frazer Hines (Jamie McCrimmon).

Cast: John Stratton (Shockeye); Jacqueline Pearce (Chessene); Laurence Payne (Dastari); James Saxon (Oscar); Carmen Gomez (Anita); Clinton Greyn (Stike); Tim Raynham (Varl); Aimee Delamain (Dona Arana); Nicholas Fawcett (Technician); Laurence Payne (Computer voice); Fernando Monast (Scientist); Jay McGrath (Dead Androgum).

Story: The Time Lords send the Second Doctor and Jamie to investigate unauthorised time travel experiments on Space Station J7. Dastari, the Station Head, has been biologically

207

'augmenting' Androgums, a race of primitive savages, such as Shockeye, the Station's ever-hungry chef. Chessene, an augmented female Androgum, has allied herself with Sontaran Group Marshal Stike, who wants the secret of the Rassilon Imprimature, a symbiotic print contained within a Time Lord's physiology that is the key to time travel. The Sontarans invade the Station, making it look like the Time Lords' work. They then take the Second Doctor to Andalusia, where they plan to dissect him. Drawn to the Station by his other self's pain, the Sixth Doctor rescues Jamie and follows the trail to Spain. Dastari implants the Second Doctor with Shockeye's genes, but the Sixth Doctor rescues him and kills Shockeye. Chessene eventually destroys the Sontarans and, reverting to her bestial nature, kills Dastari. She is disintegrated when she attempts time travel without the Imprimature.

This was Patrick Troughton's last role in *Doctor Who* before his untimely death.

Novelisation: *Doctor Who – The Two Doctors* by Robert Holmes (0 426 20201 5) first published by W H Allen (now Virgin Publishing Ltd) in 1985 with cover by Andrew Skilleter. Target library number 100.

Video tape: *The Two Doctors* (BBCV 5148) first released in 1993 with cover by Colin Howard.

(6Y) **TIMELASH**
(2 45-minute episodes)
9 March 1985 to 16 March 1985

Writer:
Glen McCoy

Director:
Pennant Roberts

Regular cast: see 6T above

Cast: JeanAnne Crowley (Vena); Eric Deacon (Mykros); Robert

Ashby (the Borad); Paul Darrow (Tekker); David Chandler (Herbert George Wells); Denis Carey (Old Man); David Ashton (Kendron); Peter Robert Scott (Brunner); Dicken Ashworth (Sezon); Tracy Louise Ward (Katz); Christine Kavanagh (Aram); Steven Mackintosh (Gazak); Dean Hollingsworth (Android); James Richardson (Guardolier); Martin Gower (Tyheer/Bandril Ambassador); Neil Hallett (Maylin Ranis).

Story: The Karfelons suffer under the rule of the Borad, a tyrant who banishes rebels through a time tunnel known as the Timelash. The Doctor, who visited Karfel in his third incarnation, is persuaded to travel to Earth to bring back Vena, a girl who inadvertently fell into the Timelash with a precious amulet. The Doctor also brings back Herbert, a man from the 19th century. The Borad turns out to be a scientist who was accidentally sprayed with M80, an unstable element, while experimenting on a Morlox, a savage, underground reptilian creature, thus becoming half-Karfelon, half-Morlox. The Borad plans to murder all the Karfelons through a war with their neighbours, the Bandrils, and repopulate the planet with creatures like himself, starting with Peri. The Doctor uses a Kontron time crystal to defeat a Borad clone, and makes peace with the Bandrils. He then gets rid of the real Borad by banishing him to ancient Scotland through the Timelash. Herbert turns out to be H. G. Wells.

Novelisation: *Doctor Who – Timelash* by Glen McCoy (0 426 20229 5) first published by W H Allen (now Virgin Publishing Ltd) in 1985 with cover by David McAllister. Target library number 105.

(6Z) **REVELATION OF THE DALEKS**
(2 45-minute episodes)
23 March 1985 to 30 March 1985

Writer:
Eric Saward

Director:
Graeme Harper

Regular cast: see 6T above

Cast: Terry Molloy (Davros); Eleanor Bron (Kara); Clive Swift (Jobel); Alexei Sayle (DJ); Jenny Tomasin (Tasambeker); William Gaunt (Orcini); John Ogwen (Bostock); Stephen Flynn (Grigory); Bridget Lynch-Blosse (Natasha); Trevor Cooper (Takis); Colin Spaull (Lilt); Hugh Walters (Vogel); Alec Linstead (Head of Stengos); Ken Barker (Mutant); Royce Mills, Roy Skelton (Dalek voices); Penelope Lee (Computer voice); John Scott Martin, Cy Town, Tony Starr, Toby Byrne (Daleks).

Story: Suspicious of the death of one of his friends, the Doctor goes to Nekros, location of the Tranquil Repose mortuary where, under the management of Jobel, dying millionaires and politicians are preserved in suspended animation. The Doctor has been lured by Davros who, as the Great Healer, has secretly taken over Tranquil Repose. Davros has been genetically reengineering the more aggressive of the deceased into a new breed of Daleks, and has turned the rest into food for a company he created and entrusted to the ambitious Kara. But Kara hires Orcini, a former Knight of the Order of Oberon, to assassinate Davros. Meanwhile, Davros manipulates Tasambeker, Jobel's spurned assistant, into murdering Jobel. Orcini fails to kill Davros and, instead, kills Kara who has betrayed him. Takis, another embalmer, calls the real Daleks, who invade Tranquil Repose and capture Davros. Orcini sacrifices himself to destroy Tranquil Repose, and the Doctor shows the survivors how to refine the local flowers into food.

Twenty-Third Season
(THE TRIAL OF A TIME LORD)

(This season was broadcast as one 14-part story entitled *The Trial of a Time Lord*, with no individual segment titles.)

Producer:
John Nathan-Turner

Script Editor:
Eric Saward

(7A) **THE MYSTERIOUS PLANET**
(4 episodes)
6 September 1986 to 27 September 1986

Writer:
Robert Holmes

Director:
Nicholas Mallett

Regular cast: Colin Baker (the Doctor); Nicola Bryant (Peri Brown).

Guest stars: Michael Jayston (the Valeyard); Lynda Bellingham (the Inquisitor).

Cast: Tony Selby (Glitz); Joan Sims (Katryca); Glen Murphy (Dibber); Tom Chadbon (Merdeen); Roger Brierley (Drathro); David Rodigan (Broken Tooth); Adam Blackwood (Balazar); Timothy Walker (Grell); Billy McColl (Humker); Siôn Tudor Owen (Tandrell).

Story: The TARDIS is drawn to a huge space station. The Doctor emerges alone to face a tribunal of Time Lords. His memory of recent events (such as the reason for Peri's absence) is gone. The prosecutor, the Valeyard, intends to prove him guilty of cosmic interference, with evidence recorded in the Matrix or through the TARDIS. The Trial begins with a screening of the Doctor and Peri arriving on Ravolox, a planet

211

once almost destroyed by a solar fireball. Ravolox turns out to be Earth, two million years in the future, moved to a different location in space. The Doctor discovers an underground civilisation ruled by Drathro, a robot whose purpose is to guard three Sleepers from Andromeda. Meanwhile, outside, Peri is captured by the Free, a tribe led by Katryca. She meets Glitz, who wants to steal the Sleepers' 'secrets' and plots to destroy the tribe's totem, a black light converter which powers Drathro. Glitz's accomplice Dibber blows up the totem, but instead, it starts a chain reaction which threatens the universe. The Free invade the underground. Drathro kills Katryca, but is destroyed when the Doctor shuts down the energy systems. Despite the Doctor's protests that the evidence is being tampered with by the Valeyard, the Trial continues, with the Doctor's life now hanging in the balance.

The answers to the mystery of who moved Earth through space and rechristened it Ravolox, and why, and the true nature of the Sleepers' 'secrets' are to be found in the season's last story.

Novelisation: *Doctor Who – The Mysterious Planet* by Terrance Dicks (0 426 20319 4) first published by W H Allen (now Virgin Publishing Ltd) in 1987 with cover by Tony Masero. Target library number 127.

Video tape: *The Trial of a Time Lord* (BBCV 5008) first released in 1993 with cover by Alister Pearson.

(7B) MINDWARP
(4 episodes)
4 October 1986 to 25 October 1986

Writer:
Philip Martin

Director:
Ron Jones

Regular cast: see 7A above

Guest stars: see 7A above

Cast: Brian Blessed (King Yrcanos); Nabil Shaban (Sil); Christopher Ryan (Kiv); Patrick Ryecart (Crozier); Alibe Parsons (Matrona Kani); Richard Henry (Mentor); Trevor Laird (Frax); Gordon Warnecke (Tusa); Thomas Branch (the Lukoser).

Story: The Valeyard presents the Doctor's most recent adventure. The travellers arrive on Thoros-Beta, home of the Mentors, reptilian financiers like Sil, who use mind-controlled humanoids as their slaves. Their leader, Kiv, has had his brain expanded but will now die unless his scientist, Crozier, finds a way to safely transplant it into another being. The Doctor is subjected to Crozier's machine and starts behaving in a more selfish way. Seemingly afraid that Crozier will use his body, he betrays Peri and collaborates with Sil. Peri escapes with the warlord king Yrcanos. They stage a rebellion, but are captured. When the Doctor finds out that Crozier plans to transfer Kiv's mind into Peri's brain, he frees Yrcanos, who destroys the mind-control centre. But the Time Lords pull the Doctor out of the time stream before he can rescue Peri. The mind transfer is successful and Kiv's mind now occupies Peri's body. Because such a technology could affect the course of universal evolution, the Time Lords manipulate Yrcanos to kill Peri, Crozier and the rest.

(The ending of this story is later revealed to be the result of the Valeyard's forgery. Yrcanos presumably killed the villains before they could destroy Peri's mind. As a result, she lived and married the warrior king.)

Novelisation: *Doctor Who – Mindwarp* by Philip Martin (0 426 20335 6) first published by W H Allen (now Virgin Publishing Ltd) in 1989 with cover by Alister Pearson. Target library number 139.

Video tape: *The Trial of a Time Lord* (BBCV 5008) first released in 1993 with cover by Alister Pearson.

Script Editor:
None listed

(7C) **TERROR OF THE VERVOIDS**
(4 episodes)
1 November 1986 to 22 November 1986

Writers:
Pip and Jane Baker

Director:
Chris Clough

Regular cast: Colin Baker (the Doctor); and introducing Bonnie Langford (Melanie Bush).

Guest stars: see 7A above

Cast: Honor Blackman (Prof. Lasky); Michael Craig (Commodore); Denys Hawthorne (Rudge); Yolande Palfrey (Janet); Tony Scoggo (Enzu/Grenville); Malcolm Tierney (Doland); David Allister (Bruchner); Arthur Hewlett (Kimber); Simon Slater (Edwardes); Barbara Ward (Mutant); Sam Howard (Atza); Leon Davis (Ortezo); Hugh Beverton, Martin Weedon (Guards); Mike Mungarvan (Duty Officer); Peppi Borza (First Vervoid); Bob Appleby (Second Vervoid); Barbara Ward (Ruth Baxter); Gess Whitfield, Paul Hillier, Bill Perrie, Jerry Manley (Vervoids).

Story: The Doctor now presents his evidence: a story from his near future, after he has met a new companion, Melanie. Following a mayday call, the TARDIS lands on the *Hyperion III* space liner *en route* from Moga to Earth. The call is from an undercover agent who, posing as a Mogarian, suspects that a dangerous criminal is on board; but the agent is poisoned. Meanwhile, the Vervoids, a vegetal life form discovered by Prof. Lasky, are released and start killing the passengers. Bruchner, one of Lasky's assistants, goes mad and tries to send the ship into a black hole. This is averted by the Mogarians, who then hijack the ship with the help of Security Officer Rudge. But Dolland, Lasky's other assistant, uses Mel to kill the Mogarians. He turns out to be the real criminal, who wants to sell the Vervoids as slave labour. The creatures rampage through the ship, killing Rudge, Dolland and finally Lasky. The Doctor uses a magnesium-like substance to accelerate their life-cycle, causing them to all wither and die. The Valeyard now accuses him of genocide.

The story of the Doctor's meeting with Melanie is never recounted, and the events of this story presumably take place in a future that is somehow parallel to that of the *Trial* storyline, and every subsequent story.

The working title for this story was *The Ultimate Foe*.

Novelisation: *Doctor Who – Terror of the Vervoids* by Pip and Jane Baker (0 426 20313 5) first published by W H Allen (now Virgin Publishing Ltd) in 1987 with cover by Tony Masero. Target library number 125.

Video tape: *The Trial of a Time Lord* (BBCV 5008) first released in 1993 with cover by Alister Pearson.

(7C) THE ULTIMATE FOE
(2 episodes)
29 November 1986 to 6 December 1986

Writers:
Robert Holmes and
Pip and Jane Baker
(episode 1: with Eric Saward,
uncredited)

Director:
Chris Clough

Regular cast: see 7A above

Guest stars: see 7A above

Cast: Anthony Ainley (the Master); Tony Selby (Glitz); Geoffrey Hughes (Popplewick); James Bree (the Keeper of the Matrix).

Story: Glitz and Mel are brought to the Tribunal as witnesses by the Master, who speaks from within the Matrix. It is revealed that it is the High Council who nearly destroyed Earth, because the planet sheltered the Andromedan Sleepers, who had stolen the Matrix's secrets. Afraid that the Doctor would find out the truth, the Council made a deal with the Valeyard to get rid of the Doctor in exchange for his remaining regenerations. The evidence against the Doctor, including Peri's death, has indeed been forged. The Valeyard is exposed as the amalgamation of the Doctor's darker side, between his twelfth and final regeneration. He flees into the Matrix, but the Doctor pursues him. With the help of Glitz and the Master, who hopes that the Doctor and the Valeyard will destroy each other, the Doctor engages the Valeyard in a mental duel. But the Valeyard, who hides behind the identity of Mr Popplewick, a Dickensian clerk, is also plotting to murder the Time Lords attending the Trial with a Particle Disseminator. Meanwhile, the Master uses Glitz to recover the Matrix's stolen secrets. Once he learns that the High Council has been deposed, he attempts to take over, but instead becomes trapped in the Matrix. The Doctor wrecks the Valeyard's plans and escapes from the damaged Matrix. The charges against him are dismissed, and he departs with Mel. The Valeyard also appears to have escaped, under the guise of the Keeper of the Matrix.

Nicola Bryant (Peri) and Brian Blessed (King Yrcanos) appear in a very brief cameo at the end of the story showing Peri being happily married to King Yrcanos.

The working title for this story was *Time, Inc.*

Novelisation: *Doctor Who – The Ultimate Foe* by Pip and Jane Baker (0 426 20329 1) first published by W H Allen (now Virgin Publishing Ltd) in 1988 with cover by Alister Pearson. Target library number 131.

Video tape: *The Trial of a Time Lord* (BBCV 5008) first released in 1993 with cover by Alister Pearson.

SEVENTH DOCTOR

SYLVESTER McCOY
1987 – 1989

Twenty-Fourth Season

Producer:
John Nathan-Turner

Script Editor:
Andrew Cartmel

(7D) TIME AND THE RANI
(4 episodes)
7 September 1987 to 28 September 1987

Writers
Pip and Jane Baker

Director:
Andrew Morgan

Regular cast: Sylvester McCoy (the Doctor); Bonnie Langford (Melanie).

Cast: Kate O'Mara (the Rani); Mark Greenstreet (Ikona); Donald Pickering (Beyus); Ridhard Gauntlett (Urak); Wanda Ventham (Faroon); John Segal (Lanisha); Karen Clegg (Sarn); Peter Tuddenham, Jacki Webb (Voices).

Story: The Rani causes the TARDIS to crash land on Lakertya, forcing the Doctor to regenerate. Disguised as Mel, she then tries to enlist his help. Meanwhile, the real Mel meets Ikona, a local rebel. The other Lakertyans collaborate with the Rani and her four-eyed Tetraps, because she holds their leader, Beyus, hostage. Beyus knows she can kill his people by releasing a swarm of deadly insects. The Rani has kidnapped the greatest geniuses in the Universe (including Einstein) to combine them into a giant brain. She plots to launch a rocket to blow up an asteroid made up of extra-dense 'strange matter'. The resulting explosion will turn the brain into a planet-size Time Manipulator, enabling the Rani to recreate the Universe. After inciting the Lakertyans to revolt, the Doctor fools the Rani into blowing up the brain, causing the rocket to miss the asteroid. Beyus sacrifices himself to save his people. The Rani escapes in her TARDIS, but is taken prisoner by the Tetraps. The Lakertyans embark on a new, more determined existence.

Novelisation: *Doctor Who – Time and the Rani* by Pip and Jane Baker (0 426 20331 3) first published by W H Allen (now Virgin Publishing Ltd) in 1987 with photomontage cover. New edition in 1991 with cover by Alister Pearson. Target library number 128.

(7E) **PARADISE TOWERS**
(4 episodes)
5 October 1987 to 26 October 1987

Writer:
Stephen Wyatt

Director:
Nicholas Mallett

Regular cast: see 7D above

Cast: Howard Cooke (Pex); Richard Briers (Chief Caretaker); Clive Merrison (Deputy Chief Caretaker); Joseph Young (Young Caretaker); Annabel Yuresha (Bin Liner); Julie Brennon (Fire Escape); Catherine Cusack (Blue Kang Leader); Astra Sheridan (Yellow Kang); Brenda Bruce (Tilda); Elizabeth Spriggs (Tabby); Judy Cornwell (Maddy); Simon Coady (Video Commentary).

Story: The Doctor and Mel arrive in Paradise Towers, a 304-storey luxury building now fallen into disrepair. The original inhabitants departed to fight a war, leaving the Towers inhabited by oldsters (Rezzies) and youngsters (Kangs), and managed by the Caretakers and the robotic Cleaners. The Doctor is mistaken for the Great Architect by the Caretakers. Meanwhile, Mel meets Pex, a self-appointed hero, who is in reality a cowardly young man who hid rather than go to fight in the war. The Cleaners, who have been secretly killing Kangs, begin to turn against all humans. They are controlled by Kroagnon, the Great Architect who designed the Towers, whose brain was buried in the basement when he tried to prevent the people from living in his creation. But Kroagnon takes over the Chief Caretaker's body, then proceeds to exterminate all human life inside the Towers. The Doctor convinces the Kangs, the Rezzies and the Caretakers that they must cooperate to survive. He lures Kroagnon out of the Caretaker HQ. Pex redeems himself by helping destroy the Great Architect, but dies in the process.

Novelisation: *Doctor Who – Paradise Towers* by Stephen Wyatt (0 426 20330 5) first published by W H Allen (now Virgin Publishing Ltd) in 1988 with cover by Alister Pearson. Target library number 134.

(7F) **DELTA AND THE BANNERMEN**
(3 episodes)
2 November 1987 to 16 November 1987

Writer:
Malcolm Kohll

Director:
Chris Clough

Regular cast: see 7D above

Cast: Don Henderson (Gavrok); Belinda Mayne (Delta); David Kinder (Billy); Sara Griffiths (Ray); Richard Davies (Burton); Stubby Kaye (Weismuller); Morgan Deare (Hawk); Hugh Lloyd (Goronwy); Johnny Dennis (Murray); Anita Graham (Bollit); Ken Dodd (Tollmaster); Leslie Meadows (Adlon); Brian Hibbard (Keillor); Martyn Geraint (Vinny); Clive Condon

(Callon); Richard Mitchley (Arrex); Robin Aspland, Keff McCulloch, Justin Myers, Ralph Salmins (The Lorells); Jessica McGough, Amy Osborn (Young Chimeron); Laura Collins, Carley Joseph (Chimeron Princess); Tracey Wilson, Jodie Wilson (Vocalists); Russell Brook, Ian McClaren, Tim Scott (Chimerons).

Story: Chimeron Queen, Delta, flees from Gavrok and his Bannermen mercenaries, who have destroyed her people. The Doctor sees her board a galactic tour bus en route to visit Disneyland in 1959. The bus hits a satellite, and instead lands near Shangri-La, a South Wales holiday camp. Delta is carrying with her an egg which hatches a young Chimeron Princess. But the Bannermen locate Delta and slaughter the tourists. With the help of Billy, a young local mechanic who has fallen in love with Delta, Ray, his would-be girlfriend, Goronwy, a local bee keeper, Shangri-La manager Mr Burton, and two US secret agents sent to collect the satellite, the Doctor foils the Bannermen. The Mercenaries are eventually defeated when the ultrasonic powers of the young Chimeron princess are broadcast over Shangri-La's public-address system. Gavrok is killed by one of his own booby traps. Billy, who has been ingesting a Chimeron substance to help him mutate, goes with Delta to help her repopulate her planet.

Novelisation: *Doctor Who – Delta and the Bannermen* by Malcolm Kohll (0 426 20333 X) first published by W H Allen (now Virgin Publishing Ltd) in 1989 with cover by Alister Pearson. Target library number 135.

(7G) **DRAGONFIRE**
(3 episodes)
23 November 1987 to 7 December 1987

Writer:
Ian Briggs

Director:
Chris Clough

Regular cast: See 7D above, and introducing Sophie Aldred (Ace).

Cast: Tony Selby (Glitz); Edward Peel (Kane); Patricia Quinn (Belazs); Tony Osoba (Kracauer); Stephanie Fayerman (McLuhan); Sean Blowers (Zed); Stuart Organ (Bazin); Nigel Miles-Thomas (Pudovkin); Shirin Taylor (Customer); Miranda Borman (Stellar); Ian Mackenzie (Anderson); Chris MacDonnell (Arnheim); Leslie Meadows (Creature); Daphne Oxenford (Archivist); Lynn Gardner (Announcer).

Story: The Doctor and Mel arrive on Ice World, a trading post on the dark side of the planet Svartos. It is ruled by the megalomaniac Kane, who can only exist in sub-zero temperatures. The Doctor teams up with Sabalom Glitz to go looking for a legendary Dragon who lives in the depths of Ice World and guards a mysterious treasure. Meanwhile, Mel befriends Ace, a 16-year-old girl from Earth with a passion for nitro-nine explosives. The Dragon turns out to be a living mechanoid, whose body hides a powerful energy crystal. Kane orders his men to kill the Dragon, then slaughters Ice World's population. The Doctor takes the crystal, but has to give it to Kane in exchange for Ace's life. Kane uses the crystal to power Ice World, which is in reality a huge spaceship. He plans to return to his home planet of Proamon, from which he was exiled 3,000 years ago. When the Doctor reveals Proamon's sun went nova 2,000 years ago, Kane commits suicide by exposing himself to direct sunlight. Glitz then takes over Ice World, and Mel decides to stay with him. Ace chooses to go with the Doctor.

  This was the 150th *Doctor Who* story.

Novelisation: *Doctor Who – Dragonfire* by Ian Briggs (0 426 20322 4) first published by W H Allen (now Virgin Publishing Ltd) in 1989 with cover by Alister Pearson. Target library number 137.

Video tape: *Dragonfire* first released in 1994 with cover by Bruno Elettori.

Twenty-Fifth Season

Producer:
John Nathan-Turner

Script Editor:
Andrew Cartmel

(7H) REMEMBRANCE OF THE DALEKS
(4 episodes)
5 October 1988 to 26 October 1988

Writer:
Ben Aaronovitch

Director:
Andrew Morgan

Regular cast: Sylvester McCoy (the Doctor); Sophie Aldred (Ace).

Cast: Simon Williams (Gilmore); George Sewell (Ratcliffe); Dursley McLinden (Mike); Pamela Salem (Rachel); Karen Gledhill (Allison); Michael Sheard (Headmaster); Harry Fowler (Harry); Joseph Marcell (John); William Thomas (Martin); Jasmine Breaks (The Girl); Peter Hamilton Dyer (Embery); Peter Halliday (Vicar); Derek Keller (Kaufman); Terry Molloy (Emperor Dalek/Davros); John Scott Martin, Cy Town, Tony Starr, Hugh Spight, David Harrison, Norman Bacon, Nigel Wild (Daleks); Royce Mills, Roy Skelton, Brian Miller, John

Leeson (Dalek Voices); Kathleen Bidmead (Mrs Smith); John Evans (Undertaker); Richie Kennedy (Milkman); Ron Berry (Gravedigger).

Story: The Doctor returns to Coal Hill Secondary School in 1963. There, an army unit headed by Group Captain Gilmore and Sgt. Mike Smith, and assisted by two scientists, Rachel and Allison, is investigating hostile aliens, which turn out to be white Imperial Daleks. The Emperor Dalek, from his orbiting mothership, has been sending Dalek Commandos through a transmat station located in the school's cellar. They are after the Hand of Omega, a quasi-living remote stellar manipulator, which the First Doctor had left behind in an undertaker's casket during his earlier visit. But renegade Daleks, led by the Black Dalek, are also after the Hand. They have enlisted the help of the fascist Ratcliffe, and use a young child mentally linked to a battle computer as their agent. Ace befriends Mike, who turns out to be in Ratcliffe's employ. Eventually the two rival Dalek factions battle each other. With the help of a 'special weapon' Dalek, the Imperial Daleks win and transport the Hand to their mothership. The Emperor Dalek is revealed to be Davros. The Doctor taunts him into using the Hand, which turns Skaro's sun into a supernova and destroys Davros' ship. When the Doctor makes him aware of the extent of the Daleks' defeat, the Black Dalek self-destructs. Mike is killed by the young child, who reverts to normal when the Black Dalek dies.

This story contains numerous references to *An Unearthly Child*, the first *Doctor Who* story, as well as a reference to Prof. Bernard Quatermass and his British Rocket Group.

Novelisation: *Doctor Who – Remembrance of the Daleks* by Ben Aaronovitch (0 426 20337 2) first published by W H Allen (now Virgin Publishing Ltd) in 1990 with cover by Alister Pearson. Target library number 148.

Video tape: *The Daleks Limited Edition Boxed Set* (BBCV 5005) first released in 1993 with cover by Alister Pearson includes *Remembrance of the Daleks* (BBCV 5007) with cover by Alister Pearson.

(7L) **THE HAPPINESS PATROL**
(3 episodes)
2 November 1988 to 16 November 1988

Writer:
Graeme Curry

Director:
Chris Clough

Regular cast: see 7H above

Cast: Sheila Hancock (Helen A); Ronald Fraser (Joseph C); David John Pope (Kandy Man); Harold Innocent (Gilbert M); Lesley Dunlop (Susan Q); Georgina Hale (Daisy K); Rachel Bell (Priscilla P); Richard D. Sharp (Earl Sigma); John Normington (Trevor Sigma); Tim Barker (Harold V); Jonathan Burn (Silas P); Philip Neve (Wences); Ryan Freedman (Wulfric); Mary Healey (Killjoy); Steve Swinscoe, Mark Carroll (Snipers); Tim Scott (Forum Doorman); Annie Hulley (Newscaster); Cy Town (Execution victim).

Story: The Doctor and Ace arrive on Terra Alpha, a future Earth colony where people are forced to be happy or die. Alpha is ruled by Helen A, with her companion Joseph C and her pet, the fierce Fifi. Her enforcer is the dreaded Kandy Man, the product of scientist Gilbert M. Opponents 'disappear', i.e. are shot by guards dubbed the 'Happiness Patrol', or are drowned in boiling candy. Ace befriends a young patroller, Susan Q. The Doctor meets Earl Sigma, another colonist stuck on Alpha, and a fan of blues music. He also encounters the pipe people, the original natives, driven underground by the human settlers. Together, they organise a revolt, and foil the Patrol by pretending to be happy. Eventually, the Kandy Man is killed beneath a flow of his own boiling candy, and Fifi is crushed under an avalanche of candy crystals. Joseph C and Gilbert M flee in a shuttle intended for Helen A, who, when she discovers Fifi's body, finally realises that happiness is nothing without sadness. Earl Sigma stays on to help Susan Q teach the blues to the newly liberated colony.

Novelisation: *Doctor Who – The Happiness Patrol* by Graeme Curry (0 426 20339 9) first published by W H Allen (now Virgin Publishing Ltd) in 1990 with cover by Alister Pearson. Target library number 146.

(7K) **SILVER NEMESIS**
(3 episodes)
23 November 1988 to 7 December 1988

Writer:
Kevin Clarke

Director:
Chris Clough

Regular cast: see 7H above

Cast: Fiona Walker (Lady Peinforte); Gerard Murphy (Richard); Anton Diffring (De Flores); Metin Yenal (Karl); Leslie French (Mathematician); Martyn Read (Security Man); David Banks (Cyberleader); Mark Hardy (Cyberlieutenant); Chris Chering (First Skinhead); Symond Lawes (Second Skinhead); Dolores Gray (American Tourist); Courtney Pine, Adrian Reid, Ernest Mothle, Frank Tontoh (Jazz Quartet); Brian Orrell, Danny Boyd, Scott Mitchell, Bill Malin, Tony Carlton, Paul Barrass (Cybermen); Dave Ould, John Ould (Walkmen); Mary Reynolds (H.M. the Queen).

Story: A rocket-powered asteroid houses validium, a deadly silver-coloured living metal, once created by Rassilon to be Gallifrey's ultimate defence. In unseen events in Windsor in 1638, the metal was shaped into a statue dubbed Nemesis by the evil Lady Peinforte. She was then thwarted by the Doctor, when he launched it back into space, where its orbit brought it near

Earth every 25 years, each time creating disasters. Nemesis lands in Windsor in 1988. It is now coveted by South American Nazis led by De Flores, who has Nemesis's bow; Lady Peinforte, who has Nemesis's arrow and has used it to travel forward in time with her man-servant Richard, and the Cybermen. The Doctor succeeds in stealing the bow and reanimates Nemesis. Lady Peinforte then attempts to blackmail him with the secret of his real identity, which she learned from Nemesis. Having failed, she merges with the statue. The Cyberleader, which has disposed of the Nazis, orders the Doctor to launch the statue towards the Cyberfleet, which has been lurking in space. But Nemesis destroys the fleet. Richard kills the Cyberleader and is returned to 1638.

This story marks the programme's twenty-fifth anniversary.

Novelisation: *Doctor Who – Silver Nemesis* by Kevin Clarke (0 426 20340 2) first published by W H Allen (now Virgin Publishing Ltd) in 1989 with cover by Alister Pearson. New edition in 1993 with cover by Alister Pearson. Target library number 143.

Video tape: *Silver Nemesis* (BBCV 4888) first released in 1993 with photomontage cover.

(7J) THE GREATEST SHOW IN THE GALAXY
(4 episodes)
14 December 1988 to 4 January 1989

Writer:
Stephen Wyatt

Director:
Alan Wareing

Regular cast: see 7H above

Cast: T.P. McKenna (The Captain); Jessica Martin (Mags);

Christopher Guard (Bellboy); Dee Sadler (Flowerchild); Ian Reddington (Chief Clown); Deborah Manship (Morgana); Ricco Ross (Ringmaster); Chris Jury (Deadbeat); Daniel Peacock (Nord); Gian Sammarco (Whizzkid); David Ashford (Dad); Janet Hargreaves (Mum); Kathryn Ludlow (Little Girl); Peggy Mount (Stallholder); Dean Hollingsworth (Bus Conductor); Alan Heap (Tumbling Clown); Paul Sadler, Philip Sadler, Patrick Ford (Clowns).

Story: An advertising satellite draws the Doctor and Ace to the Psychic Circus – the self-proclaimed Greatest Show in the Galaxy – on planet Segonax. There, they meet an assortment of odd characters, including the boastful, untrustworthy explorer Captain Cook, and his protege, Mags, who have all come to compete in a talent contest. The Circus is held in a grip of fear by the evil Chief Clown and his deadly, robotic clowns. Deadbeat, a brain-damaged labourer, is revealed to be the circus' original founder, Kingpin. Would-be performers are killed when they fail to entertain the Circus's only spectators, a mysterious family of three. The Doctor tries to uncover the Circus's secret, but is betrayed by the Captain. When they all perform together, Mags is revealed to be a werewolf, who then kills the Captain. The family turns out to be the three evil Gods of Ragnarok, with an unfulfillable craving for entertainment. Meanwhile, Ace finds the talisman which restores Kingpin's sanity. With it, the Doctor is able to turn the Gods' own power against them. The Circus is destroyed, and Kingpin plans to start a whole new one with Mags.

Novelisation: *Doctor Who – The Greatest Show in the Galaxy* by Stephen Wyatt (0 426 20341 0) first published by W H Allen (now Virgin Publishing Ltd) in 1989 with cover by Alister Pearson. Target library number 144.

Twenty-Sixth Season

Producer:
John Nathan-Turner

Script Editor:
Andrew Cartmel

(7N) **BATTLEFIELD**
(4 episodes)
6 September 1989 to 27 September 1989

Writer:
Ben Aaronovitch

Director:
Michael Kerrigan

Regular Cast: Sylvester McCoy (the Doctor); Sophie Aldred (Ace).

Guest Star: Nicholas Courtney (Brigadier Lethbridge-Stewart Retd.).

Cast: Jean Marsh (Morgaine); Christopher Bowen (Mordred); Angela Bruce (Brigadier Winifred Bambera); Marcus Gilbert (Ancelyn); Ling Tai (Shou Yuing); Angela Douglas (Doris); June Bland (Elizabeth Rowlinson); Noel Collins (Pat Rowlinson); James Ellis (Peter Warmsly); Marek Anton (the Destroyer); Dorota Rae (Lavel); Robert Jezek (Sergeant Zbrigniev); Paul Tomany (Major Husak); Stefan Schwartz (Knight Commander).

Story: Answering a distress signal, the TARDIS is drawn to Carbury, where a nuclear missile convoy, under the direction of UNIT Brigadier Winifred Bambera, is stopped. Under a neighbouring lake is an extra-dimensional spaceship containing the body of King Arthur and his sword Excalibur. Ancelyn, a knight from that other dimension, arrives on Earth to recover Excalibur, but is followed by the evil Mordred, who summons his mother, the powerful sorceress Morgaine. They all recognise the Doctor as Merlin, one of his future incarnations. A battle erupts between UNIT and Morgaine's men. Hearing of the Doctor's return, Brigadier Lethbridge-Stewart comes out of retirement, and ends up using silver bullets to kill the Destroyer, an otherworldly creature released by Morgaine to devour the Earth. Morgaine tries to trigger the explosion of the nuclear missile, but the Doctor shows her there would be no honour in such a victory. Arthur is revealed to have been dead all along. Morgaine and Mordred are remanded to UNIT's custody.

Novelisation: *Doctor Who – Battlefield* by Marc Platt (0 426 20350 X) first published by Virgin Publishing Ltd in 1991 with cover by Alister Pearson. Target library number 152.

(7Q) **GHOST LIGHT**
(3 episodes)
4 October 1989 to 18 October 1989

Writer:
Marc Platt

Director:
Alan Wareing

Regular Cast: see 7N above

Cast: Ian Hogg (Josiah Samuel Smith); Sharon Duce (Control); John Hallam (Light); Carl Forgione (Nimrod); Sylvia Syms (Mrs Pritchard); Katharine Schlesinger (Gwendoline); Michael Cochrane (Redvers Fenn-Cooper); Frank Windsor (Inspector Mackenzie); John Nettleton (Rev. Matthews); Brenda Kempner (Mrs Grose).

Story: The Doctor and Ace arrive in Perivale 1883, in Gabriel Chase, an evil house that Ace burned down in 1983. The house is built upon an ancient spaceship, and its inhabitants are under the domination of Josiah Samuel Smith, who turns out to be a reptilian alien from the ship who has evolved into a human. Smith is holding prisoner the explorer Redvers Fenn-Cooper, who went mad when he first beheld the ship's true owner, and plots to have him kill Queen Victoria to restore the British Empire to its former glory. Smith's plans are thwarted by Control, another alien who evolves into a woman; Nimrod, his Neanderthal servant; and Ace, who causes the release of a powerful alien named Light. Light once catalogued all of Earth's species, but when he learns that his catalogue has been made obsolete by evolution, he wants to destroy mankind. He disintegrates when the Doctor shows him that no one can stop evolution. Fenn-Cooper, Control and Nimrod leave in the ship.

Novelisation: *Doctor Who – Ghost Light* by Marc Platt (0 426 20351 8) first published by W H Allen (now Virgin Publishing Ltd) in 1990 with cover by Alister Pearson. Target library number 149.

Script book: *Doctor Who – Ghost Light* by Marc Platt (1 65286 477 X) first published in 1993 by Titan Books with cover by Alister Pearson.

Video tape: *Ghost Light* (BBCV 5344) first released in 1994 with a cover by Colin Howard.

(7M) THE CURSE OF FENRIC
(4 episodes)
25 October 1989 to 15 November 1989

Writer:
Ian Briggs

Director:
Nicholas Mallett

Regular Cast: see 7N above

Cast: Dinsdale Landen (Dr Judson); Alfred Lynch (Commander Millington); Tomek Bork (Sorin); Joann Kenny (Jean); Joanne Bell (Phyllis); Peter Czajkowski (Sergeant Prozorov); Nicholas Parsons (Rev Wainwright); Cory Pulman (Kathleen

Dudman); Marek Anton (Vershinin); Stevan Rimkus (Captain Bates); Marcus Hutton (Sergeant Leigh); Janet Henfrey (Ms Hardaker); Anne Reid (Nurse Crane); Mark Conrad (Petrossian); Christien Anholt (Perkins); Aaron Hanley (Baby); Cy Town (Haemovore); Raymond Trickett (Ancient Haemovore).

Story: The Doctor and Ace arrive at a secret naval base off the coast of Northumberland towards the end of the Second World War. There, Dr Judson has built the Ultima Machine, a computer designed to break German ciphers. Base commander Millington, obsessed by Norse mythology, plots to let a Russian commando unit, led by Captain Sorin, steal the Ultima core, which he has booby-trapped with a deadly toxin. Judson uses the Ultima Machine to translate ancient runes, which in turn lead to the release of Fenric, an evil entity from the dawn of time whom the Doctor trapped seventeen centuries ago in a Chinese flask. The flask was later stolen and buried by Vikings. The base is attacked by humans who have become vampiric Haemovores. Fenric takes over Judson's body to challenge the Doctor at chess, and Ace unwittingly helps Fenric win. Fenric then takes over Sorin's body, and plans to release the deadly toxins. But the Doctor succeeds in turning an Ancient Haemovore against Fenric, whose host body is killed by the toxin. The baby of a young woman whom Ace helped escape the Haemovores is revealed to be her mother.

Novelisation: *Doctor Who – The Curse of Fenric* by Ian Briggs (0 426 20348 8) first published by W H Allen (now Virgin Publishing Ltd) in 1990 with cover by Alister Pearson. Target library number 151.

Video tape: *The Curse of Fenric* (BBCV 4453) first released in 1991 with cover by Alister Pearson.

(7P) SURVIVAL
(3 episodes)
22 November 1989 to 6 December 1989

Writer:
Rona Munro

Director:
Alan Wareing

Regular cast: see 7N above

Cast: Anthony Ainley (the Master); Julian Holloway (Sergeant Paterson); Lisa Bowerman (Karra); Will Barton (Midge); Sakuntala Ramanee (Shreela); David John (Derek); Sean Oliver (Stuart); Gareth Hale (Len); Norman Pace (Harvey); Kate Eaton (Ange); Adele Silva (Squeak); Michelle Martin (Neighbour); Kathleen Bidmead (Woman).

Story: The Doctor takes Ace to Perivale because she wants to look up her old friends, but most of them seem to have disappeared. They have been transported by the cat-like kitlings to the planet of the Cheetah People, descendants of an ancient race which has reverted to savagery and has the ability to teleport through space. The Doctor and Ace are eventually transported to the planet. Ace teams up with Midge and two other old friends, while the Doctor meets the Master, who has drawn him there because he needs the Doctor's help to escape from the doomed planet, whose symbiotic nature is causing the Master to turn into an animal. Midge lets his animal side overcome him, and the Master uses him to teleport to Earth. Ace, who has almost succumbed to the attraction of a Cheetah woman, Karra, gains the same ability and takes the Doctor and the others back to Perivale. There, the Master uses Midge and his friends to go after the Doctor, but Midge dies. The Master kills Karra, who reverts to human form. Overtaken by his animal nature, he drags the Doctor back to the disintegrating Cheetah planet. The Doctor is transported back to Earth when he makes the decision to refuse to fight.

Novelisation: *Doctor Who – Survival* by Rona Munro (0 426 20352 6) first published by W H Allen (now Virgin Publishing Ltd) in 1990 with cover by Alister Pearson. Target library number 150.

EIGHTH DOCTOR
PAUL McGANN
(1996)

Executive Producers:
Philip Segal, Alex Beaton, Jo Wright

Producer:
Peter V. Ware

Writer:
Matthew Jacobs

Director:
Geoffrey Sax

Cast: Paul McGann (the Doctor), Daphne Ashbrook (Grace Holloway), Eric Roberts (the Master), Sylvester McCoy (the Seventh Doctor), Yee Jee Tso (Chang Lee), David Hurtubise (Wagg), John Novak (Salinger), Michael David Simms (Doctor Swift), Catherine Lough (Wheeler), Dolores Drake (Curtis), William Sasso (Pete), Jeremy Radick (Gareth), Eliza Roberts (Miranda), Joe Wirkkunen (Ted), Bill Croft (Policeman), Dee Jay Jackson (Security), Gordon Tipple (Old Master), Mi-Jung Lee, Joanna Piros (News Anchors).

Story: The Master is killed by the Daleks on Skaro and the Seventh Doctor is charged with taking his remains back to Gallifrey. The Master turns into a morphing snake and causes the TARDIS to land in San Francisco on the eve of the millennium. The Seventh Doctor is shot by a gang and appears to die while being operated on by Dr. Holloway. He regenerates into the Eighth Doctor. Meanwhile, the Master takes over the body of an ambulance driver and plots to use the TARDIS' Eye of

Harmony to destroy the Earth. The new Doctor succeeds in convincing Dr. Holloway he is the same man, and with her help and that of reformed gang member Chang Lee, he succeeds in foiling the Master's scheme. The evil Time Lord is sucked into the Eye of Harmony.

Novelisation: *Doctor Who* by Gary Russell, first published by BBC Books, May 1996.

Video tape: *Doctor Who (BBCV 5882)*, first released May 1996.

ADDENDUM

DOCTOR WHO: THE 'MISSING BITS'

What happens to the holes when the cheese is gone?
– Bertolt Brecht.

THE FIRST DOCTOR

THE MASTERS OF LUXOR (1963)

1. THE CANNIBAL FLOWER
2. THE MOCKERY OF MAN
3. A LIGHT ON THE DEAD PLANET

4. TABON OF LUXOR
5. AN INFINITY OF
   SURPRISES
6. THE FLOWER BLOOMS

Writer:
Anthony Coburn

Story: The TARDIS is drawn by a mysterious signal from a barren moon. It is then captured inside a crystal city, which drains its power. The city uses it to reactivate an army of robotic Derivitrons who mistake the Travellers for the Masters of Luxor. The Derivitrons' leader, the Perfect One, has stolen the lifeforce of its human Masters in a vain attempt to become alive. He now plans to steal Susan and Barbara's. Ian and the Doctor escape outside, and discover the signal's source: the body of the robot's real creator, Tabon of Luxor, held in suspended animation. They reanimate him and return to the city. The Perfect One cannot deal with his creator's hatred and seeks to destroy himself, but his death triggers an atomic device. Before the explosion, Tabon reverses the TARDIS's power drain, enabling the Travellers to flee the now-doomed moon.

Note: This story is part of a fine, ongoing collection of *Doctor Who* scripts, edited by John McElroy and published by Titan Books. As explained in its introduction, *The Masters of Luxor* was originally written by Coburn, the screenwriter of *An Unearthly Child* (A), to be the second *Doctor Who* story. However, the producers chose instead to go with Terry Nation's *The Daleks* (B). In spite of the tight continuity that exists between (A) and (B), there is no reason not to think that, somewhere, somewhen, the Doctor, Susan, Ian and Barbara took a sidestep in time to Luxor's moon before their fateful landing on Skaro.

Script book: *The Masters of Luxor* by Anthony Coburn (1 85286 321 8) first published by Titan Books in 1992 with cover by Alister Pearson.

THE THIRD DOCTOR

THE PARADISE OF DEATH
BBC Radio 5 – 5 episodes
(27 August 1993 to 24 September 1993)

Writer: **Producer/Director:**
Barry Letts   Phil Clarke

Cast: Jon Pertwee (The Doctor); Elisabeth Sladen (Sarah Jane Smith); Nicholas Courtney (Brigadier Lethbridge-Stewart); Harold Innocent (Freeth); Peter Miles (Tragan); Maurice Denham (President); Richard Pearce (Jeremy Fitzoliver); Andrew Wincott (Crestin/Bill/Radio Voice/Ambulance Man); Dominic Letts (Nobby/Kitson/Wilkins/Soldier); Brian Hall (Grebber/Reporter); Jillie Meers (Clorinda/UN General Secretary); John Harwood (General); John Fleming (Odun/Patrol Leader); Jonathan Tafler (Capt. Waldo Rudley); Jane Slavin (Onya); Emma Myant (Greckle); Michael Onslow (Rasco Hedal); David Holt (Medan/Hunter); Julian Rhind-Tutt (Guard/Rance/Board Member/Echo Location Operator/Lexhan); Trevor Martin (Kaido/Guard/Custodian of Data Store/Jenhegger); Philip Anthony (Yallett/Officer of the Day).

Story: The Doctor, Sarah and the Brigadier investigate Spaceworld, an amusement park built by the Parakon Corporation. The Doctor discovers that its leaders, chairman Freeth and his sadistic henchman Tragan, are aliens who have come with promises of commercial exchanges which will turn Earth into a paradise. While snooping around, Sarah is captured by Tragan, who takes her to the planet Parakon. The Doctor, the Brigadier and Sarah's photographer, Jeremy Fitzoliver, follow in the TARDIS. Parakon is ruled by a well-meaning but weak President, who turns out to be Freeth's father. Its population is in thrall to violent games fed through Experienced Reality, all its material needs apparently provided for by the seemingly miraculous Rapine plant. The Doctor teams up with a group of rebels led by Onya and discovers that, far from being a paradise, Parakon has been ravaged by Rapine and now requires huge supplies of fertiliser. Freeth has been engineering wars among other species in order to obtain enough bodies to process into fertiliser. While the Brigadier leads the insurrection, the Doctor is forced by Freeth into a deadly fight with games champion Jenhegger. Onya reveals the truth to the President, who stops the games. Freeth tries to kill his father, but is thrown to his death by Jenhegger. Peace returns and Onya becomes Parakon's new prime minister.

Note: This story takes place between *The Time Warrior* (UUU) and *Invasion of the Dinosaurs* (WWW).

Novelisation: *Doctor Who – The Paradise of Death* by Barry Letts (0 426 20413 1) first published by Virgin Publishing Ltd in 1994 with cover by Alister Pearson.

Audio tape: *The Paradise of Death* (catalogue number: ZBBC 1494, ISBN: 0563 401761) first released in 1993 with photo-montage cover.

THE FOURTH DOCTOR

DOCTOR WHO AND THE
PESCATONS (1976)
Argo Records (Decca)

Producer:
Don Norman

Directors:
Harvey Usill (voices)
Don Norman (FX/music)

Writer:
Victor Pemberton

Cast: Tom Baker (the Doctor/Narrator), Elisabeth Sladen (Sarah Jane Smith), Bill Mitchell (Zor).

Story: The Doctor and Sarah Jane Smith encounter the shark-like Pescatons, whose planet is threatened with destruction as its orbit gets closer to its sun. Their leader, the monstrous Zor, leads an invasion of Earth. Sarah discovers the aliens are vulnerable to high frequency sound when the Doctor plays his piccolo. The Doctor then lures Zor into a trap. Once the Pescaton leader is eliminated, the invasion falls apart and, soon afterwards, the aliens' planet is destroyed.

Note: This story was originally released as an Argo Record put out by Decca to capitalise on the popularity of Tom Baker and Elisabeth Sladen. Victor Pemberton is the writer of both script and novelisation of *Fury from the Deep* (RR), which shares certain themes with *The Pescatons*.

Novelisation: *Doctor Who – The Pescatons* by Victor Pemberton (0 426 20353 4) first published by Virgin Publishing Ltd in 1991 with cover by Pete Walbank.

THE SIXTH DOCTOR

SLIPBACK
BBC Radio 4 Special – 6 ten-minute episodes
(25 July, 1 August and 8 August 1985)

Writer:
Eric Saward

Producer:
Paul Spencer

Cast: Colin Baker (The Doctor); Nicola Bryant (Peri); Jane Carr (Computer); Jon Glover (Shellingborne Grant); Nick Revell (Bates, Snatch); Alan Thompson (Maston Mutant, Steward, Droid, Time Lord); Valentine Dyall (Slarn); Ron Pember (Seedle).

Story: The TARDIS materialises on board the *Vipod Mor*, a galactic survey ship captained by the repulsive Slarn. Grant, one of the ship's officers, turns out to be a galactic con man who tried to escape the law (in the persons of officers Seedle and Snatch) by having his brain transplanted into another man's body. Meanwhile, the ship's computer has developed a schizophrenic personality, and wants to travel back in time to put the galaxy right. The Doctor is unable to stop the computer, but later is told by renegade Time Lord Vipod Mor that the ship's explosion at the beginning of time is responsible for the Big Bang.

Note: *Slipback* was written by script editor Eric Saward in a humorous tone markedly different from that used in the television programme. The story also offers a version of the creation of the universe which conflicts with that depicted in *Terminus* (6G).

Novelisation: *Doctor Who – Slipback* by Eric Saward (0 426 20263 5) first published by W H Allen (now Virgin Publishing Ltd) in 1986 with cover by Paul Mark Tamms.

Audio tape: *Genesis of the Daleks/Slipback* (ZBBC 1020) first released in 1988 with photomontage cover.

The missing season

These three stories (known as the 'missing season') were scheduled to be produced in 1985 between *Revelation of the Daleks* (6Z) and *The Trial of a Time Lord* (7A–7C), when the programme was suddenly placed on an unexpected hiatus by the BBC. As is the case with *The Masters of Luxor*, their novelisations confer upon them an 'official nature' denied (so far) to those numerous other scripts written for *Doctor Who* during its many years of existence, but never actually produced.

THE NIGHTMARE FAIR (1985)

Writer:
Graham Williams

Story: The Doctor and Peri are drawn to Blackpool. There, the Doctor confronts the Celestial Toymaker, who is revealed to be a being from another Universe. The Toymaker is planning to use a monstrous new video game to enslave mankind. The Doctor eventually defeats the Toymaker's game, and imprisons the evil immortal in a trap powered by his own brain.

Note: The late Graham Williams was producer of *Doctor Who* during its 15th to 17th seasons. He was also co-writer of *The Invasion of Time* (4Z) and *City of Death* (5H). This story brings back, and gives an origin to, the Celestial Toymaker, a villain who had not been seen since William Hartnell's days (Y).

Novelisation: *Doctor Who – The Nightmare Fair* by Graham Williams (0 426 20334 8) first published by W H Allen (now

Virgin Publishing Ltd) in 1989 with cover by Alister Pearson and Graeme Way.

THE ULTIMATE EVIL (1985)

Writer:
Wally K. Daly

Story: The evil dwarf Mordant, one of the Salankans, a race of ruthless cosmic traders, uses a hate ray to start a war between the peace-loving nation of Tranquela and the computer-controlled society of Ameleria, in order to sell them weapons. The Doctor stumbles across the plot while looking for a good spot for a vacation, and convinces Mordant to leave by threatening him with the Time Lords' wrath, if they learn that the crystal balls Mordant gave them are spying devices.

Novelisation: *Doctor Who – The Ultimate Evil* by Wally K. Daly (0 426 20347 X) first published by W H Allen (now Virgin Publishing Ltd) in 1990 with cover by Alister Pearson.

MISSION TO MAGNUS (1985)

Writer:
Philip Martin

Story: The Doctor is forcibly drawn to the temperate world of Magnus by Anzor, a Time Lord who used to bully him at school. Magnus is a former Earth colony where a virus has decimated the male population, leaving the women to rule. The Doctor defeats a plot by the Ice Warriors to move Magnus's orbit and turn the planet into an ice world, thwarting the exiled Sil's business plans in the process. Freed of the virus, Magnus's female leaders contemplate reconciliation with the males of their brother planet, Salvak.

Note: Philip Martin, the author of *Vengeance on Varos* (6V) and *Mindwarp* (7B), brings back the villainous Sil, whom he created, and the Ice Warriors, who had not appeared in the programme since *The Monster of Peladon* (YYY).

Novelisation: *Doctor Who – Mission to Magnus* by Philip Martin (0 426 2034 X) first published by W H Allen (now Virgin Publishing Ltd) in 1990 with cover by Alister Pearson.

0-595-27618-0

CPSIA information can be obtained
at www.ICGtesting.com
Printed in the USA
LVOW08s1457061216
516056LV00001B/52/P